TRUFFLES

TRUFFLES

ULTIMATE LUXURY, EVERYDAY PLEASURE

ROSARIO SAFINA AND JUDITH SUTTON

WINE SUGGESTIONS by Joseph Scalice **PHOTOGRAPHY** by Shimon and Tammar Rothstein

Food styling by Paul Grimes

This book is printed on acid-free paper.

Published by John Wiley & Sons, Inc., Hoboken, New Jersey

Published simultaneously in Canada

Design by Vertigo Design, NYC

For general information on our other products and services or for technical support, please contact our Customer Care Department within the United States at (800) 762-2974, outside the United States at (317) 572-3993 or fax (317) 572-4002.

Wiley also publishes its books in a variety of electronic formats. Some content that appears in print may not be available in electronic books. For more information about Wiley products, visit our web site at www.wiley.com.

Library of Congress Cataloging-in-Publication Data:

Safina, Rosario.
  Truffles : ultimate luxury, everyday pleasure / Rosario Safina and Judith Sutton ; wine suggestions by Joseph Scalice ; photography by Shimon and Tammar Rothstein ; food styling by Paul Grimes.
      p. cm.
Includes bibliographical referenced and index.
  ISBN 0-471-22508-8 (alk. paper)
1. Cookery (Truffles) 2. Truffles. I. Sutton, Judith C. II.
Title.
  TX804.5 .S24 2002
  641.6'58—dc21

                                          2002002971

Printed in the United States of America

10 9 8 7 6 5 4 3 2 1

TO MY WIFE, LINDA,

WHO HAS ALWAYS BELIEVED IN MY WORK,

AND MY SON, PAOLO,

WHO LOVES THE AROMA OF BLACK TRUFFLES.

RS

TO THE MEMORY OF MY FATHER

JS

ACKNOWLEDGMENTS

There are many people I would like to thank:

Susan Wyler, our editor, who came up with the idea for the book, asked me to work on this exciting project, and has been its champion since the beginning.

Peggy Fallon, for her delicious recipes and irreverent wit.

Patricia Safina, for her enthusiasm, generosity, and humor, and Natasha Ladera, for her invaluable assistance.

All the chefs who so generously contributed their recipes: Alex Lee, Andrew Carmellini, Wayne Nish, Terry Brennan and David Cox, Frank Whittaker, Laurent Tourondel, Rick Moonen, Mario Batali, Fortunato Nicotra, Mike Anthony and Dan Barber, Cyril Renaud, Rick Tramonto, Barbara Lynch, Emeril Lagasse, Sandro Gamba, and, especially, Paul Bartolotta.

Joseph Scalice, for his thoughtful and imaginative wine suggestions.

Mickey Choate, my agent, for his enthusiastic support, patience, and love of truffles and other good food.

Paul Grimes, for his fabulous food styling, and Shimon and Tammar Rothstein, for their stunning photographs.

Vertigo Design, NYC for their sleek interior design.

Diana Cisek, Valerie Peterson, P. J. Campbell, Michele Sewell, Jeff Faust, and everyone else at Wiley who contributed to the realization of the book.

And, of course, my family and my friends.

JS

CONTENTS

TRUFFLES: AN INTRODUCTION

INTRODUCTION

PRESENTLY WE WERE AWARE OF AN ODOR GRADUALLY COMING TOWARDS US, SOMETHING MUSKY, FIERY, SAVORY, MYSTERIOUS—A HOT, DROWSY SMELL, THAT LULLS THE SENSES AND YET INFLAMES THEM—THE TRUFFLES WERE COMING.

—WILLIAM THACKERAY

Intense, earthy, seductive, hauntingly fragrant—there is nothing else in the world like a fresh truffle. The musky scent of a white truffle as it is shaved paper-thin over a plate of delicate fresh pasta, or the heady aromas that arise from a sauce perfumed with black truffles, can be intoxicating. Imbued with a sense of mystery, truffles have inspired some fanciers to rhapsodize, caused others to swoon. Called everything from a black diamond to a princess, the truffle has long reigned as the jewel of haute cuisine, a magical ingredient that classically trained chefs have elevated to the ultimate luxury.

But truffles are no longer a once-a-year treat, with indulgence limited to their short season. Today you can find an ever-increasing array of wonderful truffle products on the market, from fragrant butters and oils to intense purees and pastes. Star chefs have been stocking their kitchens with these "secret ingredients" for more than a decade, but recently they have become available to the home cook, displayed on the shelves of gourmet shops— and even in some upscale supermarkets.

With a bottle of truffle oil in your pantry or a tub of truffle butter in the refrigerator, an everyday meal can be transformed into a sensuous celebration—with almost no effort at all. Most of these products are amazingly versatile, and because they are not the rarities fresh truffles are, they can be surprisingly affordable. At the same time, many of them possess so much flavor that a little goes a long way.

Opening a bottle of white or black truffle oil can be as heady an experience as shaving slices of a fresh white or black truffle over a dish. Drizzle the oil onto grilled fish or cured meats, add it to a vinaigrette, or stir it into creamy mashed potatoes. Toss fresh pasta with truffle butter for an almost-instant gourmet meal, or slather the butter on crusty bread for an incredibly indulgent snack. Or try intense white or black truffle paste—just a teaspoon or so is enough to richly flavor a sauce or a vegetable puree. Spoon white truffle cream over vegetables or a roasted veal chop. Do be careful, though, you may find yourself seduced into eating it straight out of the jar. Truffle flour, a relative newcomer even chefs are still discovering, is so intoxicatingly fragrant that it works best as a flavoring or condiment—sprinkle a little over grilled steak or stir just a pinch into a pan sauce, and the dish will explode with flavor. Think of these new products as fabulous convenience foods. With them, you can enjoy truffles whenever you want, all year-round.

Of course, there are also times to use fresh truffles with abandon. Creamy risotto showered with shaved white truffles, for example, and glistening golden brown baby chickens cloaked in sliced black truffles are among the best dishes in the world. But when fresh truffles are not available, there is no reason not to indulge in the same irresistible taste and to indulge in many of those same dishes—because almost any one of them can be made using a prepared truffle product instead.

The first part of this book offers an introduction to truffles in all their glory. There's a brief history of the remarkable tuber, followed by a guide to the different types of fresh truffles, a description of how they grow, and a look at the future. An entire chapter tells you everything you need to know about buying and preparing fresh truffles, with a detailed glossary of truffle products, from oils and butter to pastes to honey. How to buy, store, and use all of these indispensable new pantry items is described in careful, easy-to-follow detail.

At the heart of any cookbook is its food, and *Truffles* is no exception. We offer more than 115 recipes for every part of the meal except dessert. (Although some chefs do reach a bit upon occasion to prepare desserts with truffles, we, like most cooks, would rather use them in recipes that show them off to their natural advantage.) An incredible assortment of appetizers, soups, salads, entrées, and side dishes of all sorts—as well as snacks, panini, pizzas, and brunch dishes—exploit the power of truffles to elevate the simple to the sublime. As the stunning photographs illustrate, some of these use fresh truffles, and others achieve the same luxurious effect from a variety of truffle products.

Most of the recipes we offer are simple but sophisticated, and many of them take very little time to prepare: they are easy enough for every day, but special enough for the most important guest. Although all of them are indulgent, some could be described as supreme comfort food: the ultimate "macaroni and cheese," for example, made with penne and truffle cheese. And, of course, there is more than one recipe for truffled mashed potatoes, on the theory—and our first-hand experience—that once sampled, they are forever treasured. More elaborate dishes for special ultra-indulgent meals, including some favorite recipes contributed by top chefs, balance the range of recipes.

Whenever possible, we have provided make-ahead information, to cut down on last-minute preparation. Many of the recipes also include variations, sometimes substituting a truffle product for a fresh truffle, or one product for another, other times providing elaborations on a theme.

Truffles are unique, their reputation one of mystery and myth. But cooking with them need not be intimidating. As the recipes in this book demonstrate, truffles are just as delicious in a simple contemporary dish as in an elaborate preparation from classic French cuisine. With that in mind, and with all the new truffle products to choose from, we are sure you will agree that truffles truly deserve to be an everyday pleasure.

Black Truffles

A BRIEF HISTORY OF TRUFFLES

YOU HAVE ASKED THE SCHOLARS WHAT THIS TUBERCLE IS, AND AFTER TWO THOUSAND YEARS OF DIS-CUSSION, THE SCHOLARS HAVE ANSWERED THE SAME AS THE FIRST DAY: "WE DO NOT KNOW." YOU HAVE ASKED THE TRUFFLE ITSELF AND THE TRUFFLE HAS ANSWERED YOU: "EAT ME AND ADORE GOD." TO TELL THE STORY OF THE TRUFFLE IS TO TELL THE HISTORY OF THE WORLD'S CIVILIZATION.

—ALEXANDRE DUMAS

Truffles have a history dating back to antiquity, and over the centuries they have been both revered and feared. One of their earliest fans was Cheops (the pyramid builder), and the Sumerians and others in the Fertile Crescent are known to have been fond of them. The ancient Greeks and Romans numbered truffles among their culinary delicacies; Pliny, Juvenal, and others wrote about them. One of Aristotle's disciples thought truffles were caused by thunderstorms, and many others also imagined them to be the result of lightning strikes.

More than a few recipes for truffles can be found in the first cookbook ever written, Apicius's *De re Coquinaria*, which dates to the first century A.D. Although his recipe combining truffles and garum—a Roman condiment that could be considered the precursor to Thai fish sauce—probably would not appeal to modern tastes, another of his most famous dishes, truffles wrapped in caul fat before being cooked, can still be found in one form or another in classic French restaurants today.

Perhaps not surprisingly, Nero was a lover of truffles, which he referred to as "food of the gods." But after the fall of the Roman Empire, they became a forbidden fruit. A symbol of indulgence and a reputed aphrodisiac, truffles were proscribed by the Church during the Middle Ages. Although their origins remained cloaked in mystery, they were widely considered to be the creation of the devil, or even, according to Christian Etienne's *The Magic of the Truffle*, "the manifestation of the souls of the damned…blackened by their sins."

Etienne also writes that "since man has been cooking, truffles have been regarded as quasi-sacred and attributed with magical powers." Their mystique, or aura, has hardly lessened over the centuries. Here is food writer Paula Wolfert on her first truffle:

That truffle seemed to me like earth and sky and sea. I felt at one with nature, that my mouth was filled with the taste of the earth. There was a ripeness, a naughtiness, something beyond description. A gastronomic black diamond, it was utter luxury and earthiness combined.

With the Renaissance, truffles came back into favor and were in great demand. Messibugo, a cookbook author who is considered the father of Italy's tradition of *grande cucina*, featured truffles in many of his multicourse banquet menus. In fourteenth-century France, when Pope John XXII moved from his native Dordogne to take up residence in Avignon, he had oak trees planted nearby in the hopes that truffles would come along with them. Catherine de Médicis brought her love of truffles (and her cooks, with their recipes) to France when she married Henry II. And Louis XIV, the hedonistic Sun King, certainly enjoyed them in his court.

THE APHRODISIAC TRUFFLE

An old Italian proverb warns, "Those who wish to lead a virtuous life should abstain from truffles." And Brillat-Savarin's pronouncement that "[t]he truffle is not a positive aphrodisiac, but it can upon occasion make women more tender and men more apt to love" has often been quoted. Truffles are described as seductive, musky, evocative of sex. Actually, truffles do contain testosterase, a chemical component closely related to the male hormone testosterone. It's similar to a chemical found in the saliva of male pigs, and truffles are indeed an aphrodisiac for female pigs—the reason, undoubtedly, that the sows traditionally used by truffle hunters were so good at unearthing them. However, scientifically speaking at least, testosterase does not affect human beings in the same way. Nevertheless, that has never stopped people from imagining they do.

During the eighteenth century, truffles were so abundant in Italy that there were even hunting parties organized to search for them. In 1751, the Italian king presented England's George II with two truffle hunters and a half-dozen truffle hounds so they could hunt for truffles in Windsor Park; apparently they were successful at finding some, at least. Lord Byron, or so the story goes, kept a truffle on his desk to inspire creativity.

Colette might be considered the truffle's greatest champion. She referred to them as "black princesses" and "jewels" and once said, "If I can't have too many truffles, I'll do without truffles." Fortunately, she lived in a time when truffles could still be found in quantity. It was for truffle fanciers like Colette that the first *Larousse Gastronomique* provided recipes such as a timbale filled entirely with sliced truffles. The volume also included a number of nineteenth-century truffle recipes, such as one that begins: "Take three pounds of truffles, the biggest you can find, round, smooth, firm, and very black." Those were the days.

ALBA, PERIGORD, AND BEYOND: WHITE AND BLACK TRUFFLES, AND OTHER RELATIVES

Although Italy's white truffle

and France's "black diamond" are the best known, there are, in fact, close to a hundred different varieties of truffles. In addition to these true truffles, which are all members of the *Tuber* genus, there are a few relatives that can be considered along with them. Because many truffles have been given various names, they are identified here by both their Latin names and their most popular regional names or nicknames.

White Truffles

Italy's white truffle, *Tuber magnatum* (or, more formally, *Tuber magnatum pico*), is a relative newcomer on the scene, having been discovered a mere two hundred years ago or so. And it's only been available in the United States for a few decades. Nevertheless, for many, the white truffle is the true prize. It is more delicate and more intoxicatingly fragrant than the black winter truffle, with an aroma that is variously referred to as musky, sexy (or even raunchy), and garlicky. In *Gastronomy of Italy*, Anna Del Conte describes it as tasting like "the perfect marriage between a clove of garlic and a piece of the best Parmesan."

White truffles, also referred to as Alba or Piedmont truffles, can be four to five times the price of even the best black winter truffles, in part, of course, because of their haunting fragrance, but primarily because they are much rarer than the black truffle. In a good year, the harvest may be only three tons, compared to thirty-five tons for the black. *T. magnatum* is found only in northern and parts of central Italy and in Istria, Croatia (which has been part of Italy at various times in its past). Although Alba, in the Piemonte region, is traditionally associated with white truffles, today it is actually the center of the truffle business, not of the best harvest, and many white truffles come from other parts of Piemonte, as well as from Tuscany, the Marches, Umbria, Emilia-Romagna, and regions slightly farther to the south. Nor are Istrian white truffles to be disdained—in some years, they are as good as, if not better than, the Italian harvest.

White truffles are faintly golden, beige, or pale brown, with lighter tan or cream-colored flesh marked by thin pale veins. Their color is determined to a great extent by the host tree. Pink spots or lines or a pinkish cast to their flesh, for example, indicates the oak or willow. Their skin is relatively smooth, though the truffles themselves can be bumpy or lumpy. White truffle season runs from early October to early January, with late November and December being the peak.

Most white truffles in the market are the size of a golf ball at most, often smaller, although they can grow much larger. They are graded according to size and appearance, from "super extra" to "extra grade" to "first choice." If you've wondered why the truffles you've seen in some restaurants or in books look so much finer than the ones your local gourmet market has on display, it's because they are the top grades. Super extras can be the size of an orange, or even bigger, while extra grade truffles are about the size of a large egg; first choice are walnut-sized or smaller. Restaurants that offer white truffles are usually offering extra grade. It's nice to know, though, that the aroma and taste of a small truffle can be just as potent, if not more so, as a larger one.

Black Winter Truffles

Tuber melanosporum, the black truffle so strongly associated with France's Périgord region, has been beloved by gourmands for centuries. Although it is often called the Périgord truffle, today many black truffles come from Provence and other parts of southern France, including Quercy, the Vaucluse, and even as far west as the Pyrenees. *T. melanosporum* (*T. melanosporum vittadini*, to be precise) is also found in Spain, particularly in the Catalonian region, all the way down to Valencia. And it grows in Italy too, primarily in the Marches and Um-

bria. There it is often called the Norcia truffle, after the Umbrian town of that name. However, although they are the same species, Italian black truffles are for whatever reasons generally inferior to the best French black truffles. If you're in Italy at the right time, indulge in *T. magnatum*, not *melanosporum*.

Black truffles have an earthy, intense, somewhat winy fragrance. Like white truffles, they are often described as musky—to some, they simply reek of sex. They usually range from dark brown (or even reddish) to black in color, depending on how mature they are: coal black means a ripe truffle. The bumpy skin (peridium) is most often described as warty or faceted, but one writer has aptly compared its texture to that of a dog's nose. The flesh inside is gray or purplish-black, with white veins running throughout. Black truffles are in season from late November through March and are usually at their best from December to March.

Summer Truffles

The summer truffle, *Tuber aestivum*, also called the English—or, occasionally, Saint John's—truffle, suffers somewhat unfairly from comparison to *T. melanosporum*. Although summer truffles are sometimes passed off as black truffles by unscrupulous dealers, they are quite different in both flavor and texture, and, with proper treatment, they come into their own. Summer truffles are also used in many truffle products, including cheeses and butters.

Summer truffles are far more popular in Europe than they are here, and there they are used with relative abandon—a practice made economically feasible by the fact that they are much less expensive than their cousins. Summer truffles are found in Tuscany, Umbria, and the Marches, among other regions in Italy, in France, in parts of southern Germany, and in Spain. Recent yearly harvests have ranged from seventy to eighty tons.

With their nubby black or dark brown skin, summer truffles do resemble black winter truffles at first glance. Their skin is tougher than that of *T. melanosporum*, though, and their flesh is pale beige or putty colored, with thin white veining. When they are sliced, they can be almost crumbly, and they are slightly crisp and nutty tasting.

Summer truffles have a comparatively long season, from May through October. However, they are at their best from late July onward. Harvested too early, they have about as much flavor as Styrofoam, but by late July or August, they start to have more perfume. Late-season summer truffles, from September to the end of October, are by far the most flavorful.

Brumale

Tuber brumale has a variety of confusing common names, including musk truffle and violet or magenta truffle, and an appearance very like that of *T. melanosporum*, although its interior is distinguished by more widely spaced, thicker veins. It grows in most of the same places as its cousin, throughout France, Italy, and Spain. Some brumale have an appealing truffle-musky flavor, but others have almost no fragrance at all, or worse yet, an unpleasant aroma of petroleum; some even have a bitter taste.

The season for brumale is more or less the same as for black winter truffles, but it is rarely seen fresh in this country. It is usually preserved or used in various truffle products, and processing is actually kind to most brumale, mellowing their flavor.

Bianchetti

Tuber albidum, which were until recently classified as *T. borchi*, are most commonly called bianchetti, but other names include spring truffle and Tuscan truffle. In Italy, they are found in Tuscany as well as Emilia-Romagna, Lazio, and as far south as Campania. Unlike black and white truffles, they grow under pine trees rather than broad-leafed varieties.

OREGON TRUFFLES

T. gibbosum, the Oregon white truffle, seems to inspire an impossibly wide range of reactions in those who taste it. Aficionados (James Beard, an Oregon native, was one of them) deem it worthy of comparison to *T. melanosporum*, while others describe it as tasting of petroleum. Mushroom authority Jack Czarnecki argues that because Oregon truffles are fresher than Italian white truffles, which have spent at least a few days in transit, they need to ripen for a few days after picking before they reach their peak. That may be part of it, but it seems likely that the main reason for its variable reputation is that there are actually several different varieties of *T. gibbosum*, each with its own characteristics.

In any case, the various Oregon white truffles, which can be found throughout the Pacific Northwest, do resemble small Italian white truffles in appearance. Their seasons vary according to specific type, but the winter variety, which is the most common at the present time, seems to be at its best in October and November.

Oregon black truffles are not actually members of the *Tuber* genus; instead, they belong to *Leucangium*. Until very recently they were classified as *Picoa carthusiana*, which is a European genus, and that name is still often used. The truffle that is considered to be the best, and the one most frequently harvested, is *L. carthusiana*, but there are several other known varieties in Oregon alone (as well as some, confusingly enough, that actually do belong in *Picoa*). Unlike the *Tuber* family, these "truffles" mature above ground.

Oregon black truffles have a bumpy, warty black exterior and a pale to dark brown interior, with thin white veining. They can be quite large and are often irregularly shaped. They are in season in the fall and winter. According to their fans, the best specimens can be somewhat reminiscent of black winter truffles.

Fresh Oregon truffles are available primarily from specialty purveyors in the regions where they are harvested. They are used raw or heated only briefly.

Although the word *bianchetti* translates literally as "little whites," these are not really white—though they do tend to be small. Early in the season, they look just like *T. magnatum*; later, their color is more likely to be tan or pale brown.

Bianchetti are in season from mid-January through April. Fresh, they are best raw or slightly warmed. Known as the poor man's white truffle in Italy, *T. albidum* are used in a wide variety of truffle products and are often bottled or canned.

Burgundy Truffles

Tuber uncinatum, called *truffe de Bourgogne*, or Burgundy truffle, in France, is found in Lorraine as well as Burgundy. A close relative of the summer truffle, with similar characteristics, it is in season from early October through December.

Himalayan Truffles

Several varieties of truffles are found in the lowland areas along the entire length of the Himalayas, where they grow under pine trees. The most common are *T. indicum* and *T. sinense*; a third variety is *T. himalayense*. Both *T. sinense* and *T. indicum* look like black winter truffles, ranging from chocolate brown to black on the outside. The flavor of these truffles, also called Chinese truffles, varies widely. Some have little taste at all, while others smell like petroleum; *sinense* can leave a bitter aftertaste. Fresh and at their peak, though, they can be quite good. They are best cooked, and they can be an excellent substitute for summer truffles, with less tendency to crumble when sliced.

OAK TREES AND DOGS: HOW TRUFFLES GROW AND ARE HARVESTED

Much of the pervasive mystique

associated with truffles stems from the way they grow and are harvested. Although truffles are related to mushrooms, they are quite different from them in many ways. Rather than a fungus per se, they are actually the fruiting, or reproductive, bodies of various species of what are called mycorrhizal fungi. They grow among the root systems of certain trees, in an unusual symbiotic relationship with the trees, and, unlike mushrooms, they mature underground: no wonder they have been called "the perfume of the earth itself."

Where Truffles Grow

Oak trees are one of the favorite host trees for truffles, but many other broad-leaved trees, including poplars, willows, birches, elms, and certain fruit or nut trees, such as the hazelnut, may shelter truffles within their root systems. Certain species of truffles, such as Himalayan ones, grow under pine trees. Soil conditions are also important, with chalky, humus-y alkaline earth, well aerated to allow the growth of the mycelium (the truffle's filament-like roots), offering the most hospitable environment. Although most truffles are more or less round, the condition of the soil can affect their shape. Rocks and other such impediments will result in lumpy or irregularly shaped truffles, as will compacted soil.

The term *mycorrhiza* refers to the symbiotic relationship between the mycelium of a fungus and the roots of a tree, and mycorrhizae develop as the spidery roots of the truffle become interconnected with the host tree's rootlets. The relationship meets the definition, it is a true, of a symbiotic one, because the truffle does help the tree to absorb nutrients and water from the soil, but most of the benefits are on the side of the truffle, which—dare we say it—acts more like a parasite at times.

With no chlorophyll of its own, the truffle relies on the host tree to provide nutrients, such as carbohydrates and other substances. The aroma and quality of the mature truffle depends, to a greater or lesser extent, on the tree that shelters it. Some say those found under oak trees are the best, with the strongest fragrance; others say that truffles that grow under willow or linden trees are the most aromatic. The flavor of white truffles tends to be the most strongly affected by the particular type of tree.

Eventually trees that serve as hosts to truffles are affected by the relationship and may become stunted or twisted. Nevertheless, truffles often continue to appear under the same trees for as long as seventy years.

How Truffles Grow

Truffles grow over a period of about six to eight months, with most types, other than summer truffles, maturing in the late fall to winter. Generally, truffles thrive in a fairly humid, mild climate, with August's weather in particular being a crucial determinant of their development—rain then, preferably with intermittent heavy storms, and warmth are a sign that the harvest will be good. These are the very conditions a winemaker dreads, and it is an old adage that a great year for truffles is a poor one for wine, and vice versa.

With all that said, truffles are anything but predictable. No one really knows why truffles appear year after year under the same trees but are found fitfully or only briefly in other spots. And that, in turn, helps explain the secretive world of the truffle hunters—the men known as *trifolai* or *tartufai* in Italy, *caveurs* or *les rabassiers* in France. (They are almost always men, though there has been the occasional female truffle hunter.)

The Cult of the Truffle Hunter

Fiercely protective of their knowledge of "truffle terrain," truffle hunters usually work alone, in the dark of night, with no more illumination than a flashlight. Musing on how to spot a truffle hunter, Otwald Buchner, author of *The Joy of Truffles*, says, "Well, at first you can't. His . . . is a clandestine occupation that shuns the limelight and other people. Perhaps," Buchner continues, "you can recognize him by his cunning, his shiftiness. After all, he has to fool his rivals, the taxman, and, from time to time, a customer."

Although the classic image of a truffle hunter is that of a solitary man with his loyal hound, any professional truffle hunter (in Italy, Urbani alone has five thousand *trifolai* searching for their truffles) has at least several dogs along with him. In earlier times, he might have had a trained pig rather than dogs. Pigs, especially sows, were traditionally used for truffle hunting, but they like truffles as much as people do—and feel no compunction about being selfish about their find. Dogs, on the other hand, are just as happy, or happier, to be given a special treat instead once they have located a truffle. And there is also the fact that it's much harder to load a huge pig than a dog into the car.

Actually, Italy banned the use of pigs for truffle hunting in 1975, because they tend to be so destructive of the truffles' habitats. (Wild boars still enjoy their share, however, during truffle season, another factor the truffle hunter has to deal with.) In Sardinia, odd as it seems, goats are sometimes used instead of dogs. (Since goats are known to be voracious and rather undiscriminating eaters, they no doubt indulge in their fair share of truffles.)

Truffle hounds come in many shapes and sizes—there is no favored breed, and they are often mutts. Personality tends to mean more than breed, though spaniels and beagles are familiar companions. (According to a recent article in the *New York Times* on training dogs for the USDA's "Beagle Brigade," which sniffs out suspect foods and other contraband at airports, "there is more difference in scenting ability between individual dogs than between breeds…. Nearly any dog can be trained to detect specific targets using a system of rewards.") Some truffle hunters choose white dogs because they are easier to see at night. Regardless of breed, a well-trained truffle dog is worth anywhere from $2500 to $5000. They are valuable indeed; sadly, in some years there have been distressing reports of truffle hounds being poisoned by unscrupulous truffle hunters.

Once truffle season begins, the hunters revisit the places and trees that have been fruitful before, hoping that *T. magnatum* or *melanosporum* will have flourished there once again. (Jane Grigson wrote of secret maps of truffle grounds handed down from generation to generation.) Discovering new locales depends primarily upon the dogs sniffing them out, but there are a few other things the truffle hunter looks for. One is what is called the *brûlé*, French for "burn"—a circle of scorched-looking earth at the base of a host tree. As truffles grow, they draw up all the nutrients from the soil, leaving little nourishment for most other plant life. But a *brûlé* isn't always an indication that there are truffles lurking underground; sometimes it is just the result of the mycorrhizae zapping the nutrients, with no truffles to show for it.

If there are a lot of truffles and they are large enough, there may be also be cracks in the ground, but this is a less common sign. Swarms of tiny golden flies hovering above the ground may indicate a fragrant cache of black truffles below (but these same insects are not attracted to white truffles, making them even harder to find).

When his dog has made a discovery, the truffle hunter usually takes over, although sometimes the dog may be so well trained it will gently unearth the truffle and carry it in its mouth to its master. If the dog has found a truffle that is too small or scarcely mature, the *trifolau* will carefully replace the soil, leaving the mycorrhizae intact, so that the truffle can continue to grow—something that was impossible in the days when a huge, and determined, sow had made a discovery.

Some truffle hunters have been known to find truffles on their own, without a dog to

A car park. Chill morning mist swirls over the broken asphalt. Two cars emerge out of the gloom. . . . Three men get out. Numbers, prices are muttered. French? Italian? It doesn't matter. Repeatedly the men look round them, probing the mist with their eyes. One of them silently opens the [trunk] of his vehicle. . . . He fishes out a number of plastic bags, out of which the other two extract dark fist-sized nuggets. They inspect them, smell them, turn them over in their fingers, and, satisfied, pat the supplier on the shoulder. Wordlessly, he counts their wad of banknotes and hands over the plastic bags to them. A quick hand-shake, they merge back into their cars and disappear again into the mist and gloom.

—OTWALD BUCHNER, *THE JOY OF TRUFFLES*

guide them. They look first for the telltale "scorched earth," as well as for the truffle flies. Then they get down on their hands and knees to see if they can detect that tantalizing aroma and carefully dig at the promising spot, sometimes using a trowel or small pickax. Dogs, however, make this work much easier, and the harvest of a man searching on his own is not likely to be particularly rewarding.

Dark Alleys and Back Rooms—Truffle Markets

Although there are regular truffle markets held in towns like Périgueux and Bergerac in France and Alba and Asti in Italy, much of the real business takes place out of sight of tourists and any casual buyers, often in the early dawn. Buchner's evocative description of one such transaction could apply to many of these towns—though the truffles are more often wrapped in handkerchiefs or newspaper rather than plastic bags.

Commercial truffle hunters prefer to sell to brokers and other serious buyers, and because the truffle business still tends to operate on a strictly cash basis, the last thing a hunter wants is to attract the attention of the tax authorities. At the more open markets, the truffle sellers are likely to be displaying the smaller, more misshapen of their finds—or to be bemoaning the fact that their search was fruitless. The best of their harvest remains tucked into a jacket pocket or under a lumpy sweater until a serious buyer approaches. Or an independent truffle hunter may turn up at the back door of a restaurant or shop to make his sale. Rumors and secrecy partly determine truffle prices during a given season, and they often fluctuate wildly from day to day.

The most important market in Italy is the one in Alba, which has held an annual truffle fair since the early 1930s. "You know you've come at the right time when your nostrils are assaulted by a wild, intoxicating aroma that perfumes the air," writes Carol Field in *Celebrating Italy*, and, indeed the scent of truffles lingers even after the markets have closed up for the day. Alba still dominates the truffle business, but it is no longer the center of the harvest, and there are fairs and markets held throughout the surrounding regions. Norcia's is an important market, as is that in Aqualagna—which is one of the few in Italy where both white and black truffles can be found for sale. For those traveling to Italy, truffle "hotlines" provide information about the fairs in some towns.

In France, markets are held in towns throughout the Périgord and regions beyond, including, in addition to those in Périgueux and Bergerac, Sarlat, Carpentras, and, especially, the important one at Lalbenque. These, of course, are all celebrating Colette's "jewel sprung from a poverty-stricken soil": the black winter truffle.

DEEP IN THE HEART OF TEXAS: INOCULATED TREES AND OTHER TRUFFLE EXPERIMENTS

Even by the turn of the nineteenth century, the annual truffle harvest was diminishing. Throughout France and Italy, stands of oak trees, under which truffles flourished, were being cut down to provide fuel and building material. Indiscriminate truffle hunters—not to mention wild boars and other such foragers—were destroying the intricate underground root systems that allow truffles to grow. The landscape was changing, and with it the environment, which was no longer so hospitable to the prized tubers. Overharvesting, repeated destruction of truffle environments, and pollution have continued to take their toll. Two hundred years ago, the annual truffle harvest in France reached two thousand tons or more; today, it's a shadow of that, a mere forty tons or so.

From Little Acorns . . .

Not surprisingly given their rarity and value, a lot of people have tried to find a way to raise truffles. Because of their very nature, truffles defy commercial agricultural practices, but there are ways to encourage them to grow. There are two main approaches, the first one dating back to the early nineteenth century. In 1810, with a handful or so of acorns, the enterprising Joseph Talon planted what would become the first "truffle plantation," in the Vaucluse region of France. Six years later, he found truffles under his trees. Talon may have been the first, but he was not the last, to discover that from little acorns not only mighty oaks but also truffles grow, and the practice of planting trees known to be hospitable to truffles eventually was widely adopted.

In the twentieth century, Jacques Pébeyre, following in the footsteps of his father and grandfather, became one of the leading *trufficulteurs* in France, with dozens of acres of oak trees on a farm outside Cahors devoted to truffles. Jacques is known as "the

TRUFFLES IN THE VINEYARD

When the deadly phylloxera infestation virtually destroyed the vineyards of Southwest France in the mid-nineteenth century, many of the devastated growers planted oak trees to replace their grapevines. Grapevines, oddly enough, were known to be hospitable to truffles, in part because the vines do a good job of aerating the soil so the mycorrhizae can develop. Truffles and grapevines like the same type of soil, and they grow in the same climate zones. Before phylloxera, truffles had thrived among the roots of certain grapevines, and some vintners had planted oak trees to help them along. However, it is rare to find truffled vineyards today—one of the main reasons being the truism about a good year for truffles being a poor one for wine, because good weather for truffles spells trouble for grapevines.

king of truffles" in France, and his son Pierre-Jean has joined him, continuing the trufficulture tradition. There are truffle plantations in Spain as well, the largest one on an estate near Soria, about halfway between Madrid and the Pyrenees. More recently, truffle farms have been established in New Zealand and in the Australian province of Tasmania. While some of these plantations still follow the time-honored practice of planting various species of host trees, most of them have also adopted a newer technique.

Texas Hill Country

In the late 1970s, efforts to find a more reliable method—if anything about attempting to "raise" truffles can be referred to as reliable—led to the first experiments with "inoculated trees," or "truffled seedlings." With this technique, seedlings of trees such as oaks or hazelnuts are inoculated with truffle spores before they are planted, in the hope that mycorrhizae will develop and truffles will be the result. The first truffles from inoculated trees were harvested in the Périgord in 1977, and since then inoculated trees have been planted in countries around the world. In fact, today about 35 percent of black winter truffles come from inoculated trees

Although the term "cultivated truffles" is widely used to describe the fruits of truffled trees, or of any type of truffle plantation, it is in some ways an unfortunate one. For these truffles are not "tamer" versions of the real thing, in the way that various mushrooms (or farmed fish, like salmon) are—they are the real thing. They grow from the same spores, and when conditions are right, they are the perfect black diamonds of any truffle lover's dreams.

In France, the Pébeyres are among those who have planted truffled trees. In Italy, the Urbanis, another "truffle dynasty," have been in the forefront of research into truffle cultivation. This is hardly surprising, since Urbani is the largest producer of truffles and truffle products in the world (it was the Urbani family who introduced the first truffles in the United States more than forty years ago). Urbani has a 3700-acre farm in Umbria dedicated to inoculated trees. Their seedlings have been planted in many other countries, including the United States, where there are now several notable truffle farms.

Frank Garland, of Garland Gourmet Mushrooms and Truffles, was one of the first truffle pioneers in America. On his farm in Hillsborough, North Carolina, several hundred trees are hosts to black truffles. A recent harvest produced close to fifty pounds of truffles. North of Santa Rosa, California, there's a successful truffle plantation (started with four hundred Urbani seedlings) that has been harvesting eighty to one hundred pounds of truffles each year. Demand for the truffles from both plantations is high, and most are earmarked for area chefs who have sampled them.

The most ambitious plantation in the United States, however, is one located—somewhat incongruously, it might seem—in Hext, Texas, about a hundred miles northwest of Austin. Hext is situated in the rolling hill country, which, it turns out, has the same climate as central Italy and Provence—traditionally the home of the best truffles. In 1992, partners Roy Carver and Rosario Safina planted 60,000 inoculated hazelnut trees on 180 acres of the T-Bar Ranch. (One of the crops at Carver's original T-Bar in Oregon is wasabi, the so-called "Japanese horseradish," which no one else has been able to raise in this country.) They installed an extensive irrigation system, and soil temperature and moisture are monitored by computer. Irrigation, part of any modern truffle plantation, in effect allows farmers to create the perfect rainy Augusts that truffles love. By the year 2000, the tell-tale rings of *brûlé*, the "burnt earth" indicating mycorrhizal activity, started to appear at the base of the trees on the T-Bar. (The trees, by the way, produced what seemed to be normal hickory nuts—but all the shells were empty, the needed nutrients having been stolen by the subterranean activity of the mycorrhizae.) All the signs are good for a truffle harvest, if not this year, then next.

Who harvests these truffles? You might think there would be a new system to match the sophistication of these computerized plantations. But for the moment, at least, it is still dogs that are doing the hunting. On a successful plantation, where many of the trees are sheltering truffles, their characteristic, haunting fragrance may linger in the air, but dogs are still the best at zeroing in on just where the tubers grow, without needlessly disturbing the soil and root systems. At the T-Bar, Pasquale Scricco, who grew up in the truffle-rich region of Abruzzi but now lives in New Jersey, and his dog Truffle will be leading the hunt.

The success of these experiments notwithstanding, it is unlikely that large-scale production will become a reality. (Lovers of white truffles will be disappointed to hear that farming and inoculation efforts with these have been far from promising.) Truffle plantations and farms have helped ensure that there will continue to be a supply of truffles despite the effects of urbanization, overharvesting, and pollution on their natural habitats. But the mysterious tubers are likely to remain the rare diamonds they have always been.

BUYING, STORING, AND SERVING TRUFFLES

AWAY WITH ALL THIS SLICING, THIS DICING, THIS GRATING, THIS PEELING OF TRUFFLES!... EAT IT ON ITS OWN, SCENTED AND GRAINY-SKINNED, EAT IT LIKE THE VEGETABLE IT IS, HOT AND SERVED IN MUNIFICENT QUANTITIES.

—COLETTE

Although most people know

that truffles are a seasonal delicacy, few think of them as ripening (nor are "ripe" and "underripe" terms we associate with mushrooms, their cousins). But indeed they do ripen and mature throughout their short seasons, and, while timing varies somewhat from year to year, depending on weather and other related factors, each has its peak.

Truffle Seasons

The season for black truffles runs from late November to March. However, they usually aren't ripe much earlier than early to mid-January. Immature black truffles are brownish rather than coal black. Black truffles that look slightly reddish are definitely underripe and should be avoided. The interior of the truffle should be purplish-black to dark gray, and the white veins noticeable and fairly widely spaced. (At truffle markets, responsible sellers may cut a nick in the skin to show the buyer the quality of the inside.) Just as a truffle can be immature, it can also be overripe or past its prime. If left in the ground too long, it can dry out, losing fragrance and flavor, and begin to shrink.

White truffles are in season from late September until December or into January (so that, fortunately, they are still available for New Year's Eve celebrations!). But usually, unless the weather has been particularly damp and cold, they are not at their best until about mid-October. White truffles that are picked earlier, while the ground is still hot and dry, are likely to crumble when sliced. As mentioned earlier, the particular color of a white truffle depends partly on the tree that sheltered it. Pink spots or veining, for example, indicates oak or willow—which some think host the best white truffles.

The season for summer truffles extends from early summer into the fall, beginning in late May or June and running into October or even November. But summer truffles do not reach their peak until the height of summer; early ones have little or no flavor. Starting in July and August, they can be quite good, and they can hold their own throughout the rest of the season. Summer truffles are known for their texture, but when overmature or improperly stored, they can start to resemble dried cork.

Buying Truffles

Any truffle you buy should be fragrant—after all, isn't that much of what you are paying for? The dealer should let you sniff (discreetly) before buying, and you should like what you smell. Truffles should be firm and dry, though not dried out. Sponginess or give indicates age, and either of these is a sign that the truffle may be on the point of spoiling. Fresh truffles should look plump, and white truffles in particular should show no signs of wrinkling. Although the truffles you are likely to come across in the market will generally be fairly clean, some truffle hunters have been known to resort to filling the crevices or cavities of truffles with mud to increase their weight—and selling price—so do look carefully.

Gourmet markets often like to display their truffles on a bed of rice (for more on the truffle-rice connection, see below). That may give them an attractive rustic look, but it also allows the truffles to dry out, and dehydrated truffles will have lost both perfume and weight. If shopping at a specialty market rather than from a mail-order source, choose one that has a truffle-loving clientele and, consequently, a good turnover. You don't want a truffle that has been sitting in the case for days. The manager should be able to tell you when they received the truffles.

Although some restaurant chefs, among others, consider large black and white truffles to be the best, bigger isn't always better. These may have been in the ground too long and have less fragrance and flavor than medium-sized ones.

Storing Truffles

Ideally, truffles should be used within a day or so of purchase, but, properly stored, they will keep for longer: white truffles for three to four days, black winter truffles for up to two weeks, and summer truffles for as long as three weeks. Of course, all are most fragrant when at their freshest.

Storing truffles in rice in a tightly sealed jar is often recommended, but it is not actually a good way to keep them. For one thing, truffles need to "breathe." If they are kept in an airtight container, they may rot. Furthermore, the rice will draw out moisture from the truffles, so they may dry out. And despite assertions to the contrary, the rice will not really become infused with truffle flavor—it may smell of truffles when you remove the truffle, but once you cook the rice, the elusive aroma will have disappeared. The best way to store truffles is wrapped individually in paper towels in a cardboard box, in the coldest part of the refrigerator (even better, tuck a disposable diaper around the wrapped truffles); replace the paper towels daily.

Although "truffled rice" is, for the most part, a myth, you can "truffle" some other ingredients, most notably eggs. Truffles and eggs are a favorite marriage, and if you store a few eggs in the shell together with a fragrant black truffle for even a few hours, or, better yet, for a day or two, the eggs will absorb the truffle's intense fragrance almost magically. You will then have truffled eggs that you can scramble or turn into an omelet, leaving the truffle for another dish (or add some of it to the eggs and save the rest for later). Butter also readily takes on the fragrance of both black and white truffles (for more about homemade truffle butter, see page 33).

If you have a black truffle that must be kept for longer than a week or two, store it in Cognac or other good brandy (or even bourbon, if that is your preference) in a tightly sealed jar in the refrigerator, for up to two months. The brandy, which will become infused with truffle flavor, can be used in the sauce when you do cook the truffle, or it can be added to other sauces as appropriate. The Cognac method is good when you have a few slices or bits of truffle left over; you can also infuse brandy with truffle peelings.

Fresh black truffles can be frozen, although their flavor and texture will suffer (a home freezer is nowhere near as cold as the commercial ones used for flash-freezing truffles, a different matter). Wrap the truffle (or portion of a truffle) well and place it in the coldest part of the freezer; use it within a month.

To Cook or Not to Cook Truffles

Fresh white truffles should never be cooked. They should be warmed, though; gentle heat brings out their intoxicating fragrance, but too much will destroy it. That is why white truffles are usually shaved or grated over a plate of warm pasta, or another dish, after it is set in front of the diner—the better to swoon over them!

Black winter truffles can be served raw, sliced paper-thin and incorporated into salads, for example, but their flavor is usually enhanced when they are warmed or cooked. Long cooking is not generally advised, however, because it will mute their perfume.

Although summer truffles are sometimes cooked, they are at their best raw or just warmed. And because they don't have the overpowering fragrance of white or black truffles, they really should be used in generous amounts. Some chefs boost the flavor of summer truffle dishes by adding truffle juice or garnishing them with truffle oil. Summer truffles are especially good in salads, sliced paper-thin in a shower over dressed greens and tossed with them so they absorb some of the vinaigrette.

Truffles have a remarkable affinity for a wide variety of foods, including some of the most humble. Eggs are one of the most notable, and both black and white truffles appear frequently as their companions. Perhaps because truffles grow underground, they pair well with root vegetables, from the lowly parsnip to potatoes—potatoes and truffles are one of the most satisfying pairings of all. But veal, scallops, and lobsters, as well as chicken also take to truffles, as do certain cheeses—Parmesan and Taleggio, for example—which echo the pungent, earthy flavor.

Although Colette preferred her truffles whole, in noble splendor, even she agreed that they benefited from some fat: "a score or so of smallish strips of bacon, fat, but not too fat, which will give body to the stock [in which the truffles cook]." Fat, from bacon to cream or butter to foie gras, always brings out the flavors of other ingredients. Grated or sliced black truffle simmered briefly in heavy cream makes a delicious sauce, and whole black truffles can be wrapped in pork belly or pancetta before they are baked or roasted. Classic sauce périgueux often contains foie gras in addition to the black truffles that give it its name.

Cleaning and Cutting Truffles

Fresh truffles always need to be cleaned, some more vigorously than others. They may be dusted with soil or have a few bits of earth clinging to them, or there may be sand or grit hiding in their crevices. An unused toothbrush is a handy tool for cleaning truffles. Sometimes a few good swipes with a dry toothbrush are all that is needed; other times, moistening the brush and rinsing it clean as necessary will do the trick. As white truffles are thinner-skinned than black and summer truffles, they should be treated more gently in either case. And sometimes truffles, particularly black ones, will have to be scrubbed under cold running water. Be thorough but as brief as possible.

Once they are cleaned, white truffles are ready to be used. Black and summer truffles may be peeled or not. If bumps or crevices make it difficult to clean these truffles thoroughly, they will need some trimming or peeling, but often it is a simply a matter of personal preference. And keep in mind that its crisp, crunchy texture, including that of the skin, is part of the appeal of a summer truffle.

As is true of garlic, the more finely truffles are cut or sliced, the more flavor they will contribute. Just a quarter-ounce of grated truffle, for example, can perfume an entire dish (see Green Beans with Truffle Cream, page 216). But for many dishes, more generous quantities of truffles, sliced paper-thin, are called for. And because they are used raw, white truffles are almost always shaved or sliced over the dish they will enhance.

To preserve as much of their fragrance and flavor as possible, slice or cut truffles just before you use them. The best tool for slicing truffles is a special cutter with a razor-sharp blade, which allows you to shave the truffle directly over each serving. Available at gourmet markets and from mail-order sources, truffle slicers are not expensive, but the more versatile mandoline or plastic vegetable slicers (especially the Japanese version known as a Benriner) will also do a good job. Depending on the type of slicer you are using, when garnishing a dish, you may have to slice the truffle onto a plate or cutting board, then scatter it over the food. Lacking any of these, a very sharp knife or sharp vegetable peeler will do the job. For chopping, mincing, or julienning truffles, just use a sharp knife. Truffles can be grated with a fine cheese grater, or with the newer rasp-type graters available in many gourmet shops.

TRUFFLE PRODUCTS:
AFFORDABLE LUXURIES

When fresh truffles aren't in season, and even when they are, there is an enticing array of delicious truffle products that you can use in a variety of ways. Many of these are fairly inexpensive, and often just a little—a drizzle of truffle oil or honey, a spoonful of truffle butter—goes a long way, making them a real bargain. Here is a guide to the best of them.

Truffle Oil

Truffle oil is perhaps the most versatile of all truffle products. White truffle oil in particular seems to enhance almost any dish, from simple sautéed potatoes to homemade gnocchi to grilled whole fish. A creamy soup such as cauliflower takes on a new elegance when finished with white truffle oil. Black truffle oil is especially compatible with beef dishes, including carpaccio, and cured meats such as Italian bresaola, but it too can complement a wide range of foods. Both the black and white oil can, of course, be used for a sophisticated vinaigrette (subtly or more strongly flavored with truffle depending on whether or not it's made with some regular olive oil as well).

Although truffle oils can be produced by an extraction process, most are made by infusing oil with the flavor of truffles. Truffle oils made with sunflower, grapeseed, and other oils are available, but the best are those made with olive oil. Pure or blended olive oil makes a better base than extra-virgin, which can overpower the truffle flavor. Truffle oils vary widely in quality. Some "designer" oils provide barely a hint of that heady fragrance, so choose wisely. The best oils are so intense that often only a few drops are all that are needed to perfume a dish.

When adding black or white truffle oil to hot food, it's generally best to use the oil to finish the dish or as a garnish, since heating will diminish its delightful fragrance. Stir the oil into the cooked dish at the last moment and serve immediately, or drizzle it over each serving. If you're in an especially generous mood, you could put a small cruet of truffle oil on the table as a condiment for your guests to pour as they like.

Once opened, bottles of truffle oil should be kept in a cool, dark place, but not refrigerated; chilling congeals the oil and allows the aroma to escape. Stored properly, the oil will keep for one to two months after being opened—but you will likely use it up long before that!

Truffle Butter

To coin a phrase, "almost everything tastes better with truffle butter." Once you've tried it, you may find yourself adding it to practically anything. It can be tossed with hot pasta, used in elegant sandwiches made with prosciutto di Parma, added to hot pan juices for an easy but delicious sauce, or stirred into mashed potatoes and other vegetable purees.

Most truffle butters are made with summer truffles, sometimes with white or black winter truffles or truffle "essence" or juice added. (For recipes for homemade truffle butter, see page 197.) Good-quality truffle butter is so intensely flavorful that it often makes sense, depending on the dish, to "cut" it with some regular butter. Although it is not as delicate as truffle oil, it is best to add the butter toward the end of cooking or just before serving, so it retains all its potency.

Refrigerated, truffle butter will keep well for several weeks. Wrapped in foil and then a heavy-duty plastic bag, it can be frozen for three months or longer—think of a container of truffle butter in your freezer as the ultimate convenience food.

Truffle Cheeses

Delicious "truffled cheeses" are produced in Italy's Umbrian and Piedmont regions. *Formaggio al tartufo* is the general name for truffle cheese; *caciotta al tartufo* indicates a sheep's milk cheese. Most truffle cheeses are made with sheep's milk, but some are a combination of cow's and sheep's milk. In general, these are semisoft cheeses, though some are aged or firmer. Some truffle cheeses are studded—more or less liberally, depending on the producer—with Italian black truffles, others with white truffles and/or summer truffles, or with bianchetti.

A truffled cheese can be served on its own or as part of a cheese plate. For the most intense flavor, allow the cheese to come to room temperature, then cut it into thin slices. Truffled cheese can be used to make an amazing grilled cheese sandwich (see page 45), grated over simple pasta dishes, added to frittatas or omelets, and used in myriad other ways.

Note: In Périgord, you may come across chèvres with black truffles. These are usually, if not always, made with canned truffles or truffle trimmings, and what little truffle flavor these may impart is usually overwhelmed by the goat cheese.

Frozen and Canned Truffles, and Truffle Juice

Flash-Frozen Truffles

A relatively new product, flash-frozen black truffles surpass even the best canned truffles in quality. Frozen at a very low temperature, in a process similar to that used for IQF (individually quick frozen) fruits and packaged in Cryovac, the truffles can be used in most dishes in place of fresh truffles, as well as in any recipe that calls for canned truffles.

Flash-frozen white truffles are also available, but since freezing does affect the texture, these cannot be indiscriminately substituted for fresh white truffles, which are almost always used raw. Frozen white truffles, however, are good in stuffings and fillings, such as those for ravioli, and can be added to sauces.

As long as your freezer is as cold as 10°F (-12°C)—or better yet, 0°F (-18°C) or lower—flash-frozen truffles will keep well for at least two months.

Canned Truffles

There is a wide variety of canned and bottled truffles available, and some are far better than others. The canning process by definition cooks the truffles, so they will always have lost some flavor as well as shrunk in size. Look for the words "1st cooking" on the label—these truffles have been canned in brine and then cooked only long enough to sterilize them. Other canned truffles, in contrast, are cooked first, then canned and subjected to another processing. Also look for the word "extra": this indicates the higher grade, with "first choice" designating the next lower grade; the grade below this will simply be labeled "truffles."

Canned first-cooked whole extra black truffles (*T. melanosporum*) are the best product in this category, with the most flavor and best texture. Other grades of black truffles are also canned or jarred. Canned sliced black truffles are available, as are truffle pieces and what are called "breakings." High-quality canned whole black truffles can be substituted for fresh in many recipes. In general, the pieces and bits are best used as a garnish; they will not have enough flavor or character to carry a whole dish. Do be sure to save the brine, or "juice," from canned or jarred truffles (see below).

White truffles (*T. magnatum*) can also be found canned, usually whole, but sometimes sliced. Summer truffles are available canned whole, in pieces or slices, or as breakings. Jars of white truffle "mélanges" contain *T. magnatum* and bianchetti.

Truffle Juice

Black truffle juice is a favorite of many chefs. It is not, of course, juice extracted from truffles, but brine from preserving them. Truffle juice can add flavor to sauces, broths or soups, and other dishes. It can also be used to intensify the truffle flavor in dishes made with summer truffles. And, as mentioned above, it is found in some truffle butters.

Cans of truffle juice come in various sizes, but if you have more than you need, any extra can be frozen for later use; it will keep for at least a month. A convenient method is to freeze the juice in an ice cube tray, then pop the cubes into a heavy-duty freezer bag; one or two cubes will be enough for most sauces. Save the juice from canned or jarred black truffles in the same way if you are not using it in the dish with the truffles.

Truffle Puree/Truffle Paste

Both black and white truffle purees, also called pastes, are available in tubes. Most contain pureed truffles plus oil. Some white truffle purees are made from bianchetti rather than *T. magnatum*. Just a small amount is enough to flavor a dish; stir a few teaspoons into risotto or whisk into a pan sauce for a finishing touch. Or stir some of either the white or black puree into fonduta (see page 205) if you don't have fresh white truffles on hand.

Once opened, most tubes of truffle puree keep well in the refrigerator for up to two weeks. The puree will still be good after that but will gradually lose its flavor.

Truffle Cream

Good-quality white truffle cream is a wonderfully rich delicacy. Sometimes called truffle fondue, most of these are a combination of truffles (often bianchetti) and cheese, though there are different versions. They can be served straight from the jar, but are often best slightly warmed. Be careful not to overheat them, though, or the texture and flavor will suffer.

For a somewhat retro hors d'oeuvre, a truffle cream made with cheese can be served like traditional Swiss fondue, warm with cubes of bread for dipping. It's also good as a dip for crudités. But it can play a more sophisticated role when spooned over a grilled steak or served alongside roast fillet of beef. Or stir some into comfort foods such as mashed potatoes. Once opened, most truffle creams will keep in the refrigerator for a week or so.

Truffle Sauces and Other Relatives

In addition to truffle purees and white truffle cream, there are many variations on the theme, such as truffled olive and almond puree or porcini cream with truffles. Various prepared truffle sauces are also available, which you may want to add to your pantry for a rainy day.

Truffle Honey

Truffle honey is new to this country, though it has long been a favorite in Umbria and the Piemonte. There are different brands, but most are a mild honey infused with the flavor of white truffles.

Use truffle honey in marinades or for basting grilled game birds, or drizzle it over thinly sliced prosciutto. To end a meal, truffle honey is delicious with a chunk of Parmigiano-Reggiano or a good aged pecorino or other sheep's milk cheese. It makes an unusual accompaniment for a plate of assorted strong cheeses and fruit, or simply with one fruit, such as sliced ripe pears.

Once the jar is opened, truffle honey can be kept in a cool, dark place for at least two weeks, although its fragrance will gradually diminish over time.

Truffle Flour

In an article about truffle flour in the *New York Times*, food writers Matt and Ted Lee called it "a miracle powder," and the innocuous-looking stuff is surprisingly potent. Infused with the aroma of white truffles, the flour can be used more traditionally in doughs for pasta or gnocchi (see page 134) or in crespelle (crepe) batters. But even a quarter-teaspoon or so stirred into a simple pan sauce at the last minute adds a deep truffle fragrance. It can be used as a thickener for sauces and stews, but it should usually be "cut" with regular flour for this purpose.

Truffle flour can also be sprinkled over the filling for homemade ravioli just before sealing the little packages; the dough shields the flour from the heat of the boiling water, and the cooked pasta emerges with an intense taste of truffles. The flour can even be used like a seasoning, sprinkled over a grilled steak or roasted fish at the last minute for a burst of truffle flavor.

Truffle flour comes in glass jars, which should be kept tightly sealed in a cool, dark place. Or store it in the freezer, where it will keep for months.

Truffle Powder

Truffle powder—not to be confused with truffle flour—has nothing of the intensity of porcini powder (there's a reason why you've never seen dried truffles). Skip it, and go for one of the many better choices available.

Truffle Pastas

Specialty markets and mail-order sources offer a variety of truffle pastas. Both fresh and dried are available, from truffled fettuccine or tagliatelle packaged in elegant boxes to frozen tortellini. Some have more flavor than others; you may want to sample a few to find your favorite.

Shaving Truffles

RECIPES

GRILLED VEGETABLES WITH TRUFFLE CREAM, page 64

BEEF TAGLIATA WITH BLACK TRUFFLES, page 172

POUSSIN EN DEMI-DEUIL, page 160

SHIRRED EGG WITH WHITE TRUFFLES AND FINGERLING POTATOES, page 203

BAY SCALLOPS AND FOIE GRAS RAVIOLI WITH
CIPOLLINE BOUILLON AND BLACK TRUFFLES, page 72

PAN-SEARED SALMON WITH TRUFFLED FRENCH LENTILS, page 152

TRUFFLE TARTLETS, page 56

PASTA WITH BROWNED TRUFFLE BUTTER AND FRESH SAGE, page 114

BLACK TRUFFLE RISOTTO WITH LOBSTER AND TRUFFLE BUTTER FROTH, page 130

A Note about the Recipes

You will notice that some of the recipes using fresh truffles specify the weight of the truffle (or truffles), while others simply call for "1 truffle." This is because in certain recipes, a more-or-less precise amount of truffle is essential for the success of the dish (for example, the Scallop-Truffle "Napoleons" with Creamed Leeks, where you need a truffle large enough to give you 20 slices); but in others the amount you use really depends on personal taste, and on your budget. In general, however—and we do include some recipes that use less than these amounts—we suggest a quarter-ounce of white truffle or one-half to an ounce of black truffle per person.

Truffles and Wine

While an aged Barolo is a perfect match with black truffles and white Burgundy pairs beautifully with white truffles, since all the dishes in this book feature truffle flavor, we thought it would be interesting to provide some fresh ideas and a bit of variety. Joseph Scalice is wine director and co-proprietor of March restaurant in New York City, which features the creative cuisine of Chef Wayne Nish, the other proprietor. Tasting menus are featured, and Scalice recommends original choices for each course, the aim being a synergistic effect between the food and the wine. That's why we were delighted that he agreed to select the wines for our truffle recipes.

I have made wine choices that I feel will either underline the flavors of a dish or become a dynamic ingredient in the recipe. Since I have become known for my cutting-edge pairings, some choices may seem a bit unusual, but I think your palate will appreciate what convention may not. I am less concerned with region, producer, and vintage reputation and more concerned with the attributes of the wine itself and how it marries with each dish. I have recommended specific producers and vintages because of what they bring to the table. Some wines may be hard to locate, but if you cannot find a particular label, ask your favorite wine shop to recommend a comparable selection. A lot of the fun is in the experimentation and the discovery of new food and wine sensations.

—JOSEPH SCALICE

APPETIZERS AND SMALL BITES

BAGNA CAUDA WITH WHITE TRUFFLE OIL

DEVILED QUAIL EGGS WITH TRUFFLES

NEW POTATOES STUFFED WITH TRUFFLE AIOLI

MINI GRILLED CHEESE SANDWICHES WITH TRUFFLE CHEESE

TRUFFLED FRICOS

TRUFFLED WHOLE BRIE

CROSTINI WITH CREAMY WHITE TRUFFLE-MUSHROOM TOPPING

CROSTINI WITH GARLICKY WHITE BEAN PUREE

BRUSCHETTA

TRUFFLE BRUSCHETTA WITH TOMATOES AND RED ONION

BRUSCHETTA WITH TALEGGIO CHEESE AND WHITE TRUFFLES

CATALAN TOMATO BREAD

BUTTERY TRUFFLE CRACKERS

A TRIO OF TRUFFLE TARTLETS

TRUFFLE TARTLETS WITH SMOKED SALMON AND CREME FRAICHE

TRUFFLE TARTLETS WITH A MELANGE OF WILD MUSHROOMS

TRUFFLE TARTLETS WITH MASCARPONE AND TRUFFLE PUREE

QUICK PUFF PASTRY BOUCHEES WITH TRUFFLE CREAM

TRUFFLED CHICKEN LIVER PATE

BRANDADE WITH YUKON GOLD POTATOES AND BLACK TRUFFLE

GRILLED VEGETABLES WITH TRUFFLE CREAM

MINI ARANCINI WITH TRUFFLES

FELIDIA'S ASPARAGUS FLANS WITH MORELS AND BLACK TRUFFLE SAUCE

CAULIFLOWER TERRINE WITH BLACK TRUFFLES AND MACHE SALAD

BAY SCALLOPS AND FOIE GRAS RAVIOLI WITH CIPOLLINE BOUILLON AND BLACK TRUFFLES

TRUFFLE-DUSTED SEA SCALLOPS WITH WATERCRESS SALAD AND LEMON VINAIGRETTE

RESTAURANT DANIEL'S TUNA CRUDA WITH BLACK TRUFFLE-ANCHOVY SAUCE

CARPACCIO WITH TRUFFLES

BRESAOLA WITH BLACK TRUFFLE OIL

TRUFFLED COUNTRY PATE

BAGNA CAUDA WITH WHITE TRUFFLE OIL

BAGNA CAUDA, LITERALLY, "HOT BATH," is a popular Italian antipasto, a warm dipping sauce of olive oil, butter, garlic, and anchovies served with chilled cut-up vegetables. It comes from the Piemonte region in the north, and in truffle season, a white truffle is often shaved into the sauce. We prefer to save our fresh truffles for other dishes, adding white truffle oil instead. Serve with your choice of vegetables (see the ideas below) and good crusty bread. SERVES 6 TO 8

½ **cup olive oil** [125 ml]

4 **garlic cloves,** minced

4 to 6 **anchovy fillets**

8 **tablespoons (1 stick) unsalted butter** [125 grams]

1 **tablespoon white truffle oil**

Freshly ground black pepper

VEGETABLES FOR SERVING (CHOOSE AT LEAST THREE):

Celery stalks, cut into 2- to 3-inch-long sticks [5 to 8 cm]

Fennel bulbs, halved, cored, and cut lengthwise into thin strips

Red and/or yellow bell peppers, cored, seeded, and cut into thick strips

New potatoes, cooked in boiling salted water until just tender, drained, cooled, and halved or quartered, depending on size

Cherry tomatoes

Broccoli or cauliflower florets, blanched in boiling salted water for 1 to 2 minutes, drained, and chilled in ice water

Carrots, cut into 2- to 3-inch-long sticks [5 to 8 cm]

Sugar snap peas, tough strings removed, blanched in boiling salted water for about 30 seconds, drained, and chilled in ice water

1. Combine the olive oil, garlic, and anchovies in a small heavy skillet. Warm over very low heat, stirring occasionally and mashing the anchovies with the back of a wooden spoon, until the oil is very fragrant and the anchovies have dissolved, about 5 minutes; do not let the garlic brown.

2. Add the butter and heat, stirring, until it melts. Transfer the sauce to a chafing dish (see Note below) and stir in the truffle oil and pepper to taste.

3. Serve the sauce with the vegetables, providing a small plate and a fork (long-handled ones if you have them) for each guest—and be sure to put out plenty of napkins.

NOTE: If you don't have a chafing dish or a fondue pot lurking in the back of the closet, another way to keep the dip warm is to heat a brick (new or wrapped in foil) in a hot oven for 30 minutes or so. Set it on a trivet or other heatproof surface and put the pan of sauce on top.

SOMMELIER WINE SUGGESTION | Remelluri Blanco 1998; Rioja, Spain

DEVILED QUAIL EGGS WITH TRUFFLES

USING QUAIL EGGS turns this retro favorite into a suave party hors d'oeuvre. You can serve these bite-size tidbits on the optional brioche croutons, or arrange them simply on a platter lined with baby spinach or arugula—or set each one on an individual leaf. Garnish each egg half with slivered black truffle or with chive sticks. Quail eggs are available in Chinese markets and gourmet shops. MAKES 24

6 to 8 slices of brioche, challah, or other egg bread, cut ¼ inch thick [.5 cm] (for croutons; optional)

12 quail eggs

3 tablespoons Truffle Mayonnaise (use any of the versions on page 193), plus about 1 tablespoon more if serving on croutons

1 to 2 teaspoons white or black truffle oil (optional)

Salt and freshly ground white pepper

About 2 teaspoons small slivers black truffle or twelve 1-inch-lengths chives [2.5 cm]

1. If making the croutons, preheat the oven to 325°F [160°C]. Using a 1½-inch [1-cm] round cookie cutter, cut out 24 crustless rounds from the brioche. Place on an ungreased baking sheet and bake for 6 to 8 minutes, until lightly toasted. Let cool.

2. Put the quail eggs in a large saucepan and add cold water to cover by about 1 inch [2.5 cm]. Bring just to a boil, stirring gently several times. Reduce the heat and simmer for 1 minute. Immediately remove from the heat. Let the eggs stand in the hot water for 10 minutes, then drain. Transfer to a bowl, add cold water to cover by several inches, and let stand until cool; drain.

3. To peel the eggs, tap each one sharply several times against a work surface to crack the shell in a few places, then roll the egg under the palm of your hand to help release the egg from the inner membrane. Carefully peel the eggs, rinse off any remaining bits of shell, and pat dry.

4. Cut each egg lengthwise in half. Carefully remove the yolks, and transfer to a small bowl. Add the 3 tablespoons mayonnaise and mash to a smooth paste with a fork or the back of a spoon. Stir in the truffle oil, if desired, and season with salt and pepper to taste.

5. Spoon the egg yolk mixture into a small resealable plastic bag and seal the bag. Cut a small triangle from one of the bottom corners and pipe the mixture into the egg whites, mounding it in the centers. (The eggs can be prepared up to 12 hours ahead and refrigerated.)

6. To serve, if using the croutons, spread a small amount of mayonnaise on each one and set a quail egg on top. Garnish the eggs with the black truffle, arrange on a platter, and serve.

SOMMELIER WINE SUGGESTION Hitorimusume Junmai Daiginjo "Shizuku" Sake; Japan

NEW POTATOES STUFFED WITH
TRUFFLE AIOLI

AIOLI IS A GARLICKY MAYONNAISE that is a staple of Provençal cooking, served with everything from poached fish to grilled vegetables. Our version, made with the addition of truffle oil, pairs seductively with creamy little potatoes for a luscious pick-up hors d'oeuvre. MAKES 24

12 small red potatoes (1½ inches in diameter; about 2 pounds total) [4 cm/1 kg]

Salt and freshly ground black pepper

About ⅔ cup Truffle Aïoli (page 213) [150 ml]

2 tablespoons minced chives

1. Put the potatoes in a large saucepan, add salted water to cover by about 1 inch [2.5 cm], and bring to a boil. Boil gently until tender, 12 to 15 minutes. Drain and let cool.

2. Cut the potatoes crosswise in half. Cut a thin slice from the bottom of each half so it will stand upright. Using a melon baller, remove the center from each potato half, leaving a shell about ¼ inch [.5 cm] thick (reserve the potato pulp for another use, if desired). Season the cavities with salt and pepper. (The potatoes can be prepared to this point several hours in advance, covered loosely, and set aside at room temperature.)

3. Using a small spoon or a pastry bag fitted with a medium star tip, fill the potato cavities with the aïoli. Garnish with the chives and arrange on a platter. (These are best at room temperature, but they can be covered and refrigerated for up to 1 hour; let return to room temperature before serving.)

SOMMELIER WINE SUGGESTION | Domaine Ott Blanc de Blanc 1999; Provence, France

MINI GRILLED CHEESE SANDWICHES WITH TRUFFLE CHEESE

MINIATURE GRILLED CHEESE SANDWICHES are an amusing but irresistible appetizer, and made with truffle cheese, this humble standby goes black tie. Baked rather than cooked on a griddle, these are quick and easy to prepare. MAKES 32

6 tablespoons unsalted or lightly salted butter, at room temperature [90 grams]

16 slices of firm-textured white bread, crusts removed

8 ounces truffle cheese, cut into slices about 1⁄16 inch thick [250 grams/2 mm]

1. Position a rack in the upper third of the oven and preheat the oven to 400°F [200°C]. Line a large baking sheet with aluminum foil.

2. Spread 3 tablespoons of the butter on 8 of the slices of bread. Arrange the remaining 8 slices on a work surface and top with the truffle cheese. Top with the buttered slices of bread, buttered side up, and cut each sandwich on the diagonal to make 4 triangles.

3. Arrange the triangles buttered side down on the prepared baking sheet and brush the remaining 3 tablespoons butter over the tops.

4. Bake for 3 to 4 minutes, or until the tops of the sandwiches are beginning to turn golden brown and the cheese is just starting to melt. Using tongs or a spatula, turn the sandwiches and bake for 3 to 4 minutes longer, until the tops are light golden brown. Arrange on a platter and serve.

SOMMELIER WINE SUGGESTION Sakonnet Vidal Blanc 1999; Rhode Island

TRUFFLED FRICOS

FRICOS ARE CHEESE CRISPS from Friuli, in the northeastern corner of Italy, and they are one of those foods you can't stop eating. Typically made simply with Montasio, a local cow's milk cheese, here they are much enlivened by the addition of truffle cheese. (You cannot make fricos solely with truffle cheese because it tends to be too soft for these crisps.) Montasio can be found in some cheese shops and at Italian grocers; if necessary, you can substitute Asiago or even Parmigiano-Reggiano.

Fricos are traditionally cooked in batches in a skillet or on a griddle. Baking them is much easier and streamlines the process, but be sure to use a nonstick baking sheet or line a regular baking sheet with parchment paper (or a Silpat baking liner if you have one), or they will stick to the pan. Serve the small crisps for nibbling with a chilled white wine. Larger crisps (see the variation below) can be shaped into cups to hold an herbed green salad for an elegant first course. MAKES 32

6 ounces Montasio cheese, grated [180 grams]   **2 ounces truffle cheese,** grated [50 grams]

1. Preheat the oven to 350°F [175°C]. If not using nonstick pans, line 2 large baking sheets with parchment paper.

2. Combine the cheeses in a bowl; toss to mix well. Using 1 tablespoon of the cheese for each crisp, form 2-inch [5-cm] rounds of the grated cheese about 1½ inches [4 cm] apart on the baking sheets.

3. Bake the crisps for 6 to 8 minutes, or until lightly golden and speckled with brown. Do not let them brown too much, or the cheese will become bitter. Let cool on the baking sheets for 1 to 2 minutes to firm slightly, then, using a metal spatula, transfer to paper towels to drain briefly. Serve warm or at room temperature.

VARIATION

FRICO CUPS You will need 4 glasses with a bottom diameter of about 2 inches [5 cm] to mold the cups. Put the glasses upside down on the counter. Make 4 large crisps at a time, using ¼ cup [25 g] cheese for each one and shaping the cheese into 6-inch [15-cm] rounds as directed above. Bake for about 7 minutes, until golden and speckled with brown. Let cool on the baking sheets for 2 minutes, then lift up with a spatula and drape each one over an inverted glass. Let cool completely before removing. Makes 8 cups.

SOMMELIER WINE SUGGESTION Château de Clapier Blanc 1999; Côtes du Lubéron, France

TRUFFLED WHOLE BRIE

THIS SUMPTUOUS PARTY HORS D'OEUVRE comes from our editor, Susan Wyler. For a really special occasion, splurge with a fresh white truffle. Made with white truffle puree rather than fresh truffle, the cheese will still be sublime. Serve with plain crackers or flatbread.

Note that for this recipe, it's important that the Brie be of good quality and properly ripened—an underripe one just will not have the same effect. The rind of a ripe Brie will be stippled with pale beige, rather than pure white, and the cheese should be soft to the touch. Buy it at a good cheese shop or a specialty market, where they will be able to help you choose. SERVES 24 TO 30

8 ounces mascarpone, at room temperature [15 cm]

1 to 1½ ounces fresh white truffle, finely minced, or 2 ounces white truffle puree or paste [30 to 45 grams/60 grams]

One 8½-inch wheel of Brie (about 2 pounds) [22 cm/1 kg]

1. Combine the mascarpone and minced truffle (or truffle puree) in a small bowl. Blend well, so that the truffle flavor is evenly distributed.

2. Using a long sharp knife, split the Brie horizontally in half. Spread the truffle mixture evenly over the bottom half of the cheese, leaving a ¼-inch [.5-cm] border all around. Replace the top half of the Brie and press down gently so it sits snugly on the bottom. If any of the filling leaks out, use a spatula or a fingertip to smooth the sides of the cheese. Wrap the cheese in plastic wrap and refrigerate for 4 days.

3. Let the cheese stand at room temperature for at least 3 hours before serving.

SOMMELIER WINE SUGGESTION René Bouvier, Marsannay Blanc 1998; Côte de Nuits, France

CROSTINI WITH CREAMY WHITE TRUFFLE-MUSHROOM TOPPING

A RICH MUSHROOM CREAM turns ordinary little toasts into a treasure, but you will find this simple paste an easy indulgence you can turn to whenever you crave a little something special to top eggs, baked potatoes, vegetables, or whatever you please. The amount of white truffle is up to you; you may even wish to enhance it with a few drops of white truffle oil—or, for daily indulgence, just substitute white truffle oil for the fresh truffle. SERVES 6 TO 8

1 tablespoon unsalted butter [15 grams]

1 shallot, finely chopped

8 ounces wild or cultivated mushrooms, trimmed, cleaned, and finely chopped [250 grams]

1 tablespoon Cognac or other brandy

¼ cup mascarpone [60 ml]

1 teaspoon chopped thyme

Salt and freshly ground black pepper

1 fresh white truffle, minced

White truffle oil (optional)

Crostini (recipe follows)

1. Melt the butter in a medium skillet over moderate heat. Add the shallot and cook, stirring, until softened, 1 to 2 minutes. Stir in the mushrooms and cook until the liquid they release has evaporated, about 5 minutes.

2. Add the Cognac and cook until most of it has evaporated, 2 to 3 minutes. Remove from the heat and let cool for 10 minutes.

3. Scrape the mushroom mixture into a food processor or blender. Add the mascarpone and thyme and process until well blended. Season with salt and pepper to taste. Add the truffle (and truffle oil, if using) and pulse until evenly distributed. (This makes about 1 cup [250 ml] truffle paste. It can be refrigerated in a tightly covered container for up to 4 days. Let return to room temperature before serving.)

4. Spread the mushroom paste on the crostini, arrange on a platter, and serve.

SOMMELIER WINE SUGGESTION | Colonarra Cupramontara Verdicchio Classico Cuprese 1998; Marches, Italy

CROSTINI

These little toasts can be made up to 3 days in advance and stored in an airtight container at room temperature. MAKES 24

24 slices of baguette, cut ¼ to ⅜ inch thick [.5 to 1 cm]

¼ cup extra-virgin olive oil [60 ml]

1. Preheat the oven to 400°F [200°C].
2. Arrange the bread on a baking sheet and brush generously with the olive oil. Bake for 5 to 7 minutes, until lightly toasted and golden brown. Let cool before using.

CROSTINI WITH GARLICKY WHITE BEAN PUREE

IT'S NOTHING SHORT of a Cinderella story: Shave a bit of white truffle over warm mashed white beans (a favorite crostini topping throughout Italy), and you've got an appetizer fit for Prince Charming. But on days when the glass slipper doesn't quite fit, white truffle oil will also effect a magical transformation on the rustic bean puree. SERVES 6 TO 8

1 tablespoon unsalted butter [15 grams]

1 tablespoon extra-virgin olive oil

1 garlic clove, minced

Pinch of crushed hot pepper flakes

1½ cups cooked cannellini beans or 1 can (about 15 ounces) cannellini beans, rinsed and drained [250 grams/425 grams]

1 teaspoon fresh lemon juice, or to taste

Salt and freshly ground black pepper

Crostini (page 49)

1 fresh white truffle or white truffle oil

1. Preheat the oven to 325°F [160°C].

2. Melt the butter with the olive oil in a medium skillet over moderately low heat. Add the garlic and hot pepper and cook, stirring, until the garlic is fragrant, about 30 seconds. Add the beans and lemon juice and cook, stirring and breaking up the beans with a wooden spoon (mash them gently, leaving some of them whole—the puree should remain somewhat coarse) until well blended and heated through, 3 to 5 minutes. Season with salt and pepper to taste and add additional lemon juice if needed. Remove from the heat.

3. Meanwhile, place the crostini on a baking sheet and heat in the oven until warmed through, about 5 minutes.

4. Spread about 2 teaspoons of the warm bean mixture over each crostini. Shave a sliver of truffle over each one (or drizzle with truffle oil). Arrange on a platter and serve warm or at room temperature.

> **SOMMELIER WINE SUGGESTION** | E. Burn, Pinot Blanc 1997; Alsace, France

BRUSCHETTA

BRUSCHETTA IS THE ORIGINAL GARLIC BREAD: thick slices of crusty country bread, grilled over a wood fire just until crisp on the outside, rubbed liberally with garlic, and drizzled with olive oil—or, in this case, truffle oil. The basic recipe can be served as is, like garlic bread, as an accompaniment to a meal, but the toasts take well to a variety of toppings, from a rustic tomato and red onion mixture to an indulgent white truffle and cheese combo. If serving the bruschetta plain, opt for the thicker slices of bread; if topping the bread, you may want to use ½-inch [1-cm]-thick slices. When serving bruschetta on its own, you will want two slices (at least) per person; with most toppings, one toast makes a good appetizer portion. MAKES 8

8 slices of good country bread, cut ½ to ¾ inch thick [1 to 2 cm]

3 garlic cloves, halved

2 teaspoons black truffle oil, or more to taste

Coarse sea salt, kosher salt, or fleur de sel

1. Prepare a moderately hot fire in a grill or preheat the broiler.

2. Place the bread on the grill or on a baking sheet under the broiler about 4 inches [10 cm] from the heat and toast, turning once, until lightly golden on both sides, 1 to 2 minutes per side.

3. Immediately rub one side of the warm slices of toast with the garlic cloves. Drizzle generously with the truffle oil, and sprinkle lightly with salt. Serve warm.

VARIATION

BRUSCHETTA WITH BLACK TRUFFLE PUREE Omit the truffle oil. Drizzle the toasts lightly with good olive oil, then spread ½ teaspoon black truffle puree or paste on each one and sprinkle with salt.

| SOMMELIER WINE SUGGESTION | Bortoluzzi "Isanzo del Friuli," Pinot Grigio 2000; Friuli, Italy

TRUFFLE BRUSCHETTA WITH TOMATOES AND RED ONION

CHOPPED TOMATOES with red onion and parsley is a traditional topping for these toasts in Italy, but here truffle puree adds another dimension. Be sure to use ripe heirloom or other flavorful tomatoes.

SERVES 4

2 ripe medium tomatoes, halved, seeded, and diced

1 tablespoon minced red onion

1 packed tablespoon minced flat-leaf parsley, plus extra for garnish

Salt and freshly ground black pepper

4 Bruschetta with Black Truffle Puree (page 51), still warm

1. Combine the tomatoes, onion, and parsley in a small bowl and stir gently to mix. Season with salt and pepper to taste. (The topping can be made up to 2 hours in advance, covered, and set aside at room temperature.)

2. Spoon the tomato topping onto the bruschetta, mounding it slightly. Garnish with chopped parsley and place on individual plates. Serve with forks and knives.

SOMMELIER WINE SUGGESTION Serringer Schloss Saarsteiner Spätlese 1999; Germany

BRUSCHETTA WITH TALEGGIO CHEESE AND WHITE TRUFFLES

TALEGGIO IS A STRONGLY FLAVORED Italian soft-ripened cheese that will appeal to anyone who loves Reblochon or Pont l'Evêque. For a less regal but still delicious variation, omit the fresh truffle and drizzle white truffle oil over the toasts. Or, if you're feeling especially extravagant, omit the cheese and shave a generous shower of white—or black—truffle directly over the still-warm bruschetta, as they do in some parts of Italy when the harvest is in full swing. SERVES 4

4 ounces Taleggio, rind trimmed cheese thinly sliced [120 grams]

Bruschetta (page 51), prepared with mild olive oil instead of truffle oil

½ to ¾ ounce fresh white truffle [15 to 25 grams]

1. Preheat the broiler. Arrange the cheese slices on the bruschetta, covering the toasts. Place on a baking sheet and broil just until the cheese is warm and beginning to melt, 1 to 2 minutes.

2. Transfer the bruschetta to serving plates. Shave the truffle over the toasts and serve immediately.

SOMMELIER WINE SUGGESTION   La Casuccia Chianti Classico 1994; Tuscany, Italy

CATALAN TOMATO BREAD

KNOWN THERE AS *PA AMB TOMAQUET,* tomato bread is served all over Spain's Catalonian region as a tapa. It is also nibbled on as a snack, or even used to make sandwiches. There are countless individual versions, but good ripe tomatoes are always essential. In Spain, a fruity olive oil is used for drizzling—but since tomato bread could be thought of as a Spanish version of bruschetta, there's no reason not to finish it off with Italian black truffle oil.

The bread is often topped with slivers or slices of serrano or other cured mountain ham or with salt-cured anchovies. Add one of these, or even thinly sliced prosciutto if you like, before drizzling on the truffle oil. MAKES 8

8 slices of good country bread, cut ½ inch thick [1 cm]

2 garlic cloves, halved

2 medium or 4 small ripe tomatoes, halved crosswise

1 to 2 teaspoons black truffle oil, or more to taste

Salt and freshly ground black pepper

1. Prepare a moderately hot fire in a grill or preheat the broiler.
2. Place the bread on the grill or on a baking sheet under the broiler and toast, turning once, until golden brown on both sides, 1 to 2 minutes per side.
3. Immediately rub one side of the warm slices of toast with the garlic cloves. Rub the toasts with the cut sides of the tomatoes (using ½ medium tomato for each 2 slices, or ½ small tomato per toast), squeezing the tomatoes so the bread absorbs the juices and is coated with a thin layer of pulp and a few seeds (discard the tomato skins).
4. Drizzle with the truffle oil, and season generously with salt and with pepper. Serve warm.

SOMMELIER WINE SUGGESTION | Bodegas Dios Baco Fino Sherry; Jerez, Spain

BUTTERY TRUFFLE CRACKERS

SERVE THESE UNUSUAL, delectable crackers with drinks, or put out a small basket of them to accompany soup. They are easy to make—mix, freeze, and then just slice and bake—and the dough will keep for at least 2 weeks in the freezer, ready for unexpected guests. MAKES ABOUT 36

1¼ cups all-purpose flour [150 grams]

½ teaspoon salt

½ cup finely shredded (not grated) Parmigiano-Reggiano [25 grams]

4 tablespoons truffle butter, cut into ½-inch cubes and chilled [60 grams/1 cm]

4 tablespoons unsalted butter, cut into ½-inch cubes and chilled [60 grams/1 cm]

¼ cup milk [60 ml]

1. Combine the flour and salt in a food processor and pulse to blend. Add the cheese and pulse briefly to mix. Scatter both butters over the flour and pulse 10 to 15 times, until the butter is in pea-sized and smaller pieces. Add the milk and pulse until the dough just starts to come together.

2. Turn the dough out onto a sheet of plastic wrap. Wrap loosely in the plastic wrap and gently knead for a few seconds, just until it comes together. Shape the dough into a 9-inch [23-cm] log about 1½ inches [4 cm] in diameter, and wrap in the plastic. Freeze for at least 2 hours, or until firm. (Well-wrapped, the dough can be frozen for up to 2 weeks.)

3. Preheat the oven to 350°F [175°C]. Using a sharp knife, cut the dough into ¼-inch [.5-cm]-thick slices and place 1 inch [2.5 cm] apart on ungreased heavy baking sheets.

4. Bake for 12 to 14 minutes, or until the edges of the crackers are deep golden brown; do not underbake. Transfer the baking sheets to wire racks to cool for 2 to 3 minutes, then transfer the crackers to the racks and let cool completely. Store in an airtight container at room temperature.

SOMMELIER WINE SUGGESTION | A. Lageder "Kolbenhof" Gewürztraminer 2000; Alto Adige, Italy

A TRIO OF TRUFFLE TARTLETS

YOU CAN FILL THESE DELECTABLE truffle-butter tartlet shells with any number of fillings. In addition to the three we offer here, you might try a creamy savory mousse or pâté, such as the Truffled Country Pâté on page 80, or even a dollop or two of ripe Brie. The fillings in the recipes below each make enough for 24 tartlets, but you could halve the amounts and serve two types (or, of course, make more tartlet shells to fill for a larger gathering).

TRUFFLE TARTLETS WITH SMOKED SALMON AND CREME FRAICHE

Crème fraîche is a traditional accompaniment to smoked salmon. Here we've combined finely chopped salmon with crème fraîche and chives to make an easy tartlet filling. (If you can't get crème fraîche, you can substitute sour cream.) MAKES 24

⅔ **cup crème fraîche** [150 ml]

2 ounces thinly sliced smoked salmon, finely chopped [60 grams]

1½ teaspoons minced chives, plus extra for garnish

Salt and freshly ground white pepper

24 mini-tartlet shells made with Truffle-Butter Tart Dough (page 58), baked and cooled

1. Combine the crème fraîche, smoked salmon, and chives in a small bowl. Stir to mix well. Season with salt and white pepper. Cover and refrigerate for 1 hour, or until the filling has thickened slightly.

2. Taste the filling and add additional salt and/or white pepper if necessary. Spoon a generous teaspoon of the filling into each tartlet shell and garnish with minced chives. Serve immediately.

SOMMELIER WINE SUGGESTION Cristalino Jaume Serra Cava Brut NV; Rioja, Spain

TRUFFLE TARTLETS WITH A MELANGE OF WILD MUSHROOMS

Almost any kind of mushroom works well for this filling—morels or porcini would be sublime on their own, or choose a combination of whatever looks best at the market, preferably a mix of wild and cultivated. Cremini and oyster mushrooms are a good duo, but even a sauté of just cremini will be good; also try chanterelles, portobellos, shiitakes, or other more exotic varieties. Depending on the type of mushrooms you use, you may have a bit of filling left over—save it to add to an omelet or stir into sautéed green beans. MAKES 24

1½ tablespoons unsalted butter [25 grams]

1 large garlic clove, minced

8 ounces mixed wild and cultivated mushrooms, or a single type (see above), trimmed (stems discarded if using shiitakes), cleaned, and cut into ¼-inch dice [250 grams/.5 cm]

⅛ teaspoon salt

A generous pinch of freshly ground black pepper

1 tablespoon minced flat-leaf parsley or 1 teaspoon thyme leaves

1½ teaspoons white truffle oil

24 mini-tartlet shells made with Truffle-Butter Tart Dough (page 58), baked and cooled

1. Preheat the oven to 350°F [175°C].

2. Melt the butter in a large skillet over moderate heat. Add the garlic and cook, stirring, until fragrant, about 1 minute. Add the mushrooms, season with the salt and pepper, and cook, stirring occasionally, until they release their liquid, 1 to 2 minutes. Increase the heat to moderately high and cook, stirring frequently, until most of the liquid has evaporated. Stir in the parsley and adjust the seasoning if necessary. Remove from the heat, and stir in the truffle oil.

3. Arrange the tartlet shells on a baking sheet. Spoon about 1 teaspoon of the mushroom filling into each tartlet shell and place in the oven for 3 to 5 minutes, until the tartlet shells are warm and the filling is hot. Serve warm.

> **SOMMELIER WINE SUGGESTION** Cristalino Jaume Serra Cava Brut NV; Rioja, Spain

TRUFFLE TARTLETS WITH MASCARPONE AND TRUFFLE PUREE

If you don't happen to have truffle puree on hand, make an herbed mascarpone filling instead by adding 1½ tablespoons finely minced fresh basil, or a combination of herbs such as basil and chives, to the mascarpone; season well, cover, and refrigerate for about an hour to allow the flavors to mellow before using. MAKES 24

⅔ cup mascarpone [150 ml]

1 teaspoon white truffle puree or paste

Salt and freshly ground white pepper

24 mini-tartlet shells made with Truffle-Butter Tart Dough (recipe follows), baked and cooled

1. Combine the mascarpone and truffle puree in a small bowl, stirring until well blended. Season with a generous amount of salt and with white pepper.

2. Spoon a generous teaspoon of the filling into each tartlet shell, and serve immediately.

> SOMMELIER WINE SUGGESTION   O. Raffault "Champ-Chenin" Chinon Blanc 2000; Loire, France

TRUFFLE-BUTTER TART DOUGH

A wide variety of fillings can be used with this fragrant truffle-flavored dough, which turns even a simple savory tart into an extraordinary appetizer or first course. Our Trio of Tartlets (page 56) offers several ideas. The pastry is so delicious you may want to roll out and bake any scraps of dough to nibble on as a cook's treat. MAKES 24 MINI-TARTLET SHELLS OR ONE 9-INCH [23-CM] TART SHELL

1¼ cups all-purpose flour [150 grams]

½ teaspoon salt

3 tablespoons truffle butter, cut into ½-inch cubes and chilled [45 grams/1 cm]

3 tablespoons unsalted butter, cut into ½-inch cubes and chilled [45 grams/1 cm]

2 to 3 tablespoons ice water

1. Combine the flour and salt in a food processor and pulse to blend. Scatter the truffle butter and unsalted butter over the flour and pulse 10 to 15 times, until the butter is in pea-sized and slightly smaller pieces. Add 2 tablespoons ice water and pulse until the dough just starts to come together, adding up to 1 tablespoon more ice water, 1 teaspoon at a time, if necessary. Do not overprocess; the dough should not form a ball in the machine, or the pastry will be tough.

2. Turn the dough out onto a work surface and gather it together in a ball.

   IF MAKING TARTLET SHELLS, shape the dough into a cylinder about 1 inch [2.5 cm] thick.

   IF MAKING A TART SHELL, shape the dough into a disk. Wrap the dough in plastic wrap and refrigerate for at least 30 minutes, or until firm. (The dough can be made up to 1 day ahead; if necessary, let soften briefly at room temperature before proceeding.)

3. TO MAKE INDIVIDUAL TARTLET SHELLS, set out two 12-cup mini-muffin pans. Cut the cylinder of dough in half, then cut each half into 12 equal pieces. Roll each piece into a ball and flatten between your palms into a round about 2 inches [5 cm] in diameter. Fit 1 round into each muffin cup, pressing the dough gently up the sides with your fingertips so that it reaches the rim of the cup; trim off any excess dough if necessary. Refrigerate for 15 to 30 minutes, until the dough is firm.

   TO MAKE A LARGE TART SHELL, roll out the dough on a lightly floured surface to a 12-inch [30-cm] round. Fit the dough into a 9-inch [23-cm] fluted tart pan with a removable bottom, without stretching it. Run the rolling pin over the top of the tart pan to remove any excess dough. Refrigerate for 20 to 30 minutes, until the dough is firm.

4. Preheat the oven to 350°F [175°C] for tartlet shells, 375°F [190°C] for a tart shell.

5. TO BAKE TARTLET SHELLS, prick the bottom of each shell 2 or 3 times with a fork. Bake for 15 to 17 minutes, until the shells are light golden brown. Transfer the pans to wire racks and let cool. (The tartlet shells can be made ahead and stored in an airtight container at room temperature for up to 1 day.)

   TO BAKE A TART SHELL, line the shell with aluminum foil. Fill it with dried beans, rice, or pie weights. Bake for 15 minutes. Remove the foil and weights and bake for 8 to 10 minutes longer, or until the dough is light golden brown. Transfer the tart pan to a wire rack and let cool. (The tart shell can be made ahead and stored, well wrapped, at room temperature for up to 1 day.)

QUICK PUFF PASTRY BOUCHEES
WITH TRUFFLE CREAM

A WARM PUFF PASTRY SHELL, known in French as a *bouchée,* makes an appropriately snazzy receptacle for a dollop of truffle cream. Some bakeries carry freshly baked bouchées, but these little "mouthfuls" (the literal translation of their name) are easily made from prepared puff pastry. Sheets of frozen all-butter puff pastry are available at gourmet shops and some upscale grocery stores. MAKES ABOUT 30

1 package (14 ounces) frozen all-butter puff pastry, thawed as directed on the package [400 grams]

About ⅓ cup truffle cream or fonduta [70 ml]

1. Line a baking sheet with parchment paper. On a lightly floured work surface, roll out the dough to about ⅛ inch [3 mm] thick. Using a 1½-inch [4-cm] biscuit cutter or round cookie cutter, cut out as many rounds as you can and arrange 1 inch [2.5 cm] apart on the lined baking sheet. Refrigerate the pastry rounds until firm, about 15 minutes.

2. Using a ¾-inch [2-cm] biscuit or round cookie cutter, make an indentation in the center of each pastry round, being careful not to cut all the way through the dough. Refrigerate until firm, 10 to 15 minutes.

3. While the pastry is chilling, preheat the oven to 375°F [190°C].

4. Bake the pastry rounds for 12 to 15 minutes, until puffed and golden brown. Transfer the baking sheet to a wire rack. Using a small fork or the tip of a sharp knife, remove the puffed lids from the warm bouchées; set aside. Remove and discard the soft centers from the pastry shells, and arrange the shells on a serving platter.

5. Spoon a heaping ½ teaspoon truffle cream into each warm pastry shell and replace the lids. Serve at once.

NOTE: The bouchées can be baked well in advance. Let cool on a rack, then store in an airtight container at room temperature for up to 2 days. Or freeze, well wrapped, for up to 2 weeks. Before serving, arrange the bouchées, with their lids, on a baking sheet and place in a preheated 375°F [190°C] oven for about 5 minutes, or about 7 minutes if frozen, until hot and crisp.

SOMMELIER WINE SUGGESTION Au Bon Climat Pinot Blanc 1999; California

TRUFFLED CHICKEN LIVER PATE

ONE DISTINCTIVE QUALITY of this chicken liver pâté is its relative leanness—just a tablespoon each of butter and oil in place of the usual stick of butter. Just a tad of white truffle puree, however, adds plenty of richness. For a slightly more traditional version, you could substitute minced black truffle for the puree. Serve on Crostini (page 49) or crackers. SERVES 6 TO 8

1 tablespoon unsalted butter [15 grams]

1 tablespoon olive oil

½ cup finely chopped onion [70 grams]

8 ounces chicken livers, rinsed and trimmed [250 grams]

¼ cup dry Marsala [60 ml]

½ teaspoon white truffle puree or paste

Salt and freshly ground black pepper

1. Melt the butter with the olive oil in a large skillet over moderate heat. Add the onion and cook, stirring, until softened, about 3 minutes. Increase the heat to moderately high, add the chicken livers, and cook, stirring occasionally, until lightly browned but still slightly pink inside, about 5 minutes.

2. Increase the heat to high and pour in the Marsala. Cook, stirring and scraping up the browned bits from the bottom of the pan, until all but about 2 teaspoons of the liquid has evaporated. Transfer to a medium bowl and let cool for 10 minutes.

3. Using the tines of a fork, mix the truffle puree into the chicken livers, coarsely crushing them. Continue mixing until a coarse paste forms. Season with salt to taste and a generous amount of pepper. Cover and refrigerate for at least 30 minutes to blend the flavors. (The pâté will keep well for up to 2 days.)

SOMMELIER WINE SUGGESTION Dole Balavaud "Germaine-Balavaud" 1997; Valais, Switzerland.

BRANDADE WITH YUKON GOLD POTATOES AND BLACK TRUFFLE

BRANDADE IS A MUCH-LOVED Provençal specialty made with salt cod, olive oil, and mashed potatoes. Adding a sliced black truffle to the creamy puree makes it especially luscious. Serve with crostini, garlic toast, or breadsticks for dipping or spreading. Salted and dried cod can be found in Italian or Spanish markets, as well as some fish markets and supermarkets; *baccalà* is the Italian name, *bacalao* the Spanish. It is sometimes packed in little wooden crates. Salt cod is sold as whole fillets or portions of fillets, with the skin or not; skinless salt cod is easier to prepare. Look for fish that is white (not grayish, an indication of age), and choose thicker fillets or pieces, rather than the thinner tail sections. Be sure to soak it as directed to soften the fish and remove the excess salt, leaving it with its clean distinctive taste. SERVES 8 TO 10

1 pound boneless, skinless salt cod
[500 grams]

1 medium onion, halved

1 bay leaf

12 ounces Yukon Gold or russet potatoes,
peeled and cut into ¾-inch chunks [350 grams/2 cm]

2 to 3 garlic cloves, coarsely chopped

⅓ cup extra-virgin olive oil [70 ml]

¼ cup heavy cream [60 ml]

Freshly ground white pepper

1 black truffle, cut into julienne strips

1. Put the cod in a colander, set in the sink, and rinse under cold running water for 5 minutes. Transfer to a bowl, cover with cold water, and refrigerate for 24 hours, changing the water at least 3 times.

2. Rinse the cod thoroughly and cut it into 4 or 5 pieces. Place in a large saucepan and add the onion, bay leaf, and enough cold water to cover by 1 inch [2.5 cm]. Bring to a boil over moderately high heat, reduce the heat to low, and cook until the cod is opaque throughout and flakes easily, about 10 minutes. With a slotted spoon, remove the cod and set aside.

3. Add the potatoes to the cooking liquid and bring to a boil over moderately high heat. Cook until the potatoes are tender when pierced with the tip of a sharp knife, about 15 minutes. Drain; discard the onion and bay leaf.

4. Preheat the oven to 425°F [220°C]. Lightly butter a 9-inch [23-cm] gratin dish or other shallow ovenproof serving dish.

5. Combine the cod and garlic in a food processor and pulse until the cod is finely ground. With the machine on, gradually add the olive oil, processing until blended. Add the potatoes and pulse just until blended (do not overprocess, or the potatoes will become gluey). Add the cream and pulse once or twice, just to blend. Season with pepper to taste, then transfer the brandade to a bowl and stir in the truffle.

6. Scrape the brandade into the prepared dish and smooth the top. Bake for about 15 minutes, until lightly browned on top and heated through. Serve hot.

SOMMELIER WINE SUGGESTION Clos Ste. Madeleine Cassis Blanc 1998; Provence, France

GRILLED VEGETABLES WITH TRUFFLE CREAM

GRILLED VEGETABLES with truffle cream for drizzling or dipping are a perfect easy summer appetizer, or serve them as a side dish with steak or other simple grilled meats. Add other favorite vegetables to the mix, if you like. Any leftover vegetables make great open-faced sandwiches—drizzle slices of crusty bread with olive oil, top with the vegetables, and run under the broiler for a minute or so, then spoon some truffle cream over each one. SERVES 4

2 red or yellow bell peppers (or one of each)

2 zucchini, cut lengthwise into ¼-inch-thick slices [.5 cm]

2 yellow squash, cut lengthwise into ¼-inch-thick slices [.5 cm]

2 tablespoons olive oil, plus extra for brushing

2 tablespoons finely minced basil

Salt and freshly ground black pepper

1 small red onion

2 large portobello mushroom caps

2 ripe tomatoes, cut in half

4 to 8 thick slices of crusty bread

½ cup truffle cream or fonduta [125 ml]

1. Prepare a hot fire in a grill.

2. Place the peppers on the grill and grill, turning occasionally, for about 10 minutes, or until charred on all sides. Transfer to a medium bowl, cover tightly with plastic wrap, and set aside to steam and cool for about 10 minutes.

3. Meanwhile, combine the zucchini and yellow squash on a large deep platter. Drizzle the oil over the slices, tossing to coat, then sprinkle with 1½ tablespoons of the basil and season with salt and pepper to taste; toss again.

4. Cut the onion lengthwise in half, then cut each half into 4 wedges, keeping the wedges attached at the root end. Brush the onion, portobellos, and tomatoes with olive oil and season with salt and pepper to taste.

5. To grill the vegetables, arrange the zucchini, yellow squash (set the platter aside), and onion on the grill and grill, turning occasionally, until lightly charred and tender, 10 to 12 minutes for the zucchini and yellow squash, 7 to 9 minutes for the onion. Place the mushrooms gill side down

on the grill and grill, turning once or twice, until juicy and tender, 5 to 7 minutes. Add the tomatoes cut side down and grill just until lightly charred, about 2 minutes, then turn and cook for 2 minutes longer, or until softened. As the vegetables are done, put them on the platter and cover loosely with foil to keep them warm.

6. Meanwhile, once the bell peppers have cooled slightly, pull off the skin. Cut them lengthwise in half and remove the core and seeds, then cut into ½-inch [1-cm]-wide strips; set aside.

7. Shortly before all the vegetables are done, brush the bread on both sides with olive oil and grill, turning once, until toasted. Heat the truffle cream in a small saucepan over low heat, stirring frequently, just until warm, then transfer to a small serving bowl.

8. While they are still warm, cut the portobellos into quarters. Cut the onion wedges apart. Arrange all the vegetables on the platter. Serve with the truffle cream and grilled bread.

SOMMELIER WINE SUGGESTION | Alban "Central Coast" Viognier 1999; California

MINI ARANCINI WITH TRUFFLES

YOU COULD ALMOST THINK of this as deep-fried risotto. Adding the essence of aromatic truffle to these miniature croquettes (their name means "little oranges" in Italian) makes this classic Sicilian appetizer hard to resist. Serve on small plates with forks. MAKES 24 TO 30

8 cups chicken stock, or 2 to 3 cans (14½ ounces each) low-sodium chicken broth plus enough water to make 8 cups [2 liters/400 gram cans]

8 tablespoons (1 stick) unsalted butter [125 grams]

1 small onion, minced

2 cups Arborio, Carnaroli, or Vialone Nano rice [400 grams]

½ teaspoon salt

1 tablespoon extra-virgin olive oil

¼ cup homemade or canned tomato puree or sauce [60 ml]

¾ cup freshly grated Parmigiano-Reggiano [40 grams]

2 large eggs, beaten

Freshly ground black pepper

1 cup finely diced Italian Fontina or mozzarella cheese (about 4 ounces) [120 grams]

2 teaspoons black truffle puree or paste

2 cups dry bread crumbs, plus extra if needed [150 grams]

About 6 cups peanut oil or other oil for deep-frying [1.5 liters]

1. Bring the stock to a simmer in a large saucepan. Reduce the heat to low and keep warm.

2. Melt the butter in a large saucepan over moderate heat. Stir in half of the onion and cook until softened, 2 to 3 minutes. Add the rice and cook, stirring often, until it is coated with butter and translucent, about 2 minutes.

3. Add 4 cups [1 liter] of the stock and the salt and increase the heat to moderately high. Cook, stirring constantly, until almost all the liquid is absorbed, about 10 minutes. Continue adding the stock 1 cup [250 ml] at a time, stirring, until the mixture is creamy and the rice is just tender, about 20 minutes from the time you first added stock. Remove from the heat and let cool to room temperature. (You can speed the process by spreading the rice out on a baking sheet.)

4. Meanwhile, in a small skillet, heat the olive oil over moderate heat. Add the remaining onion and cook until softened, 2 to 3 minutes. Stir in the tomato sauce and remove from the heat. Let cool completely.

5. Add the Parmesan and eggs to the cooled rice, stirring to blend well. Season with pepper to taste. Stir the Fontina and truffle puree into the onion-tomato sauce mixture. Spread the bread crumbs on a plate or in a pie pan.

6. Moisten your hands with water and scoop up about 3 tablespoons of the rice mixture. Shape it into a ball, than flatten it in the palm of your hand into an even round. Place a scant table-spoon of the truffle mixture in the center of the rice, and gently squeeze your hand closed to encase the filling in the rice. Roll the stuffed rice between both hands into a ball, and roll it in the bread crumbs to coat well. Repeat with the remaining rice, truffle mixture, and bread crumbs. (The arancini can be assembled up to 12 hours in advance. Place on a baking sheet, cover, and refrigerate. If the coating becomes damp, roll the arancini in bread crumbs again before deep-frying.)

7. Preheat the oven to 250°F [120°C].

8. Heat the oil in a large heavy saucepan or deep-fryer over moderate heat until it reaches 350°F [175°C] on a deep-fat thermometer. Working in batches, without crowding, add the arancini to the hot oil and cook, turning occasionally, until uniformly golden brown, about 2 minutes. Drain on paper towels. Keep the first batches of arancini warm on a baking sheet in the oven while you cook the remainder. Serve warm.

SOMMELIER WINE SUGGESTION Gran Fuedo Bodegas Julian Chivite 1999; Navarra, Spain

FELIDIA'S ASPARAGUS FLANS WITH MORELS AND BLACK TRUFFLE SAUCE

WHEN THE FIRST ASPARAGUS and morels appear in the early spring, while black truffles are still in season, Chef Fortunato Nicotra of New York City's Felidia restaurant prepares this dish. The flans are rich and yet surprisingly light in texture, almost ephemeral. Creamy braised morels complement the flavor of the asparagus, and a quick Marsala and truffle sauce provides the finishing touch. SERVES 4

FLANS

1 pound asparagus, trimmed [500 grams]

3 large eggs

Pinch of freshly grated nutmeg

½ teaspoon salt

⅛ teaspoon freshly ground black pepper

¼ cup chopped chives [60 ml]

2 small sage leaves

¼ cup freshly grated Parmigiano-Reggiano [20 grams]

1½ cups heavy cream [375 ml]

SAUCE

1 fresh or flash-frozen black truffle (about 1 ounce) [30 grams]

¼ cup dry Marsala [60 ml]

1½ tablespoons grapeseed or other neutral vegetable oil

Salt and freshly ground black pepper

Ragout of Morels (recipe follows)

1. Preheat the oven to 300°F [150°C]. Generously butter four 8-ounce [250-ml] ramekins and place them in a 9 by 13-inch [23 cm by 33-cm] baking dish or other pan that holds them comfortably.

2. To make the flans, bring a large pot of salted water to a boil. Add the asparagus and cook just until tender, 3 to 5 minutes, depending on size. Using a large wire skimmer or tongs, transfer the asparagus to a bowl of ice water to cool, then drain and pat dry.

3. In a small bowl, whisk the eggs, nutmeg, salt, and pepper together until well blended. Combine the asparagus, chives, and sage in a food processor and process until the asparagus is very finely chopped, about 2 minutes. Add the egg mixture and Parmesan cheese and process for 1 to 2 minutes, or until thoroughly combined and smooth. Add the cream and process to blend.

4. Transfer the flan mixture to a large glass measuring cup or a bowl with a spout, and pour it into the ramekins, filling them almost to the top. Pour enough hot water into the baking pan to come halfway up the sides of the ramekins.

5. Bake for 45 to 50 minutes, or until the flans are just set (the centers should feel firm when lightly touched with a finger). Let stand in the water bath for 10 minutes before serving.

6. Meanwhile, make the sauce: Combine the truffle and Marsala in a small saucepan, bring to a simmer, and simmer for 5 minutes. Remove from the heat and let cool.

7. Remove the truffle from the Marsala and set the pan aside. Using a mandoline or a Japanese vegetable slicer, shave off about one-quarter of the truffle, then shave off another quarter from the opposite side of the truffle. Wrap the remaining truffle in plastic wrap and reserve for garnish. Put the shaved truffle in a blender and add the Marsala. With the machine on, add the oil in a thin, steady stream. Season with salt and pepper to taste.

8. Make the ragout of morels; keep warm.

9. Remove the flans from the water bath and wipe the ramekins dry. Run a paring knife around the sides of each ramekin to release the flan, and invert each one onto a plate. Spoon the ragout of morels on top of the flans and drizzle the truffle sauce around them. Shave the reserved truffle over the top and serve immediately.

SOMMELIER WINE SUGGESTION Château d'Auvernier Pinot Gris 2000; Neuchâtel, Switzerland

RAGOUT OF MORELS

SERVES 4

1 tablespoon unsalted butter [15 grams]

1 tablespoon finely chopped shallots

8 ounces fresh morels, trimmed and cleaned [250 grams]

Salt and freshly ground black pepper

½ cup chicken stock or canned low-sodium chicken broth [125 ml]

½ cup heavy cream [125 ml]

1. Melt the butter in a large skillet over moderately high heat. Add the shallots and cook, stirring, until softened, about 2 minutes; do not allow the shallots to brown. Add the morels, season lightly with salt and pepper, and cook, stirring occasionally, until they are tender and most of the liquid they release has evaporated, 5 to 7 minutes.

2. Add the stock and simmer until it has reduced by three-quarters. Add the cream and simmer until slightly reduced and thickened, about 2 minutes. Season with additional salt and pepper to taste, remove from the heat, and set aside in a warm place. Reheat over low heat before serving if necessary.

CAULIFLOWER TERRINE WITH BLACK TRUFFLES AND MACHE SALAD

SERVE THIS INTRIGUING first course as chef Sandro Gamba does at NoMI in the Park Hyatt Chicago—accompanied by a thick slice of warm, toasted country-style bread slathered with truffle butter. At the restaurant, the terrine is served with a sauce of truffled beef jus—making this a good first course when you're cooking a beef roast to supply the juices—but here we've substituted more readily available beef stock. If you don't have homemade stock on hand, you can find good-quality prepared stock at many gourmet markets. SERVES 4

1 medium head of cauliflower (about 1½ pounds) [750 grams]

3 tablespoons crème fraîche

¾ teaspoon salt, or more to taste

About 4 drops hot pepper sauce, such as Tabasco

1 envelope (¼ ounce) unflavored gelatin [7 grams]

2 fresh or flash-frozen black truffles

1 cup unsalted rich beef stock [250 ml]

2 teaspoons balsamic vinegar

Pinch of freshly ground black pepper

1½ tablespoons extra-virgin olive oil

6 cups mâche (lamb's lettuce) or mixed baby lettuces [1.5 liters]

1. Cut out the core from the cauliflower and separate the cauliflower into 1½-inch [4-cm] pieces. Add the cauliflower to a large pot of boiling salted water and cook until very tender, 7 to 10 minutes. Drain in a colander, rinse under cold water, and drain again.

2. Transfer the cauliflower to a food processor or blender and process until smooth. Add the crème fraîche and process until well blended. Season with ⅛ teaspoon salt, or more to taste, and the hot pepper sauce.

3. Put 2 tablespoons cold water in a medium heatproof bowl, sprinkle the gelatin over it, and let soften for 5 minutes. Set the bowl over a saucepan of simmering water and heat, stirring occasionally, until the gelatin has dissolved, about 3 minutes. Remove from the heat and add the cauliflower puree, stirring until well blended.

4. Grease a 5¾ by 3¼ by 2-inch [15 cm by 8 cm by 5-cm] mini-loaf pan or 2-cup [500-ml] terrine mold. Scrape the cauliflower mixture into the pan and smooth the top. Rap the pan several times against the work surface to deflate any air bubbles. Cover with plastic wrap and refrigerate until set, at least 4 hours, or up to 1 day.

5. Shortly before serving, finely dice one of the truffles. Bring the beef stock to a boil in a small saucepan over moderately high heat and boil until reduced to ½ cup [125 ml]. Remove from the heat, stir in the diced truffle, and set aside.

6. In a medium bowl, whisk together the vinegar, the remaining ¼ teaspoon salt, and the pepper. Gradually whisk in the olive oil until blended. Add the mâche and toss to coat.

7. Unmold the terrine onto a cutting board and cut it into 8 slices. Arrange 2 slices in the center of each of 4 large salad plates and mound the salad on top. Shave the remaining truffle over the salads. Drizzle the truffled beef stock around the salads and serve at once.

SOMMELIER WINE SUGGESTION Chateau Yvonne Samur Blanc 1999; Loire, France

BAY SCALLOPS AND FOIE GRAS RAVIOLI WITH CIPOLLINE BOUILLON AND BLACK TRUFFLES

CHEF LAURENT TOURONDEL created this exquisite combination of sweet bay scallops and creamy foie gras. The ravioli can be prepared with either fresh foie gras or purchased foie gras terrine; we have substituted easy-to-use wonton wrappers for the fresh pasta dough used at Cello. Cipolline are small, flattish Italian onions, available at farmers' markets and many specialty produce shops; if necessary, substitute white onions. SERVES 6

BOUILLON

1 tablespoon unsalted butter

1 tablespoon olive oil

2 slices bacon, cut into small dice

10 ounces cipolline onions, finely chopped (about 1½ cups) [280 g]

1 garlic clove, minced

2 tablespoons sugar

2 tablespoons sherry wine vinegar

3 cups chicken stock or low-sodium chicken broth [700 mililiters]

Sprig of thyme

1 bay leaf

Salt and freshly ground black pepper

2 teaspoons olive oil

30 bay scallops, preferably Nantucket Bay (about 6 ounces) [200 g]

Salted freshly ground black pepper

Foie Gras Ravioli (recipe follows)

18 toasted walnut halves (about ½ cup) [125 g]

3 tablespoons walnut oil

1 large fresh or flash-frozen black truffle (about 2 ounces) [60 g]

1. To make the bouillon, melt the butter with the olive oil in a medium saucepan over moderate heat. Add the bacon and cook, stirring occasionally, until it has rendered its fat, 3 to 5 minutes. Add the onions, garlic, and sugar and cook, stirring, until the onions are soft and browned, about 7 minutes.

2. Add the sherry vinegar, increase the heat to moderately high, and bring to a boil, stirring to dissolve the browned bits on the bottom of the pan. Boil until the vinegar is reduced to a glaze. Add the stock, thyme, and bay leaf, bring to a boil, and boil until the liquid is reduced by half. Season with salt and pepper to taste. Strain through a fine-mesh strainer into a saucepan and set aside. (The bouillon can be made up to 2 days ahead, covered, and refrigerated.)

3. Bring a large pot of salted water to a boil; reduce the heat to a gentle simmer. Skim off and discard the fat that has come to the top of the bouillon. Bring the bouillon to a simmer over moderate heat; reduce the heat to low and keep warm.

4. Heat a large nonstick skillet over moderately high heat until hot. Add the 2 teaspoons olive oil and heat until hot. Season the scallops with salt and pepper. Add the scallops to the pan and cook just until browned on the first side, about 1 minute. Turn the scallops over and cook until just barely translucent in the center, about 1 minute longer.

5. Meanwhile, add the ravioli to the boiling water and cook, stirring occasionally so the ravioli don't stick together, just until the wonton wrappers are al dente, about 3 minutes. Remove the ravioli with a wire skimmer or slotted spoon and drain briefly in a colander.

6. Arrange 3 ravioli and 5 scallops in each of 6 shallow soup bowls. Scatter the walnuts over the top, and ladle in the broth. Drizzle the walnut oil over the broth, shave the truffle over the top, and serve immediately.

SOMMELIER WINE SUGGESTION Chateau de Beaucastel Chateauneuf-du-Pape Blanc 1999; Rhone, France

FOIE GRAS RAVIOLI

MAKES 18 RAVIOLI; SERVES 6

Cornmeal, for dusting

18 wonton wrappers

3 ounces fresh duck foie gras, trimmed and cut into ¼-inch dice, or foie gras terrine, cut into ¼-inch dice [90 grams/.5 cm]

Sprinkle a large baking sheet with cornmeal. Lay the wonton wrappers out on a work surface. Place about 1½ teaspoons of the foie gras in the center of each wrapper. One at a time, using a pastry brush or your fingertips, moisten the uncovered portion of each wrapper with water, than fold the wrapper over the filling to make a rectangle and press the edges firmly together to seal. If desired, use a fluted pastry wheel or a 2½-inch [6-cm] round cutter to cut the ravioli into half-moon shapes. Transfer the ravioli to the baking sheet. (The ravioli can be made early in the day, covered loosely with plastic wrap, and refrigerated.)

TRUFFLE-DUSTED SEA SCALLOPS WITH WATERCRESS SALAD AND LEMON VINAIGRETTE

PEPPERY WATERCRESS SALAD provides a lovely counterpoint to delicate truffled scallops, seared until they are golden brown. For a more elaborate presentation, serve the scallops on individual potato "galettes"; see the variations below. The "diver's scallops" called for here, which are also sometimes referred to as "dry scallops," have a much cleaner flavor and better texture than the more commonly available type, which have been soaked in a preservative to extend their shelf life. Look for diver's scallops at good fish markets. SERVES 4

1½ teaspoons fresh lemon juice

Salt and freshly ground black pepper

3½ tablespoons extra-virgin olive oil

12 ounces large diver's sea scallops (about 16 "dry" scallops), tough side muscles removed [350 grams]

1 tablespoon plus 1½ teaspoons truffle flour

1 tablespoon plus 1 teaspoon all-purpose flour

2 packed cups tiny watercress sprigs (from 1 small bunch) [500 ml]

4 tablespoons unsalted butter, cut into 4 pieces [60 grams]

1. To make the vinaigrette, combine the lemon juice, ⅛ teaspoon salt, a pinch of pepper, and 1½ tablespoons of the olive oil in a small jar, seal tightly, and shake vigorously until well blended. (The vinaigrette can be made up to 2 days ahead and refrigerated; let return to room temperature before using.)

2. Slice each scallop horizontally in half. Combine 1 tablespoon of the truffle flour and all of the all-purpose flour in a small bowl and whisk to blend. Set a fine strainer over a bowl.

3. Just before cooking the scallops, toss the watercress with the vinaigrette in a small bowl. Arrange a small mound of the salad in the center of each of 4 salad plates.

4. Heat 2 large heavy skillets, preferably nonstick, over moderately high heat until hot. Add 1 tablespoon of the remaining oil to each pan and heat until very hot but not smoking. Meanwhile, season the scallops generously on both sides with salt and pepper. In batches, toss the scallops in the flour mixture to coat lightly on both sides, than toss in the strainer to remove any excess.

5. Add half the scallops to each pan and cook until golden brown on the bottom, 1 to 2 minutes. Turn the scallops over and cook until they are browned on the second side but still slightly translucent in the center, about 1 minute longer. Transfer the scallops to a shallow bowl.

6. Pour off the oil from one of the pans, wipe the pan out with a paper towel, and return to moderate heat. Add the butter to the pan. As soon as it starts to melt, add the remaining ½ teaspoon truffle flour and cook, whisking, until the butter is foamy and just starting to color, about 2 minutes. Remove from the heat.

7. Arrange the scallops, overlapping them slightly, in a ring around each salad. Whisk any accumulated juices in the bowl into the butter sauce, then drizzle the sauce over the scallops. Serve immediately.

VARIATIONS

TRUFFLE-DUSTED SEA SCALLOPS WITH HERBS Omit the vinaigrette and watercress, and proceed as directed above. Arrange the scallops in the centers of 4 plates, overlapping them slightly, drizzle the sauce over them, and sprinkle with 1 tablespoon tiny chervil sprigs or 2 teaspoons finely chopped chives.

TRUFFLE-DUSTED SEA SCALLOPS ON POTATO GALETTES Omit the vinaigrette and watercress. Make the potato galettes as described below and cover loosely to keep warm while you cook the scallops. Place a galette on each serving plate, arrange the scallops on top, and sprinkle with chervil or chives, as in the variation above.

POTATO GALETTES

MAKES 4

1 medium baking potato	**Salt and freshly ground black pepper**
1½ tablespoons unsalted butter, melted [25 grams]	

1. Preheat the oven to 400°F [200°C]. Generously grease a large heavy baking sheet with butter.

2. Peel the potato. Using a mandoline or Japanese vegetable slicer or a very sharp knife, cut the potato into paper-thin slices; you will need a total of 36 slices. Toss the slices with the melted butter.

3. Arrange the potatoes on the baking sheet to make 4 galettes: For each, start with 1 slice in the center, then arrange 8 more slices in an overlapping circle around the center slice. Sprinkle with salt and pepper

4. Bake for about 15 minutes, or until the edges of the galettes are beginning to brown and the potatoes are cooked through. Serve hot.

SOMMELIER WINE SUGGESTION Chablis J. Dauvissat "Vaillons"; Chablis, France

RESTAURANT DANIEL'S TUNA CRUDA
WITH BLACK TRUFFLE-ANCHOVY SAUCE

AT RESTAURANT DANIEL IN NEW YORK, chef de cuisine Alex Lee garnishes this stunning dish with a few leaves of deep-fried flat-leaf parsley. There may also be a bit of the truffled anchovy sauce left over, but it would be delicious as a dip for crudités—or serve it with a grilled steak or roasted fish. Sushi-quality tuna is increasingly available at good fish shops and gourmet markets—look for a bright red color and glistening sheen; if possible, buy a large chunk (up to 2 inches thick) rather than a thinner steak. SERVES 4

2 ounces fresh or flash-frozen black truffle [60 grams]

2 tablespoons extra-virgin olive oil

2 anchovy fillets, rinsed and finely chopped

1 small garlic clove, minced

1 tablespoon finely chopped flat-leaf parsley

Pinch of hot red pepper flakes

1 tablespoon fresh lemon juice

6 tablespoons homemade mayonnaise (such as Truffle Mayonnaise, page 193, made without truffles)

Salt and freshly ground black pepper

1½ tablespoons fruity extra-virgin olive oil, preferably Ligurian

About ⅛ teaspoon Meyer lemon juice or regular lemon juice, or to taste

A few drops of black truffle oil

12 ounces sushi-grade tuna, preferably 1½ to 2 inches thick, cut across the grain into 12 slices [350 grams/4 to 5 cm]

12 tiny radishes, trimmed, or 4 small radishes, trimmed and cut into thin wedges or slices

Generous 1 cup thinly sliced fennel, preferably baby fennel [100 grams]

½ cup thinly sliced tender inner celery stalks [50 grams]

2 ounces baby arugula or other small salad greens (about 2 cups loosely packed) [60 grams/500 ml]

Fleur de sel or coarse sea salt (optional)

1. Mince half the truffle(s); reserve the remaining truffle for garnish. Heat the olive oil in a small saucepan over low heat. Add the anchovies and cook, stirring, until they dissolve. Add the garlic and cook, stirring, until fragrant, about 1 minute. Add the minced truffle, parsley, and hot pepper flakes, remove from the heat, and let stand for 5 minutes.

2. Stir the 1 tablespoon fresh lemon juice into the olive oil mixture, then stir in the mayonnaise until thoroughly blended. Season to taste with salt and pepper.

3. Combine the fruity olive oil, the ⅛ teaspoon lemon juice, and the truffle oil in a small bowl. Season this vinaigrette with a generous pinch of salt.

4. In a shallow bowl, toss the tuna with enough of the vinaigrette to coat lightly. In a medium bowl, combine the radishes, fennel, celery, and arugula. Add enough of the remaining vinaigrette to coat lightly, tossing to mix.

5. Arrange 3 slices of the tuna in a row down each of 4 rectangular plates, or arrange it "flower-petal fashion" on each of 4 round plates. Scatter the arugula mixture and the remaining vegetables around the tuna slices, or mound most of it in the centers of the round plates, and scatter the rest around the tuna. Spoon 1 to 1½ tablespoons of the anchovy sauce around the tuna on each plate. Shave the reserved truffle over the plates, sprinkle a little fleur de sel over the tuna, if desired, and serve.

SOMMELIER WINE SUGGESTION Remelluri Blanco 1997; Roja, Spain

CARPACCIO WITH TRUFFLES

CARPACCIO, PAPER-THIN SLICES of raw beef, was first served at Harry's Bar in Venice. There it is garnished with a lemony mayonnaise spiked with Worcestershire, but the dish takes well to many accompaniments, including black truffle oil and, if they're in season, grated fresh summer truffles.

Chilling—but not freezing—the beef will make it easier to slice it paper-thin. Alternatively, ask your butcher to slice the beef for you, but wrap it well before refrigerating and serve it as soon as possible. SERVES 4

12 ounces well-trimmed beef tenderloin
[350 grams]

1 lemon, halved

1 tablespoon black truffle oil, or more
to taste

**Coarse salt, preferably fleur de sel, and
freshly ground black pepper**

One 1- to 2-ounce summer truffle (optional)
[30 to 60 grams]

1½ tablespoons minced flat-leaf parsley

1. Carefully trim the beef of any remaining fat or membrane. Wrap in plastic wrap and place in the freezer for about 30 minutes, until chilled; do not freeze.

2. Using a very sharp thin knife, slice the beef paper-thin. Arrange the slices on large salad plates, overlapping them as necessary. Squeeze lemon juice to taste over the beef. Drizzle with the truffle oil, and sprinkle with coarse salt and pepper.

3. If using the summer truffle, grate it over the beef. Garnish with the parsley and serve immediately.

VARIATION

CARPACCIO WITH TRUFFLES AND AGED CHEESE Using a Japanese vegetable slicer or a vegetable peeler, shave 2 ounces [60 grams] Parmigiano-Reggiano or aged provolone over the carpaccio before garnishing it with the parsley. (Or use a mandoline to shave the cheese, then scatter it over the carpaccio.)

| SOMMELIER WINE SUGGESTION | Luigi Coppo "Camp du Rouss" Barbera d'Asti 1995; Piedmont, Italy

BRESAOLA WITH BLACK TRUFFLE OIL

BRESAOLA, SALT-CURED, air-dried beef—usually made with fillet—is a specialty of Italy's Lombardy region. It is served thinly sliced as an appetizer, garnished only, if at all, with olive oil, perhaps lemon juice, and black pepper. Like other cured meats, bresaola goes well with truffles. Add a squeeze or two of lemon juice if you like, and, if the beef is not especially salty, a sprinkling of just a few grains of flavorful fleur de sel.

Look for bresaola in specialty Italian and other gourmet markets. Store it well wrapped in the refrigerator and plan to use it within a day; it dries out quickly once sliced. SERVES 4

6 to 8 ounces thinly sliced bresaola [200 to 250 grams]

1 to 1½ tablespoons black truffle oil

Fleur de sel or other coarse salt (optional)

Coarsely ground black pepper

2 tablespoons minced flat-leaf parsley

Arrange the bresaola "flower petal" fashion, overlapping the slices slightly in the center as necessary, on 4 salad plates. Drizzle with the truffle oil, and sprinkle with a little fleur de sel, if using. Season with coarse black pepper, garnish with the parsley, and serve at once.

SOMMELIER WINE SUGGESTION Calera "Central Coast" Pinot Noir 1996; California

TRUFFLED COUNTRY PATE

PATES SEEM TO DRIFT in and out of fashion, but one thing remains constant: even the most fickle palate cannot resist a hearty country terrine dotted with black truffle. As the great food writer M. F. K. Fisher once said, "There is nothing much better in the Western world than a fine, unctuous truffled pâté."

Weighting the cooked terrine as it rests ensures a firm texture that makes slicing easier. Serve the terrine slightly chilled, cut into slices, with a crusty baguette, cornichons, and coarse-grained mustard. SERVES 12 TO 16

1 medium to large fresh or flash-frozen black truffle, finely chopped	**1 tablespoon chopped fresh thyme or 1 teaspoon dried**
2 tablespoons Cognac or other brandy	**¼ teaspoon ground allspice**
12 ounces sliced bacon [350 grams]	**⅛ teaspoon freshly grated nutmeg**
1 tablespoon unsalted butter [15 grams]	**Dash of ground cloves**
1 medium onion, finely chopped	**1 teaspoon salt**
1 pound ground pork [500 grams]	**½ teaspoon freshly ground black pepper**
8 ounces ground veal [250 grams]	**2 large eggs,** beaten
8 ounces chicken livers, rinsed, trimmed, and chopped [250 grams]	**½ cup heavy cream** [125 ml]
2 large garlic cloves, minced	**4 ounces thinly sliced cooked ham,** cut into ¼-inch-wide strips [125 grams/.5 cm]
2 tablespoons chopped flat-leaf parsley	**1 bay leaf**

1. Combine the truffle and Cognac in a small bowl. Set aside to macerate for 5 to 10 minutes.

2. Preheat the oven to 350°F [175°C]. Line a 2-quart [2-liter] terrine or loaf pan with most of the bacon, draping the strips crosswise over the bottom and up the sides. Reserve a few slices for the top.

3. Melt the butter in a medium skillet over moderate heat. Add the onion and cook, stirring occasionally, until softened, 3 to 5 minutes. Transfer to a large bowl.

4. Add the pork, veal, chicken livers, garlic, parsley, thyme, allspice, nutmeg, cloves, salt, pepper, eggs, and cream to the onion. Mix with your hands or a wooden spoon until well combined. Stir in the chopped truffle, with the Cognac.

5. Pack half of the meat mixture into the bacon-lined terrine. Cover with the ham strips. Fill the terrine with the remaining meat mixture and lay the reserved bacon slices over the top. Place the bay leaf in the center and cover the terrine with a lid or heavy-duty aluminum foil.

6. Set the terrine in a larger baking pan and add enough hot water to reach halfway up the sides of the terrine. Bake for 1¼ to 1½ hours, until an instant-read thermometer inserted into the center registers 165° to 170°F [75°C].

7. Remove the terrine from the water bath. If you used a lid, remove it and cover the top of the terrine with foil. Cut a piece of sturdy cardboard to fit inside the top of the terrine and put it on top of the pâté. Place 2 or 3 heavy cans or other heavy weights on top of the cardboard. Let the pâté cool completely, then refrigerate for at least 2 hours, or for up to 1 week, before serving.

SOMMELIER WINE SUGGESTION Bandol Domaine Tempier "La Migoua Cuvée Speciale" 1989; Provence, France

SOUPS

CREAM OF CAULIFLOWER
SOUP WITH WHITE TRUFFLE

HAUTE POTATO-LEEK SOUP

TRUFFLED MUSHROOM
BROTH EN CROUTE

WILD MUSHROOM BISQUE
WITH WHITE TRUFFLE OIL

CREAMY JERUSALEM ARTICHOKE
SOUP WITH BLACK TRUFFLE

WINTER SQUASH SOUP
WITH BLACK TRUFFLE

FLEUR DE SEL'S PARSNIP SOUP
WITH CHESTNUT RAVIOLI AND
WHITE TRUFFLE OIL

CREAM OF CAULIFLOWER SOUP
WITH WHITE TRUFFLE

CAULIFLOWER is one of those humble ingredients—like potatoes and eggs—that is elevated to another realm when teamed with truffles. This elegant cream soup is laced with truffle oil. If you should happen to have a little fresh white truffle on hand, shave it over the top for good measure. SERVES 4

1 tablespoon unsalted butter [15 grams]

1 small onion, minced

2 cups chicken stock or 1 can (14½ ounces) low-sodium chicken broth plus enough water to make 2 cups [500 ml/can is 400 grams]

3 cups small cauliflower florets (about ½ large cauliflower) [270 grams]

1 small Yukon Gold or waxy potato, peeled and coarsely chopped

½ teaspoon salt, or more to taste

Generous pinch of freshly ground white pepper

1 cup heavy cream or half-and-half [250 ml]

1 tablespoon white truffle oil, plus extra for drizzling

Tiny chervil or flat-leaf parsley sprigs, for garnish

1. Melt the butter in a large heavy pot over moderate heat. Add the onion and cook, stirring frequently, until soft and translucent, about 5 minutes.

2. Add the stock, cauliflower, potato, salt, and white pepper and bring to a boil over high heat. Reduce the heat and boil gently, stirring occasionally, until the cauliflower and potato are very soft, 17 to 20 minutes. Remove from the heat.

3. Puree the soup, in batches if necessary, in a blender or food processor. (The soup can be made ahead to this point, covered, and refrigerated for up to 1 day.)

4. Return the soup to the pot and stir in the cream. Heat over moderately low heat, stirring frequently, until hot; do not boil. Season with additional salt to taste. Remove from the heat and stir in the truffle oil until well blended.

5. Ladle the soup into bowls and drizzle a little extra truffle oil over the top of each one. Garnish with chervil and serve.

HAUTE POTATO-LEEK SOUP

SERVED COLD, IT'S VICHYSSOISE; served hot, it's even better…and a final swirl of truffle butter makes this satisfying soup worthy of the most VIP of guests. SERVES 4

2 tablespoons unsalted butter [30 grams]

2 medium leeks (white and tender green parts), coarsely chopped and thoroughly rinsed

½ teaspoon salt, or more to taste

2 medium baking potatoes (about 1 pound), peeled and thinly sliced [500 grams]

2 cups chicken stock or 1 can (14½ ounces) low-sodium chicken broth plus enough water to make 2 cups [500 ml/can is 400 grams]

1 cup heavy cream [250 ml]

1 to 2 tablespoons truffle butter

1 tablespoon chopped chives

1. Melt the unsalted butter in a large pot over moderately low heat. Add the leeks and salt and cook, stirring frequently, until the leeks are softened, 5 to 7 minutes. Add the potatoes, stock, and ½ cup water, increase the heat to high, and bring to a boil. Reduce the heat to low and cook until the potatoes are very soft when pierced with the tip of a sharp knife, 12 to 15 minutes. Remove from the heat.

2. Puree the soup, in batches if necessary, in a blender or food processor. (The soup can be made in advance to this point, covered, and refrigerated for up to 2 days.)

3. Return the soup to the pot, stir in the cream, and heat over low heat, stirring occasionally, until hot; do not boil. Season with additional salt if necessary. Add the truffle butter, stirring just until it melts. Ladle the soup into bowls and garnish with the chives.

TRUFFLED MUSHROOM BROTH EN CROUTE

FRENCH CHEF PAUL BOCUSE is known for his extravagant truffle and foie gras soup, served in crocks topped with rounds of puff pastry. Our simpler but still supremely elegant version is made with a truffle-enhanced mushroom broth. When each golden puff pastry dome is broken open at the table, your guests will swoon over the haunting aroma of fragrant broth.

    The flavorful broth can be made a few days ahead (you might also want to make a double batch and freeze half for later). For a more substantial offering, sauté some wild mushrooms in butter and add to the soup before covering with the pastry. SERVES 4

2 medium onions, unpeeled, well rinsed, and cut into large chunks

3 celery stalks with leafy tops, coarsely chopped

1 large tomato, halved and seeded

1 large carrot, coarsely chopped

1 ounce dried shiitake mushrooms, rinsed [30 grams]

2 garlic cloves, smashed

4 sprigs of parsley

3 sprigs of thyme

1 bay leaf

1 teaspoon black peppercorns

Salt

1 package (14 ounces) frozen all-butter puff pastry, thawed according to the package directions [400 grams]

1 egg

1 tablespoon heavy cream or milk

1 fresh or flash-frozen black truffle, cut into julienne strips

1. Combine the onions, celery, tomato, carrot, dried mushrooms, garlic, parsley, thyme, bay leaf, peppercorns, and 6 cups [1.5 liters] cold water in a medium pot and bring to a boil over moderate heat, skimming off the foam that rises to the top. Reduce the heat to low and simmer, uncovered, for 30 minutes.

2. Remove the broth from the heat and let stand, partially covered, for 30 minutes to intensify the flavors.

3. Strain the broth through a fine sieve, discarding the solids; if necessary, strain again, until the broth is clear. Season to taste with salt. (The broth can be made up to 3 days in advance, covered, and refrigerated. Bring to room temperature before proceeding.)

4. Preheat the oven to 450°F [230°C]. Line a baking sheet with parchment paper. Place 4 deep oven-proof soup bowls (each with a 1½- to 2-cup [375- to 500-ml] capacity) on another baking sheet.

5. Lay the pastry sheet on a lightly floured work surface. If necessary, roll out the dough so it's no thicker than ⅛ inch [3mm]. Using a plate or a pan lid as a guide, cut out 4 rounds at least 1 inch larger than the tops of the bowls. Arrange the pastry rounds on the parchment-lined baking sheet. If desired, cut out various shapes from some of the dough scraps to use as decoration and lay them on the baking sheet. Refrigerate the pastry rounds until firm, about 15 minutes.

6. In a small bowl, beat the egg with the cream to make an egg wash. Divide the truffle strips among the soup bowls and ladle in the broth. Brush a chilled puff pastry round with some of the egg wash, then invert over a soup bowl. Press the edges of the pastry snugly against the bowl to seal, pleating the dough as necessary. Repeat with the remaining pastry rounds. Brush the pastry all over with the egg wash. Decorate with the pastry cutouts, if you made them, and brush again. Cut a small vent in the center of each pastry round to allow steam to escape.

7. Bake for 15 minutes. Reduce the heat to 350°F [175°C] and bake for 10 to 15 minutes longer, until the pastry is puffed and golden. Turn off the oven and let the soup stand in the hot oven for 5 minutes before serving.

WILD MUSHROOM BISQUE WITH WHITE TRUFFLE OIL

NOTHING SUITS AN ELEGANT DINNER PARTY better than a luxurious soup, especially one that can be made in advance and reheated. Plain white button mushrooms, with a few dried porcini for enhancement, make a fine stock. Select the mushrooms for the bisque itself with an eye to what is best in the market. SERVES 4

3 tablespoons unsalted butter [45 grams]

1 tablespoon olive oil

½ pound cremini mushrooms, trimmed, cleaned, and halved or quartered [250 grams]

½ pound mixed wild or cultivated mushrooms, such as porcini, (stemmed) shiitakes, oyster mushrooms, and/or chanterelles, trimmed, cleaned, and halved or quartered [250 grams]

1 shallot, minced

Leaves from 2 sprigs of fresh lemon or regular thyme, or ½ teaspoon dried thyme

Salt

Dash of cayenne

2 teaspoons fresh lemon juice

1 medium leek (white and tender green parts), quartered lengthwise, thoroughly rinsed, and thinly sliced

1 tablespoon truffle flour

Mushroom Stock (recipe follows)

⅓ cup heavy cream [75 grams]

1 tablespoon white truffle oil

1 small fresh white truffle (optional)

1. Melt 1 tablespoon of the butter with the olive oil in a large skillet over moderately high heat. Add the mushrooms and cook, tossing, until they begin to give up their juices, 3 to 5 minutes. Add the shallot and continue to cook until the mushrooms are lightly browned and the shallot is soft, 2 to 3 minutes. Season with half the thyme, ¼ teaspoon salt, the cayenne, and lemon juice. Set aside.

2. Melt the remaining 2 tablespoons [30 grams] butter in a large heavy pot over moderately low heat. Add the leek (with any water that clings to it), cover, and cook for 5 minutes. Uncover, raise the heat to moderate, and cook until the leek is soft and almost golden, about 5 minutes longer.

3. Sprinkle on the truffle flour and cook, stirring, for 1 minute. Pour in the mushroom stock and bring to a boil, stirring to make sure the flour combines with the liquid. Add half the sautéed mushrooms and the remaining thyme, reduce the heat to a bare simmer, and cook for 10 minutes to blend the flavors.

4. Puree the soup in a blender or food processor, in batches if necessary. Return to the pot. Add the remaining mushrooms and the cream. Season with salt and cayenne to taste, bring to a simmer, and simmer gently for 5 minutes. Stir in the truffle oil, and ladle into bowls. If you have the fresh truffle, shave it over the top. Serve immediately.

MUSHROOM STOCK

MAKES ABOUT 6 CUPS [1.5 LITERS]

1 tablespoon olive oil

8 ounces button mushrooms (mushrooms that are starting to brown are fine), trimmed, cleaned, and coarsely chopped [250 grams]

1 shallot, chopped

3 sprigs of fresh thyme or ½ teaspoon dried thyme

¼ cup (about ¼ ounce) dried porcini mushrooms, rinsed [7 grams]

6 parsley stems

Salt and freshly ground black pepper

1. Heat the olive oil in a large saucepan over moderately high heat. Add the fresh mushrooms and cook, stirring occasionally, until beginning to brown, 8 to 10 minutes.

2. Add the shallot and thyme and cook for 1 to 2 minutes longer, until the shallot is softened. Add 8 cups (2 liters) water, the dried mushrooms, and parsley and bring to a boil. Reduce the heat to a simmer, partially cover, and cook for 20 to 30 minutes, until the stock is intensely flavored. Strain through a fine-mesh sieve, pressing down with a wooden spoon to extract as much liquid as possible from the mushrooms. Season with salt and pepper to taste. (The stock can be made ahead and refrigerated for up to 3 days or frozen for up to 2 months.)

CREAMY JERUSALEM ARTICHOKE SOUP WITH BLACK TRUFFLE

JERUSALEM ARTICHOKES, sometimes called sunchokes, are generally available from October through April. The knobby appearance of this tuber is reminiscent of fresh ginger, but its mild flavor definitely says globe artichoke heart. Like many other root vegetables, Jerusalem artichokes are enhanced by the flavor of truffles. SERVES 4

1 fresh or flash-frozen black truffle, cut into thin julienne strips

⅔ cup heavy cream [150 ml]

1 pound Jerusalem artichokes [500 grams]

3 tablespoons unsalted butter [45 grams]

1 large onion, chopped

2 celery stalks, tough strings removed, chopped

4 cups chicken stock or 2 cans (14½ ounces each) low-sodium chicken broth plus enough water to make 4 cups [1 liter/can is 400 grams]

⅛ teaspoon cayenne

Salt and freshly ground black pepper

1 tablespoon minced flat-leaf parsley

1. Wrap 4 of the truffle strips in plastic wrap and reserve for garnish. Combine the cream and the remaining truffle in a small bowl and set aside.

2. Fill a medium bowl with cold salted water. Peel the Jerusalem artichokes and cut into ½-inch [1-cm]-thick slices, dropping them into the water as you work to prevent discoloration.

3. Melt the butter in a large heavy pot over moderate heat. Add the onion and celery and cook, stirring, until softened, 3 to 5 minutes.

4. Drain the Jerusalem artichokes and add to the pot. Add the chicken stock and bring to a boil over moderately high heat. Reduce the heat to low and cook, partially covered, until the vegetables are very tender, about 30 minutes. Remove from the heat.

5. Puree the soup, in batches if necessary, in a blender or food processor. (The soup can be made ahead to this point, covered, and refrigerated for up to 1 day; cover and refrigerate the truffle-cream mixture as well.) Return to the pot and set over low heat. Gently stir in the reserved truffle-cream mixture and the cayenne and cook, stirring occasionally, until heated through, about 5 minutes. Season with salt and pepper to taste. Stir in the parsley.

6. Ladle the soup into bowls, garnish with the reserved truffle, and serve.

WINTER SQUASH SOUP WITH BLACK TRUFFLE

BUTTERNUT SQUASH IS PARTICULARLY SWEET, but you can use any winter squash—Buttercup, acorn, sugar pumpkin, or one of the more unusual heirloom varieties displayed at farmers' markets and specialty produce shops. Earthy black truffles complement the flavor of the hearty soup best. Lacking a truffle, stir a teaspoon or two of black truffle oil into the soup, or drizzle a little over each bowl when you serve it. SERVES 4

1 medium butternut squash (1½ to 1¾ pounds) [750 to 875 grams]

2 tablespoons unsalted butter [30 grams]

1 onion, finely chopped

1 small garlic clove, finely chopped

2 small carrots, thinly sliced

1 celery stalk, thinly sliced

⅜ teaspoon salt

2 cups chicken stock or 1 can (14½ ounces) low-sodium chicken broth plus enough water to make 2 cups [500 ml/can is 400 grams]

Freshly ground black pepper

1 small fresh, flash-frozen, or canned black truffle, cut into thin julienne strips

1. Using a sharp heavy knife, cut off the "neck" of the squash. Cut the neck and the remaining squash lengthwise in half and scrape out the seeds. Cut each piece of squash in half again and using a sharp paring knife, peel the squash. Cut into ¾-inch [2-cm] chunks.

2. Melt the butter in a large pot over moderate heat. Add the onion, garlic, carrots, celery, and salt. Cook, stirring often, until the onion is soft and translucent, 5 to 7 minutes. Add the squash and stock and bring to a simmer. Reduce the heat, partially cover, and simmer gently until the squash is very tender, about 15 minutes. Remove from the heat.

3. Puree the soup, in batches if necessary, in a blender or food processor until smooth. (The soup can be made ahead to this point, covered, and refrigerated for up to 1 day.)

4. Return the soup to the pot, add pepper to taste, and reheat, stirring occasionally, over moderate heat. Taste the soup and add salt if you think it needs it. Ladle into bowls, and garnish with the truffle.

FLEUR DE SEL'S PARSNIP SOUP WITH CHESTNUT RAVIOLI AND WHITE TRUFFLE OIL

CHEF CYRIL RENAUD OF FLEUR DE SEL in New York City ingeniously pairs humble parsnips with rich chestnuts and black and white truffles for a memorable mélange of flavors. At the restaurant, he makes diminutive ravioli with fresh pasta dough; we've used wonton wrappers instead for a shortcut version of the original. Good-quality vegetable stock is available in many gourmet markets, but chicken stock can be substituted if necessary. SERVES 4

2¼ pounds parsnips [1 kg]

6 cups vegetable stock [1.5 liters]

¼ cup crème fraîche or heavy cream [60 grams]

Salt and freshly ground black pepper

3½ tablespoons extra-virgin olive oil

2 tablespoons white truffle oil

Chestnut Ravioli (recipe follows)

1 small fresh, flash-frozen, or canned black truffle (optional)

1. Peel the parsnips. Cut 2 of the parsnips lengthwise in half (these will be used for the garnish). Thinly slice the remaining parsnips. Fit a large pot with a steamer rack, add water to come to just below the rack, and bring to a boil. Add the sliced parsnips to the steamer rack, place the parsnip halves on top, cover, and steam over moderate heat until the sliced parsnips are very tender and the halved parsnips are just tender, 8 to 10 minutes. Set the halved parsnips aside.

2. In batches, combine the sliced parsnips with the vegetable stock in a blender and puree until smooth. Transfer to a bowl and whisk in the crème fraîche. Season to taste with salt and pepper, cover, and refrigerate until ready to serve. (The soup can be made up to 1 day ahead.)

3. Preheat the oven (or a toaster oven) to 450°F [230°C]. Cut the reserved parsnip halves crosswise into ¾-inch [2-cm] pieces. Place them in a small baking pan, add 1½ tablespoons of the olive oil, and toss to coat. Season with salt and pepper. Roast, stirring occasionally, for about 20 minutes, until golden brown. Transfer to a small plate and set aside at room temperature.

4. Combine the remaining 2 tablespoons olive oil and the truffle oil in a wide shallow bowl. In a large saucepan, bring the soup to a simmer over moderate heat.

5. Meanwhile, bring a large pot of salted water to a boil; reduce the heat to a gentle boil. Add the ravioli to the boiling water and cook, stirring occasionally so the ravioli don't stick together, until the wrappers are al dente, about 3 minutes. Remove with a wire skimmer or slotted spoon and drain briefly in a colander, then toss the ravioli in the truffled oil.

6. Scatter the roasted parsnips over the bottom of 4 large shallow soup bowls. Add the ravioli and ladle the soup over them. Drizzle the remaining truffle oil mixture over the top and shave the optional black truffle over the soup. Serve immediately.

CHESTNUT RAVIOLI

MAKES 12

2 tablespoons unsalted butter

4 ounces (about 12) vacuum-packed cooked peeled chestnuts (see Note), finely chopped (about ½ cup) [125 grams]

Salt and freshly ground black pepper

1 medium fresh white truffle (about 1 ounce), cut into small dice, or ¾ teaspoon truffle flour

3 tablespoons freshly grated Parmigiano-Reggiano

Cornmeal, for dusting

12 wonton wrappers

1. To make the filling, melt the butter in a small skillet over moderate heat. Add the chestnuts, season with salt and pepper, and cook, stirring occasionally, until lightly browned, 3 to 5 minutes. Transfer to a medium bowl and let cool slightly. Add the diced truffle (or truffle flour) and the Parmesan to the chestnuts; toss to mix well.

2. To assemble the ravioli, sprinkle a large baking sheet with cornmeal. Lay the wonton wrappers out on a work surface. Place 1½ to 2 teaspoons of the filling in the center of each wrapper. One at a time, using a pastry brush or your fingertips, moisten the exposed portion of each wrapper with water, then fold the wrapper over the filling diagonally to make a triangle and press the edges firmly together to seal. If desired, use a fluted pastry wheel or a 2½-inch [6.5-cm] round cutter to cut the ravioli into half-moon shapes. Transfer the ravioli to the baking sheet. (The ravioli can be made early in the day, covered loosely with plastic wrap, and refrigerated.)

NOTE: Vacuum-packed cooked peeled chestnuts are available in some gourmet markets and through mail-order sources (see Sources, page 234).

SALADS

HERBED MIXED GREENS WITH
BLACK TRUFFLE VINAIGRETTE

WATERCRESS AND ENDIVE SALAD
WITH WALNUTS AND PERSIMMON

FENNEL SALAD WITH FRISEE,
FONTINA, AND BLACK TRUFFLE

FAVA BEAN AND ARTICHOKE
SALAD WITH LEMON AND
WHITE TRUFFLE OIL

ROASTED BEET SALAD WITH
BLACK TRUFFLE AND GOAT
CHEESE

SUMMER TRUFFLE SALAD
WITH AGED PROVOLONE

ROASTED WILD MUSHROOM
SALAD WITH TRUFFLE OIL
AND HERBS

SEARED SEA SCALLOPS WITH
PORCINI MUSHROOMS AND
TRUFFLED GREENS

SMOKED DUCK SALAD WITH
PANCETTA, WARM RICOTTA
SALATA, AND BLACK TRUFFLE

PROSCIUTTO WITH FRISEE AND
TRUFFLE OIL

HERBED MIXED GREENS WITH BLACK TRUFFLE VINAIGRETTE

USE A GOOD-QUALITY MESCLUN MIX that contains a variety of different baby greens for this salad. The truffle oil vinaigrette is wonderfully fragrant on its own, but do add the optional black truffle to the salad if you're feeling indulgent. Blue cheese and black truffle makes an especially felicitous combination. SERVES 4

4 ounces haricots verts [125 grams]

6 ounces mesclun mix (about 8 cups) [175 grams]

½ cup packed finely chopped mixed herbs, such as basil, tarragon, chervil, and flat-leaf parsley (including no more than 2 tablespoons tarragon) [125 ml]

1 fresh, flash-frozen, or canned black truffle, cut into thin julienne strips or very thinly sliced (optional)

Black Truffle Vinaigrette (recipe follows)

2 ounces Danish blue cheese or other mild blue cheese, crumbled (about ½ cup) [60 grams]

Finely chopped chives, for garnish

1. Bring a large saucepan of salted water to a boil. Add the haricots verts and cook until crisp-tender, about 5 minutes. Drain and rinse briefly under cold water until cold. Pat the beans dry with paper towels and cut into 1- to 1½-inch [2.5- to 4-cm] lengths. (The beans can be prepared early in the day, covered, and refrigerated.)

2. Put the greens in a large bowl, add the herbs, and toss to mix well. Add the beans and the truffle, if using, then add the vinaigrette, tossing to coat. Add the cheese and toss gently.

3. Arrange the salad on 4 salad plates. Sprinkle the chives around the salads and serve.

BLACK TRUFFLE VINAIGRETTE

While this vinaigrette can be used on any type of salad, the black truffle oil makes it especially appropriate for those containing assertive greens, stronger cheeses, and smoked or cured meats. The white truffle oil version (see the variation below) is best suited to salads made with soft, tender leaves and more delicate flavors. This recipe is easily doubled.

MAKES ABOUT ¼ CUP [60 ML]

1 tablespoon white wine vinegar

⅛ teaspoon Dijon mustard

¼ teaspoon salt

⅛ teaspoon freshly ground black pepper

2 tablespoons black truffle oil

1 tablespoon extra-virgin olive oil

Whisk the vinegar, mustard, salt, and pepper together in a small bowl. Slowly whisk in the truffle oil and then the olive oil in a thin, steady stream until well blended and emulsified. (The vinaigrette can be covered and refrigerated for up to 1 day; bring to room temperature before using.)

VARIATION

WHITE TRUFFLE VINAIGRETTE Make the vinaigrette as directed above, but substitute white truffle oil for the black truffle oil.

WATERCRESS AND ENDIVE SALAD WITH WALNUTS AND PERSIMMON

BURSTING WITH COLOR AND TEXTURE, this salad captures the lively flavors of fall. Tomato-shaped Fuyu persimmons, unlike the teardrop-shaped Hachiya variety, are best eaten when firm rather than soft-ripe. If they are not in season, substitute a good crisp apple, such as a Fuji or Granny Smith. SERVES 4 TO 6

½ cup walnuts [50 grams]

2 teaspoons sherry vinegar

½ teaspoon black truffle puree or paste

2 tablespoons extra-virgin olive oil

1 tablespoon walnut oil

Salt and freshly ground black pepper

1 large bunch of watercress, tough stems removed (about 4 cups loosely packed) [75 grams]

2 medium heads of endive, cut crosswise into ¼-inch slices [.5 cm]

1 small head of radicchio, cored and thinly sliced or shredded

1 Fuyu persimmon, peeled and cut into thin julienne strips

A small chunk of Parmigiano-Reggiano (about 2 ounces), at room temperature [60 grams]

1. Preheat the oven to 350°F [175°F]. Spread the walnuts on a small baking sheet. Toast in the oven, stirring once or twice, until lightly browned and fragrant, 5 to 7 minutes. Let cool slightly, then coarsely chop.

2. In a large bowl, whisk together the vinegar and truffle puree until blended. Whisking constantly, slowly add the olive oil and then the walnut oil in a thin, steady stream until well blended and emulsified. Season with salt and pepper to taste. (The vinaigrette can be made early in the day, covered, and set aside at room temperature.)

3. Add the watercress, endive, radicchio, persimmon, and walnuts to the vinaigrette. Toss to coat well.

4. Mound the salad on 4 plates. Using a vegetable peeler, shave the Parmesan over the top, and serve at once.

FENNEL SALAD WITH FRISEE, FONTINA, AND BLACK TRUFFLE

FRESH FENNEL, sometimes called finocchio, its Italian name, has a flavor reminiscent of licorice and a refreshing crunchy texture not unlike celery. The visual contrast of black truffle against palest green is a showstopper. When truffles are not in season, a drizzle of truffle oil over each serving is sure to satisfy the senses. SERVES 4

2 small fennel bulbs (about 1 pound total) [500 grams]

2 tablespoons white wine vinegar

½ teaspoon salt

Freshly ground black pepper

6 tablespoons extra-virgin olive oil

1 cup coarsely torn frisée [250 grams]

4 ounces Italian Fontina, shredded (about 1 cup) [125 grams]

1 small fresh or flash-frozen black truffle, cut into thin julienne strips

1. Cut off and discard the fennel stalks if still attached; reserve about ¼ cup [60 ml] of the feathery fennel fronds. Remove the outer layer from each bulb if it looks tough or stringy (or use a vegetable peeler to trim any tough, stringy parts as necessary). Trim the base of each bulb and with a sharp paring knife, remove most of the tough core. Using a mandoline or a sharp knife, cut the fennel into thin matchsticks.

2. In a large bowl, whisk together the vinegar, salt, and pepper to taste. Whisking constantly, add the olive oil in a thin, steady stream until well blended and emulsified. (The vinaigrette can be made early in the day, covered, and set aside at room temperature.)

3. Add the fennel, reserved fennel fronds, frisée, and Fontina to the vinaigrette. Toss gently to coat.

4. Arrange the salad on 4 plates. Scatter the truffle over the top and serve.

FAVA BEAN AND ARTICHOKE SALAD WITH LEMON AND WHITE TRUFFLE OIL

IN ITALY, THE ARTICHOKES are usually left raw for this salad and shaved paper-thin. However, a brief blanching highlights the nutty-sweet flavor of the hearts. Blanching the fava beans lightly makes it easy to peel them, but you want to be sure they are not so soft that they fall apart—adjust the timing according to the size of the shelled beans. SERVES 4

2 large globe artichokes	**1 garlic clove,** crushed and halved
½ lemon	**Pinch of coarse salt or fleur de sel**
2 tablespoons fresh lemon juice	**Coarsely ground black pepper**
2½ tablespoons fruity extra-virgin olive oil, such as unfiltered Sicilian	**1½ cups shelled fava beans (1½ to 2 pounds in the pods)** [200 grams/750 grams to 1 kg]
2 teaspoons white truffle oil	**A small chunk of pecorino Romano or Parmigiano-Reggiano**

1. Fill a medium bowl with water and squeeze the juice of the half lemon into it; set the lemon aside. One at a time, using a sharp knife, cut off the stem of each artichoke. (As you work, rub the trimmed parts of the artichokes with the lemon half to prevent discoloration.) Starting at the bottom of the artichoke and working your way around it, bend back and snap off the green leaves until you reach the pale yellow inner cone of leaves. Discard the green leaves. Cut off the yellow cone of leaves. Using a sharp-edged teaspoon or a grapefruit spoon, scrape out the hairy choke from the center of the artichoke. Trim off all the green or tough parts from the bottom of the artichoke. As you finish each artichoke, put it in the bowl of lemon water.

2. Bring a medium saucepan of salted water to a boil. Add any juice remaining in the lemon half to the water, then add the artichoke hearts and cook for 5 minutes. Drain and rinse under cold water until cool. Cut into very thin slices.

3. In a medium bowl, gently toss the artichoke slices with the lemon juice, the olive oil, and 1 teaspoon of the truffle oil. Add the garlic, salt, and a generous grinding of pepper.

4. Bring a medium saucepan of salted water to a boil. Add the fava beans and cook for 2 to 3 minutes, depending upon size. Drain and immediately transfer to a bowl of ice water to cool; drain again. To peel the fava beans, pinch the skin open at one side and squeeze out the bean. Add the favas to the artichokes. Toss gently.

5. Divide the salad among 4 salad plates. Drizzle the remaining 1 teaspoon truffle oil on top. Using a vegetable peeler, shave the cheese over the top. Finish with an extra grind of pepper and serve.

ROASTED BEET SALAD WITH BLACK TRUFFLE AND GOAT CHEESE

ROASTING BRINGS OUT all the natural sweetness of beets. Because the scarlet root vegetable and black truffles have such a fine affinity for each other, marinating the sliced beets briefly in a truffle vinaigrette permeates them almost magically with that earthy flavor. Creamy goat cheese adds a tangy but smooth counterpoint. SERVES 4

2 large bunches of beets (about 3 pounds, weighed with greens) [2.5 kg]

Scant 1 tablespoon red wine vinegar

3 tablespoons olive oil

⅛ teaspoon Dijon mustard

Salt and freshly ground black pepper

1 fresh or flash-frozen black truffle (¾ to 1 ounce) [20 to 30 grams]

4 ounces baby spinach leaves (about 2 cups) [125 grams/500 ml]

About 1 teaspoon chives cut into ½-inch lengths [1 cm]

2 ounces mild soft goat cheese [60 grams]

1. Preheat the oven to 375°F [190°C]. Trim the beets, leaving the roots and about ½ inch [1 cm] of the stems attached; reserve the greens for another use, if desired. Scrub the beets under cold running water. Put them in a small baking pan, add ¼ cup [60 ml] water, and cover the pan with aluminum foil. Roast until the beets are tender when pierced with a knife, 45 to 60 minutes, depending on size. Transfer to a plate and let cool.

2. In a small jar, combine the vinegar, olive oil, mustard, ¼ teaspoon salt, and ⅛ teaspoon pepper. Seal tightly and shake the jar until the vinaigrette is well blended and emulsified. (The vinaigrette can be made up to 1 day ahead and refrigerated; bring to room temperature before proceeding.)

3. Cut slightly more than three-quarters of the truffle into paper-thin slices. Mince the remaining truffle, wrap tightly in plastic wrap, and reserve for garnish.

4. Rub the skin off the beets and cut them into ¼-inch[.5-cm]-thick slices. Combine the beets and sliced truffle in a bowl, tossing gently to distribute the truffle. Add half the vinaigrette and toss gently to coat. Cover and set aside to marinate at room temperature for 30 minutes.

5. Put the spinach in a bowl and add just enough of the remaining vinaigrette to lightly coat the leaves. Arrange the spinach in the centers of 4 large salad plates.

6. Season the beets with salt and pepper. Add the chives and toss gently to mix. Arrange the beets in small mounds on top of the spinach and crumble the goat cheese over the top. Scatter the reserved minced truffle around the salads and serve.

SUMMER TRUFFLE SALAD WITH AGED PROVOLONE

A HIGH-QUALITY IMPORTED PROVOLONE—slightly aged, but not a provolone *piccante*—or a young Parmigiano-Reggiano both shows off and echoes the nutty quality of fresh summer truffles. Choose a mesclun mix that includes some pigment greens, such as baby arugula, mizuna, mustard greens, and the like.

For more truffle intensity, you can substitute Black Truffle Vinaigrette (page 97) for the simple lemon juice and olive oil dressing included here. SERVES 4

3 tablespoons extra-virgin olive oil

1 tablespoon fresh lemon juice

¼ teaspoon salt

⅛ teaspoon freshly ground black pepper

6 ounces high-quality mesclun mix (about 8 cups; see headnote) [175 grams]

1 large or 2 smaller summer truffles (3 to 4 ounces total), very thinly sliced [90 to 125 grams]

2 ounces imported provolone or Parmigiano-Reggiano [60 grams]

1. In a small jar, combine the olive oil, lemon juice, salt, and pepper. Seal tightly with the lid and shake until the dressing is well blended and emulsified. (The dressing can be made up to 1 day ahead and refrigerated; let return to room temperature before using.)

2. Put the greens in a large bowl and add enough of the dressing to coat lightly; toss gently. Add the truffle, drizzle the remaining vinaigrette over the salad, and toss carefully to mix without breaking the truffle slices.

3. Arrange the salad on 4 plates. Using a vegetable peeler or a mandoline, thinly slice the cheese. Arrange the slices of cheese on the salads and serve.

ROASTED WILD MUSHROOM SALAD WITH TRUFFLE OIL AND HERBS

A JUMBLE OF WOODSY FLAVORS gains subtle depths from white truffle oil. Crostini (page 49) spread with soft goat cheese would make a nice accompaniment for this earthy salad. Serve it as a first course or—with the crostini—as a light but most elegant lunch. SERVES 4

1 pound mixed wild and cultivated mushrooms, such as chanterelles, porcini, morels, shiitake, portobellos, oyster, and/or cremini, trimmed (stems discarded if using shiitake), rinsed briefly, and thickly sliced [500 grams]

¼ cup store-bought garlic olive oil or extra-virgin olive oil [60 ml]

1 tablespoon finely chopped thyme

1½ teaspoons finely chopped rosemary

Salt and freshly ground black pepper

1 tablespoon finely chopped flat-leaf parsley

1 tablespoon fresh lemon juice

¼ cup pine nuts [30 grams]

3 ounces high-quality mesclun mix or other young salad greens (about 4 cups) [15 grams]

2 teaspoons white truffle oil, or more to taste

1. Preheat the oven to 450°F [230°C]. On a large baking sheet, toss the mushrooms with 3 tablespoons of the oil, the thyme, and rosemary. Season with ¼ teaspoon salt and pepper to taste. Spread the mushrooms out in an even layer and roast, stirring once or twice, until lightly browned and fragrant, about 10 minutes.

2. Toss the mushrooms with the parsley and 2 teaspoons of the lemon juice, and set aside to cool to room temperature.

3. Meanwhile, toast the pine nuts in a small dry skillet over moderately low heat, shaking the pan often, until very lightly browned, 2 to 3 minutes. Let cool.

4. Put the greens in a medium bowl and add the remaining 1 tablespoon oil and 1 teaspoon lemon juice. Toss to coat. Season lightly with salt and pepper.

5. Arrange the greens on 4 salad plates. Mound the mushrooms over the greens and scatter the pine nuts on top. Drizzle the truffle oil over the salads and serve.

SEARED SEA SCALLOPS WITH PORCINI MUSHROOMS AND TRUFFLED GREENS

FOR THIS EXTRAVAGANT WARM SALAD, Chef Paul Bartolotta, formerly of Spiaggia in Chicago, who is known for his creativity with truffles, dresses delicate mâche and more assertive frisée with an unusual vinaigrette that combines sherry and balsamic vinegars with truffle oil and browned butter. The greens make a bed for the seared scallops (be sure to use large diver's scallops, also called "dry" scallops) and sautéed porcini, garnished with a generous shower of white truffle. SERVES 4

Browned Butter Vinaigrette (recipe follows)

1 tablespoon unsalted butter [15 grams]

4 large porcini mushrooms, trimmed, cleaned, and thinly sliced

Salt

8 very large diver's ("dry") sea scallops (about 2½ ounces each), tough side muscles removed [70 grams]

Freshly ground black pepper

1 tablespoon olive oil

3 heads of frisée, tender inner yellow leaves only (reserve the green for another use)

3 ounces mâche (about 3 cups) [90 grams]

8 large paper-thin slices of Parmigiano-Reggiano (sliced with a vegetable peeler)

1 small to medium fresh white truffle

4 chervil sprigs

1. Make the browned butter vinaigrette, and set aside in a warm place.

2. Heat the butter in a large skillet over moderately high heat until melted and golden. Add the porcini, season with salt, and sauté, tossing frequently, until golden brown, about 5 minutes. Remove from the heat and set aside in a warm place.

3. Season the scallops on both sides with salt and pepper. In a large heavy skillet, preferably non-stick, heat the olive oil until very hot. Add the scallops and cook until golden brown on the bottom, 2 to 3 minutes. Turn the scallops over, reduce the heat to moderate, and cook until golden brown on the second side and just barely cooked through, about 2 minutes longer.

4. Meanwhile, combine the frisée and mâche in a large bowl and toss to mix. Arrange a bed of the greens on each of 4 large plates. Quickly reheat the porcini if necessary, and spoon the mushrooms onto the lettuce.

5. Arrange the scallops on top of the salads and drizzle the vinaigrette over all. Garnish with the Parmesan and shave the white truffle over the top. Garnish each salad with a chervil sprig and serve immediately.

BROWNED BUTTER VINAIGRETTE

MAKES ½ CUP [125 ML]

2 tablespoons unsalted butter [30 grams]

1 tablespoon sherry vinegar

1 tablespoon balsamic vinegar, preferably *balsamico tradizionale*

2 tablespoons white truffle oil

2 tablespoons extra-virgin olive oil

Salt and freshly ground black pepper

1. Melt the butter in a small saucepan over moderately high heat. Cook the butter until fragrant and golden brown, about 2 minutes. Remove from the heat.

2. Combine the sherry vinegar and balsamic vinegar in a small bowl. Whisk in the browned butter. Whisking constantly, slowly add the truffle oil and then the olive oil in a thin, steady stream until the vinaigrette is well blended and emulsified. Season with salt and pepper to taste. Keep warm until ready to use.

SMOKED DUCK SALAD WITH PANCETTA, WARM RICOTTA SALATA, AND BLACK TRUFFLE

UNLIKE THE MORE FAMILIAR FRESH RICOTTA, ricotta salata, a specialty of southern Italy, is a snowy white sheep's milk cheese that is lightly salted, pressed, and aged until it is firm enough to slice or crumble. Black truffle and smoked duck make an opulent combination. Smoked duck is available at specialty butchers and some gourmet markets. SERVES 4

---

12 ounces haricots verts or other small green beans [350 grams]

2 tablespoons extra-virgin olive oil

8 ounces pancetta or smoky slab bacon, cut into ½-inch dice [250 grams/1 cm]

6 ounces ricotta salata, in one piece [175 grams]

1 boneless smoked duck breast (about 8 ounces), skin removed, trimmed of fat, and thinly sliced [250 grams]

1 small head of Napa (Chinese) cabbage, shredded

2 tablespoons minced flat-leaf parsley

Truffle–Honey Mustard Vinaigrette (recipe follows)

1 fresh black truffle

---

1. Bring a large saucepan of salted water to a boil. Add the haricots verts and cook until crisp-tender, about 5 minutes. Drain the beans and rinse under cold running water until cool; drain well.

2. Heat 1 tablespoon of the olive oil in a medium skillet over moderate heat. Add the pancetta and cook, stirring occasionally, until browned but not crisp, 5 to 7 minutes. With a slotted spoon, transfer to paper towels to drain.

3. Preheat the oven to 450°F [230°C]. Grease a medium baking pan (about 9 by 12 inches [23 by 30 cm]) with the remaining 1 tablespoon olive oil.

4. Cut the cheese into 4 equal slices, then cut each slice on the diagonal into 2 triangles. Arrange the cheese triangles in the prepared baking pan. Bake until the cheese is nicely browned and crisp at the edges, 6 to 8 minutes.

5. Meanwhile, in a large bowl, combine the green beans, pancetta, duck breast, cabbage, and parsley; toss gently to mix. Add the vinaigrette and toss to coat.

6. Arrange the salad on 4 large plates. Using a metal spatula, place 2 slices of warm cheese over each salad. Shave the truffle over the top and serve at once.

TRUFFLE-HONEY MUSTARD VINAIGRETTE

MAKES ABOUT ¼ CUP [60 ML]

1 tablespoon fresh lemon juice

1 tablespoon minced shallots

½ teaspoon honey Dijon mustard

¼ cup extra-virgin olive oil [60 ml]

½ teaspoon black truffle oil, or more to taste

Salt and freshly ground black pepper

In a small bowl, whisk together the lemon juice, shallots, and mustard. Whisking constantly, add the olive oil in a thin, steady stream until well blended and emulsified. Whisk in the truffle oil. Season with salt and pepper. (The vinaigrette can be made up to 1 day ahead, covered, and refrigerated. Let return to room temperature before using.)

PROSCIUTTO WITH FRISEE AND TRUFFLE OIL

AT HARRY'S BAR IN VENICE, they serve a simple appetizer of gossamer-thin slices of prosciutto draped over chopped arugula—no dressing at all. You could present this in the same way, arranging the prosciutto over the frisée salad—allow a little of the greens to peek out in the center for some color. (For another presentation, see the variation below.) SERVES 4

1½ teaspoons white wine vinegar

⅛ teaspoon Dijon mustard

1½ tablespoons extra-virgin olive oil

Scant ⅛ teaspoon salt

Freshly ground black pepper

4 cups frisée torn into bite-size pieces
(about 3 ounces) [90 grams]

6 ounces very thinly sliced imported
prosciutto (see page 109) [175 grams]

2 teaspoons white or black truffle oil,
or more to taste

1. In a small jar, combine the vinegar, mustard, olive oil, salt, and a pinch of pepper. Seal tightly with the lid and shake until well blended and emulsified. (The vinaigrette can be made up to 1 day ahead and refrigerated; let return to room temperature before using.)

2. Put the frisée in a medium bowl and add just enough vinaigrette to coat it lightly. Toss gently.

3. Arrange the prosciutto on 4 large salad plates, overlapping the slices as necessary and covering each plate completely. Place a small mound of frisée in the center of each and drizzle the truffle oil over the prosciutto. Grind black pepper over the prosciutto, if desired, and serve.

VARIATION

PROSCIUTTO-FRISÉE "BUNDLES" WITH TRUFFLE OIL Arrange one-quarter of the prosciutto on a work surface, overlapping the slices as necessary to make a rough circle about 7 inches in diameter. Mound one-quarter of the frisée in the center and bring the edges of the prosciutto up over the salad to form a small bundle about 3 inches in diameter. Using a wide spatula, carefully transfer the bundle to a salad plate, seam side down. Repeat with the remaining prosciutto and frisée. Drizzle the truffle oil around the bundles and grind black pepper over the top.

PROSCIUTTO

PROSCIUTTO is salt-cured, air-dried aged ham. Prosciutto di Parma, sometimes called Parma ham, is the Italian prosciutto that is most familiar in this country. It comes from the Emilia-Romagna region and is succulent and delicious, but there are other excellent choices as well. Prosciutto di San Daniele, from the Friuli-Venezia region, has a slightly sweeter taste. And prosciutto di Carpegna, from a small mountain town in the Marches district, has long been a favorite of Italian gourmands. This less common ham, which is especially fragrant and delicate, has recently become available in the United States, where it has quickly acquired a devoted following.

PASTA, RICE, AND POLENTA

AFTER-THE-OPERA SPAGHETTI
WITH BLACK TRUFFLE OIL

MIDNIGHT PASTA WITH TRUFFLE
BUTTER

PASTA WITH BROWNED TRUFFLE
BUTTER AND FRESH SAGE

TAGLIATELLE WITH WHITE
TRUFFLES

RAVIOLO WITH WHITE TRUFFLES
AND GOLDEN BUTTER

FAVA BEAN RAVIOLI IN
PARMESAN BROTH

TRUFFLE-SCENTED BUTTERNUT
SQUASH RAVIOLI

BAKED PENNE WITH TRUFFLE
CHEESE

BOW TIES WITH TRUFFLES,
MORELS, AND FOIE GRAS

RISOTTO WITH ASPARAGUS,
BLACK TRUFFLES, AND PROSECCO

TRU'S BLACK TRUFFLE RISOTTO
WITH LOBSTER AND TRUFFLE
BUTTER FROTH

RISOTTO WITH FRESH WHITE
TRUFFLES

NO. 9 PARK'S WHITE-TRUFFLE
GNOCCHI WITH LOBSTER,
CHANTERELLES, AND PEAS

TRUFFLED RICE TORTA

CREAMY POLENTA WITH TALEGGIO
CHEESE AND WHITE TRUFFLE

AFTER-THE-OPERA SPAGHETTI WITH BLACK TRUFFLE OIL

WHAT COULD MAKE a better late-night supper than this simple but stylish black-tie dish? Truffle oil takes *aglio e olio*, the garlic and olive oil pasta sauce beloved throughout Italy, to a new dimension. In Rome, this dish is always made with spaghetti, but you can substitute linguine or spaghettini. For a more assertive garlic taste, finely mince the garlic and leave it in the oil. SERVES 4 AS A FIRST COURSE

---

12 ounces spaghetti [350 grams]

3 tablespoons olive oil

2 to 3 garlic cloves, crushed

3 tablespoons minced flat-leaf parsley

1½ to 2 teaspoons black truffle oil

Salt and freshly ground black pepper

---

1. Bring a large pot of salted water to a boil. Add the pasta and cook until al dente.

2. Meanwhile, combine the olive oil and garlic in a small heavy skillet and heat over low heat, stirring and mashing the garlic occasionally, until the oil is very fragrant and the garlic is light golden brown, about 5 minutes. Remove from the heat and set aside.

3. Drain the pasta and return it to the pot. With a slotted spoon, remove the garlic from the oil and discard. Add the garlic oil and parsley to the pasta and toss to coat. Drizzle on the truffle oil and season with salt and pepper. Serve immediately.

SOMMELIER WINE SUGGESTION Howard Park Riesling 1999; Denmark, Australia

MIDNIGHT PASTA WITH TRUFFLE BUTTER

ANY TIME CAN BE THE TIME for romance if you decide to whip up this quick, luscious pasta. It makes a great midnight supper by itself or a luxurious side dish to a grilled steak with a sliced tomato salad. If you keep truffle butter on hand in the freezer, this dish can be tossed together on the spur of the moment. Good truffle butter is so fragrant and flavorful that just a small amount perfumes the entire dish.

SERVES 4 AS A FIRST COURSE OR SIDE DISH

8 ounces fettuccine [250 grams]

3 tablespoons unsalted butter, at room temperature [45 grams]

2 teaspoons truffle butter, at room temperature

2 tablespoons freshly grated Parmigiano-Reggiano, plus extra for serving

Salt and freshly ground black pepper

1. Bring a large pot of salted water to a boil. Add the pasta and cook until al dente; drain.

2. Return the pasta to the pot, add the unsalted butter, and toss gently to coat. Add the truffle butter and toss until it melts. Add the cheese and toss just to mix. Season with salt and pepper to taste and serve immediately. Pass extra cheese at the table.

VARIATION

PASTA WITH TRUFFLE BUTTER AND HERBS Add 1 tablespoon minced flat-leaf parsley or 2 teaspoons minced chives along with the cheese.

| SOMMELIER WINE SUGGESTION | Barolo Bricco Rocche Ceretto "Prapo" 1994; Piedmont, Italy

PASTA WITH BROWNED TRUFFLE BUTTER AND FRESH SAGE

SAGE-INFUSED BROWNED BUTTER is a classic Italian pasta sauce, often served over gnocchi as well. Here truffle butter transforms a simple dish into a superlative treat. SERVES 4 AS A FIRST COURSE OR SIDE DISH

8 ounces farfalle or fusilli [250 grams]

4 tablespoons unsalted butter [60 grams]

About 16 small sage leaves

Generous 1 tablespoon truffle butter,
at room temperature

Salt and freshly ground black pepper

Freshly grated Parmigiano-Reggiano,
for serving

1. Bring a large pot of salted water to a boil. Add the pasta and cook until al dente.

2. Meanwhile, melt the unsalted butter in a small skillet over moderate heat. Continue to cook until the butter is golden, about 3 minutes. Add the sage leaves and cook, stirring once or twice, until the butter is a deep golden brown, about 2 minutes longer. Remove from the heat. When the butter has stopped foaming, add the truffle butter and stir until it is melted.

3. Drain the pasta and return it to the pot. Pour the browned butter with the sage leaves over the pasta and toss to coat. Season with salt and pepper to taste. Transfer to a warm serving bowl or individual plates and serve at once. Pass a bowl of grated Parmesan at the table.

> **SOMMELIER WINE SUGGESTION** Bollenberg Château d'Orschwihr Pinot Blanc 1999; Alsace, France

TAGLIATELLE WITH WHITE TRUFFLES

FRESH TAGLIATELLE tossed with cream and butter and finished with a shower of white truffles is considered by many the ultimate way to enjoy fresh truffles. It is served in restaurants all over Italy when they are in season. Tagliatelle is just fettuccine by another name; it is also called *tajarìn* in the Piedmont region, where this dish is especially popular. SERVES 4 AS A FIRST COURSE

One 2-egg batch Pasta Dough (recipe follows), rolled out and cut into fettuccine as directed on page 117, or 8 ounces store-bought fresh fettuccine [250 grams]

⅔ cup heavy cream [150 ml]

3 tablespoons unsalted butter [45 grams]

¼ cup freshly grated Parmigiano-Reggiano [15 grams]

Salt and freshly ground black pepper

1 to 1½ ounces fresh white truffle [30 to 45 grams]

1. Bring a large pot of salted water to a boil. Add the pasta and cook until just tender, 2 to 3 minutes; drain.

2. Meanwhile, combine the cream and butter in a large deep skillet and bring just to a simmer over moderate heat. Simmer until the cream has reduced slightly, 1 to 2 minutes.

3. Add the pasta to the cream and butter, toss gently to coat, and reduce the heat to low. Cook, stirring occasionally, for 1 to 2 minutes to allow the pasta to absorb some of the sauce. Add the cheese, toss well, and season to taste with salt and pepper.

4. Divide the pasta among 4 warm plates and shave the truffle over the top. Serve immediately.

VARIATION

TAGLIATELLE WITH PORCINI AND WHITE TRUFFLES To gild the lily, you can add porcini mushrooms to the above dish. In a small bowl, soak 1 ounce [30 grams] dried porcini in 1 cup [250 ml] warm water until softened, about 30 minutes. Lift out the mushrooms, reserving the soaking liquid, and rinse under cold running water to remove any grit; squeeze out any excess liquid. Coarsely chop the mushrooms. Strain the soaking liquid through a fine sieve or a strainer lined with a paper towel or coffee filter.

Melt the butter in a large deep skillet. Add the porcini, then stir in the reserved soaking liquid and the cream. Bring to a simmer and cook for 3 minutes to blend the flavors. Reduce the heat to low, add the pasta to the sauce as in Step 3 above, and proceed as directed.

SOMMELIER WINE SUGGESTION Meursault Bitouzet-Prieur "Charmes" 1995; Côte de Beaune, France

PASTA DOUGH

Homemade pasta is infinitely better than the so-called "fresh" pasta found in the supermarket or the often-too-thick fresh pastas that tend to be offered by even the best gourmet markets.

MAKES ABOUT 9 OUNCES DOUGH, ENOUGH FOR 4 FIRST-COURSE SERVINGS [250 GRAMS]

1 cup all-purpose flour, plus more as needed [125 grams]

2 large eggs, lightly beaten

MAKES ABOUT 14 OUNCES DOUGH, ENOUGH FOR 4 MAIN-COURSE SERVINGS [390 GRAMS]

1½ cups all-purpose flour, plus more as needed [190 grams]

3 large eggs, lightly beaten

1. Mound the flour on a work surface and make a well in the center. Add the eggs to the well and using a fork, gradually draw the flour into the eggs, starting from the inside walls and being careful not to let the eggs spill out. When you have a rough mass of dough, set it to one side of the work surface and scrape the work surface clean. Wash your hands.

2. Lightly sprinkle the work surface with flour. Knead the dough, sprinkling it lightly with more flour as needed, until it is smooth and elastic; if you stick your finger into the center of the dough, it should no longer be sticky. (The dough can be made ahead, wrapped in plastic, and refrigerated for up to 8 hours.)

3. TO ROLL OUT THE DOUGH: Cut the pasta in half if you made a 2-egg batch, or into 3 equal pieces if you made a 3-egg batch. Work with one piece of dough at a time, keeping the remaining dough covered with plastic wrap.

4. Set the rollers of the pasta machine at the widest opening. Flatten the piece of dough with your hands and roll it through the machine. Fold the dough into thirds, gently press it together, and roll it though the same setting of the pasta machine, starting from an open end of the dough. Fold and roll the dough 2 more times, dusting it very lightly with flour if necessary to prevent sticking. Adjust the rollers of the pasta machine to the next setting and roll the pasta through it. Continue to roll the pasta, without folding it, through the successive settings of the machine until you reach the next-to-the-thinnest setting, lightly flouring the dough as necessary to prevent sticking. Lay the pasta sheet on a lightly floured surface and repeat with the remaining dough.

5. If using the dough to make ravioli or another filled pasta, it should be used immediately. If cutting the dough into fettuccine or capellini, let the sheets of dough dry until no longer moist or sticky on top, about 10 minutes. Turn the pasta over and let dry until no longer moist and sticky but still soft; do not allow the dough to stand so long that the edges start to crack.

6. TO CUT THE DOUGH: Using the fettuccine or capellini cutter on the pasta machine, cut each sheet of dough into strips. Separate the noodles and arrange on a floured work surface or baking sheet. The pasta can be cooked immediately or dried and stored for several days.

7. TO DRY THE PASTA: Spread the noodles out to allow air to circulate around them and let dry thoroughly—depending on the dough and the humidity, this may take as long as 12 hours. Transfer to a heavy-duty plastic bag or an airtight container and refrigerate for up to 3 days. Dried fresh pasta will take a minute or two longer to cook.

NOTE: To make the dough in a food processor, put the flour in the processor bowl. In a glass measuring cup or small bowl with a spout, whisk the eggs until blended. With the food processor on, slowly add eggs through the feed tube. Continue to process just until the dough forms a ball. Turn the dough out onto a lightly floured work surface and knead briefly, as directed above.

VARIATION

TRUFFLED PASTA DOUGH Beat 1½ to 2 teaspoons black truffle puree or paste into the eggs for the 2-egg batch, or 2 to 2½ teaspoons for the 3-egg batch, and proceed as directed.

RAVIOLO WITH WHITE TRUFFLES AND GOLDEN BUTTER

THESE RAVIOLI ARE SO LARGE AND RICH, only one is served per person. They are stuffed with a spinach and ricotta filling surrounding a whole egg yolk and sauced with browned butter and fresh Parmesan cheese. When you cut into the ravioli, the warm, runny egg yolk becomes part of the truffle-flecked butter sauce. This heady delight, from Chef Paul Bartolotta, who served this as one of his signature dishes at both New York City's SanDomenico restaurant (where it is still on the menu) and Chicago's Spiaggia, is fit for a king. In fact, the recipe, created in the 1930s, was originally handed down from the private chef to the last king of Italy, Vittorio Emanuele III.

      Although the recipe may look complicated, it's actually quite easy to prepare, and the results are stunning. It may just be the best white truffle pasta dish you've ever tasted. For his ultra-tender pasta dough, Chef Bartolotta uses Italian "00" flour, a soft wheat flour that can be found at Italian grocers and specialty markets (or through mail-order; see Sources, page 234).

SERVES 4 AS A FIRST COURSE

8 ounces spinach, trimmed and washed [250 grams]

1 large egg

½ cup ricotta cheese [125 ml]

¾ cup freshly grated Parmigiano-Reggiano [40 grams]

Pinch of freshly grated nutmeg

Salt and freshly ground white pepper

One 2-egg batch Pasta Dough (page 116), preferably made with Italian "00" flour, with a pinch of salt added to the flour

Cornmeal, for dusting

¼ ounce fresh white truffle, grated or sliced paper-thin (optional)

4 large egg yolks (do not separate the whole eggs until just before using; see below)

6 to 8 tablespoons unsalted butter [90 to 125 grams]

1 fresh white truffle (about 1 ounce [30 grams])

1. To make the filling, heat a large nonreactive pot over moderate heat. Add the spinach in batches, stirring and turning it (this is easy to do with tongs) until it is thoroughly wilted but still bright green, 2 to 3 minutes. Drain in a strainer, pressing against the spinach with a wooden spoon to release as much water as possible. Let cool.

2. A handful at a time, squeeze the spinach between your palms to remove as much of the remaining moisture as possible. Finely chop the spinach.

3. Lightly beat the egg in a medium bowl. Add the ricotta, a scant ¼ cup [10 grams] of the Parmesan cheese, and the spinach and stir to mix well. Season with the nutmeg, ⅛ teaspoon salt, and white pepper to taste. Cover the filling and set aside while you roll out the dough.

4. Cut the dough in half and roll it out to the next-to-last setting on a pasta machine, as directed on page 117. Cut each sheet of dough into 4 squares about 6 inches [15 cm] across.

5. Lightly dust a large baking sheet with cornmeal. Place one of the pasta squares on a lightly floured work surface (keep the remaining pasta covered with plastic wrap as you work). Using a pastry bag fitted with a large plain tip, pipe one-quarter of the filling into a ring in the middle of the pasta square, leaving a circle in the center just large enough to hold an egg yolk. Or spoon the filling onto the square and use the back of the spoon to create a hollow for the egg yolk.

6. Carefully place 1 of the egg yolks in the center of the filling and season the yolk with a pinch each of salt and white pepper. Scatter one-quarter of the optional grated truffle over the egg yolk. Using a pastry brush or your fingertips, moisten the exposed edges of the pasta with water. Place another pasta square on top and seal the edges, pressing out any air bubbles and being careful not to break the egg yolk. Using a fluted pastry wheel or a sharp paring knife, trim the edges to make a large round raviolo; there should be a plain border of pasta at least ½ inch wide all around the filling. Transfer the raviolo to the cornmeal-dusted baking sheet and repeat with the remaining ingredients to make 3 more large ravioli.

7. Bring a large pot of salted water to a boil over high heat. Reduce the heat to keep the water at a gentle boil. Meanwhile, melt the butter in a small saucepan over moderate heat. Continue to cook until the butter is fragrant and golden brown, 2 to 3 minutes. Remove from the heat and set aside in a warm spot.

8. Carefully add the ravioli to the boiling water, stirring once or twice if necessary to separate them. Return the water to a gentle boil and cook the pasta for 3 minutes (no longer, or the egg yolks will be overcooked). Just before the ravioli are done, reheat the butter over low heat.

9. Using a large wire skimmer or slotted spoon, lift each raviolo from the water, draining it well, and place on a warm serving plate. Shave the truffle over the raviolo, scatter the remaining cheese over the top, and drizzle the browned butter generously over each plate. Serve immediately.

SOMMELIER WINE SUGGESTION Shafer "Red Shoulder Ranch" Chardonnay 1998; Carneros, Napa, California

FAVA BEAN RAVIOLI IN PARMESAN BROTH

WONTON SKINS (see headnote, page 122) make instant ravioli wrappers. An easy Parmesan-flavored broth provides a flavorful backdrop for the rich, creamy fava bean puree in these pillows of ravioli. Both filling and broth are laced with fragrant white truffle oil. If fava beans are not in season, you can use frozen favas (see Sources, page 234), but do not substitute canned beans; they are not delicate enough for this dish. Frozen fava beans do not need to be blanched before they are peeled.

SERVES 4 AS A FIRST COURSE OR LIGHT LUNCH

Fava Bean Ravioli (recipe follows)

1¼ cups chicken stock or canned low-sodium chicken broth [300 ml]

2½ tablespoons unsalted butter [40 grams]

1½ tablespoons freshly grated Parmigiano-Reggiano

Salt and freshly ground white pepper

2 teaspoons white truffle oil, plus extra for drizzling

1. Bring a large pot of salted water to a boil over high heat; reduce the heat slightly to keep the water at a gentle boil. Meanwhile, bring the stock to a boil in a large skillet over high heat. Reduce the heat to moderate and boil until reduced to ¾ cup [175 ml]. Remove from the heat.

2. Add the ravioli to the pot of boiling water and cook until the wrappers are al dente, 2 to 3 minutes. With a large wire skimmer or slotted spoon, transfer to a colander to drain briefly.

3. Meanwhile, bring the reduced stock to a simmer over moderately high heat. Reduce the heat to moderate and, whisking constantly, add the butter about ½ tablespoon [250 ml] at a time, whisking until the sauce is creamy and emulsified. Reduce the heat to moderately low and gradually whisk in the Parmesan. Season with salt and pepper to taste. Remove from the heat and whisk in the truffle oil.

4. Arrange the ravioli in 4 warm shallow bowls and spoon the broth over them. Drizzle with additional truffle oil, and serve immediately.

SOMMELIER WINE SUGGESTION Chateau Fuissé J. J. Vincent 1999; Maconnais, France

FAVA BEAN RAVIOLI

MAKES 20; SERVES 4

1¼ cups shelled fava beans (about 1½ pounds in the pod) [165 grams/750 grams]

½ cup heavy cream [125 ml]

1½ tablespoons freshly grated Parmigiano-Reggiano

¼ teaspoon salt, or more to taste

Freshly ground white pepper

1 teaspoon white truffle oil

Cornmeal, for dusting

20 wonton wrappers

1. To make the ravioli filling, blanch the fava beans in a medium saucepan of boiling water for about 30 seconds, just to loosen the skin. Drain, transfer to a bowl of ice water to cool, and drain again. To peel the favas, pinch open the skin at one side of each bean and squeeze out the bean.

2. Combine the fava beans and cream in a small heavy saucepan and bring to a simmer over moderate heat. Reduce the heat and simmer gently until the beans are very tender, 12 to 14 minutes.

3. Transfer the beans and cream to a food processor and process to a puree. Add the Parmesan, salt, and white pepper to taste and process to blend well. Transfer to a bowl and let cool. Stir in the white truffle oil. Cover and refrigerate for 1 hour, or until ready to assemble the ravioli. (The filling can be made up to 1 day ahead.)

4. To assemble the ravioli, sprinkle a large baking sheet with cornmeal. Lay out 10 of the wonton wrappers on a work surface. Using a pastry bag fitted with a medium plain tip or a small spoon, pipe or place about 1½ teaspoons of the filling in the center of each wrapper. One at a time, using a pastry brush or your fingertips, moisten the edges of each wrapper with water, then fold the wrapper over the filling to make a triangle and press the edges firmly together to seal. Transfer the ravioli to the baking sheet and repeat with the remaining wrappers and filling. (The ravioli can be made early in the day, covered loosely with plastic wrap, and refrigerated.)

TRUFFLE-SCENTED BUTTERNUT SQUASH RAVIOLI

TRUFFLE FLOUR is the magic dust that gives this ravioli its haunting flavor. Using wonton wrappers is much easier than making fresh pasta dough. The wrappers are available in the refrigerator or freezer section of Asian markets and in some supermarkets or specialty grocers, as well as through mail-order (see Sources, page 234). SERVES 4 AS A FIRST COURSE OR LIGHT LUNCH

1½ cups chicken stock or canned low-sodium chicken broth [375 ml]

2 tablespoons unsalted butter, cut into bits, at room temperature [30 grams]

1½ teaspoons chopped fresh thyme

Salt and freshly ground pepper

Butternut Squash Ravioli (recipe follows)

White truffle oil, for drizzling

Freshly grated Parmigiano-Reggiano

1. Bring a large pot of salted water to a boil over high heat. Reduce the heat slightly to keep the water at a gentle boil.

2. Meanwhile, bring the stock to a boil in a large skillet over high heat. Reduce the heat to moderate and boil until reduced to 1 cup. Whisking constantly, add the butter about ½ tablespoon [250 ml] at a time, whisking until the broth is creamy and emulsified. Reduce the heat to low. Season with the thyme and salt and pepper to taste. Remove the sauce from the heat and cover to keep warm.

3. In 2 batches, add the ravioli to the pot of boiling water and cook until the wrappers are al dente, 2 to 3 minutes. Carefully remove with a slotted spoon and drain in a colander.

4. Quickly reheat the sauce in the skillet. Add the ravioli and toss gently to coat. Divide the ravioli among 4 warm shallow bowls or plates. Spoon any sauce remaining in the skillet over the ravioli, drizzle truffle oil over the top, and serve at once. Pass Parmesan cheese at the table.

SOMMELIER WINE SUGGESTION | Leon Beyer Pinot Blanc de Blancs 1997; Alsace, France

BUTTERNUT SQUASH RAVIOLI

MAKES 20; SERVES 4

1 pound butternut squash [500 grams]

2½ tablespoons olive oil

Salt

1 tablespoon finely chopped shallots

¾ cup freshly grated Parmigiano-Reggiano [40 grams]

⅛ teaspoon freshly grated nutmeg

Freshly ground black pepper

1 large egg yolk

Cornmeal, for dusting

40 wonton wrappers (from a 12-ounce package) [350 grams]

About 1¼ teaspoons truffle flour

1 egg white, beaten with 1 tablespoon water

1. Preheat the oven to 375°F [190°C]. Cut the squash lengthwise in half. Scrape out all the seeds and strings. Brush 1 tablespoon of the olive oil over the cut surfaces and season lightly with salt. Place the squash cut side down in a baking dish and cover the dish tightly with aluminum foil. Bake until the squash is very tender when pierced with a sharp knife, 45 to 60 minutes. Let the squash stand until cool enough to handle.

2. With a large spoon, scrape out the flesh from the squash, discarding the skin. Mash the squash with a fork or pass it through the coarse disk of a food mill.

3. Heat the remaining 1½ tablespoons olive oil in a medium skillet over moderate heat. Add the shallots and cook, stirring occasionally, until softened, 1 to 2 minutes. Add the mashed squash and cook, stirring to blend, for 2 to 3 minutes. Remove from the heat and let cool, then stir in the Parmesan and nutmeg. Season with salt and pepper. Add the egg yolk and blend well.

4. To assemble the ravioli, sprinkle a large baking sheet with cornmeal. Lay out half the wonton wrappers on a work surface. Place a scant tablespoon of the squash mixture in the center of each and top with a generous pinch of truffle flour. One at a time, using a pastry brush or your fingertips, moisten the edges of each wrapper with the beaten egg white. Cover with another wrapper, pressing the edges firmly together to seal. Transfer the ravioli to the baking sheet and set aside. (The ravioli can be prepared up to a day in advance. Cover tightly with plastic wrap and refrigerate.)

BAKED PENNE WITH TRUFFLE CHEESE

IN THE LAST FEW YEARS, macaroni and cheese has been showing up on the menus of even upscale restaurants. This is probably the most luxurious version you will ever taste. Serve it as a vegetarian main course or as an accompaniment to a simple grilled steak or a roast.

You can add a tablespoon or so of minced flat-leaf parsley to the dish for color, if you like. Avoid other herbs, which would overpower the delicate flavor of the cheese. SERVES 4 AS A MAIN COURSE OR 4 TO 6 AS A FIRST COURSE OR SIDE DISH

8 ounces penne or other short tubular pasta [250 grams]

3 tablespoons unsalted butter [45 grams]

3 tablespoons all-purpose flour

2 cups milk [500 ml]

8 ounces grated truffle cheese [240 grams]

¾ teaspoon salt

⅛ teaspoon freshly ground black pepper

2 to 4 tablespoons freshly grated Parmigiano-Reggiano

1. Preheat the oven to 350°F [175°C]. Butter a 1½-quart [1.5-liter] baking dish.

2. Bring a large pot of salted water to a boil. Add the pasta and cook until just barely al dente.

3. Meanwhile, melt the butter in a medium heavy saucepan over moderate heat. Add the flour and cook, stirring constantly with a wooden spoon, until the mixture is smooth and bubbling, 2 to 3 minutes. Whisking constantly, gradually add the milk and bring to a boil, still whisking. Cook, whisking, until the sauce thickens slightly, 2 to 3 minutes. Reduce the heat to low and gradually add the truffle cheese, whisking until smooth. Remove from the heat and season with salt and pepper.

4. Drain the pasta and return it to the pot. Add the cheese sauce and stir until well mixed. Scrape the pasta into the prepared baking dish and sprinkle the Parmesan evenly over the top.

5. Bake the pasta for 25 to 30 minutes, or until the sauce is bubbling and the top is lightly browned. Let stand for about 5 minutes before serving.

SOMMELIER WINE SUGGESTION Icardi l'Aurora Cortese 1999; Piedmont, Italy

BOW TIES WITH TRUFFLES, MORELS, AND FOIE GRAS

BLACK TRUFFLES AND MORELS make a felicitous combination indeed. Adding sautéed cubes of foie gras is a wonderful extravagance, but the dish is luxurious even without them. If morels are not in season, use other wild mushrooms. Or substitute 2 ounces [60 grams] dried morels for the fresh (see page 127 for instructions on "reconstituting" wild mushrooms). A good-quality imported pasta is essential; look for the smaller bow ties some producers offer. SERVES 4 AS A FIRST COURSE

1½ tablespoons unsalted butter [25 grams]

1 large shallot, finely minced

8 ounces morels, trimmed, cleaned, and halved or quartered, depending on size [250 grams]

Salt and freshly ground black pepper

½ cup chicken stock or canned low-sodium chicken broth [125 grams]

8 ounces bow tie pasta (farfalle) [250 grams]

8 ounces fresh duck foie gras, trimmed and cut into ½-inch cubes [250 grams/1 cm]

⅔ cup heavy cream [150 ml]

½ to 1 ounce black truffle, cut into thin julienne strips [15 to 30 grams]

2 tablespoons finely chopped flat-leaf parsley

1. Melt the butter in a Dutch oven or large deep skillet over moderately high heat. Add the shallot and cook, stirring frequently, until softened and translucent, about 2 minutes. Add the morels, season with salt and pepper, and cook, stirring occasionally, until most of the liquid they have released has evaporated, about 5 minutes. Add the stock, bring just to a boil, and cook until most of the stock has evaporated. Remove from the heat.

2. Bring a large pot of salted water to the boil. Add the pasta and cook until al dente; drain.

3. Meanwhile, about 5 minutes before the pasta is done, heat a large heavy skillet over moderately high heat until hot. Season the foie gras with salt and pepper. Add to the pan and cook, stirring and turning frequently, just until beginning to brown, about 1 minute. Immediately remove from the heat and, using a slotted spoon, transfer to paper towels to drain.

4. Set the Dutch oven over moderate heat, add the cream, and bring to a simmer. Add the truffle and simmer, stirring once or twice, until the cream reduces and thickens slightly, about 2 minutes. Stir in the parsley and reduce the heat to low. Add the pasta and heat, stirring once or twice, until it has absorbed some of the sauce, about 1 minute. Add the foie gras, toss gently, and serve.

SOMMELIER WINE SUGGESTION ‖ Morey St. Denis, Domaine J. Perrot-Minot 1994; Côte de Nuits, France

MORELS AND PORCINI

There are two types of mushrooms that are more than worthy of the company of truffles: morels and porcini. Although they star on their own in many dishes, of course, they also pair well with truffles—morels particularly with the black, porcini with the white.

MORELS Morels are found in both Europe and the United States, usually in dark woodsy areas, although they can turn up in unexpected spots as well. They often appear after a forest fire, though no one knows why they find scorched trees and earth so attractive. Characterized by their distinctive honeycombed appearance, morels may have caps that are pointed or round, depending on the type. In size, they can range from one inch to as much as four or five inches long. The most highly regarded varieties are the black morel (*Morchella angusticeps*) and the yellow (*M. esculenta*); the yellow morel is considered the best by most connoisseurs. Black morels are dark gray to black when at the height of their season, paler when young, and eventually turning pale blond when very mature. Morels are in season from spring to early summer. Cultivated morels, which are good but less intense than wild morels, are available for much of the year.

Morels have tough stems, which should be well trimmed before using; those that have already been trimmed, of course, are the best buy. Insects and other such invaders like to hide in the crevices of morels, and the mushrooms can sometimes harbor sand or grit as well, so they should be thoroughly rinsed before cooking. If you will be braising the morels and they seem to be sheltering unwanted visitors, you can soak them for 10 minutes or so in warm salted water to flush out the pests; then rinse them well.

Morels are always cooked. They can be braised in flavorful stock and served on their own, or added to sauces and other dishes. They love cream, and *poulet aux morilles*, chicken with a creamy morel sauce, is a French classic.

PORCINI Porcini (*Boletus edulis*) have been called the king of mushrooms, and king bolete is one of their common names. *Porcini* (which means "piglets") is their Italian name, *cèpes* is what they are called in French. They are usually referred to by one of these names in English too, or occasionally as ceps. Members of the larger family of boletes, they are undeniably its royal branch. Their biggest season is the fall, but fresh porcini can be found, at times in limited quantities, from the spring right through December.

Porcini have brown caps and pale tan stems; unlike most mushrooms, the underside of the cap is distinguished by pores, or tiny tubes, rather than gills. The caps should be firm and dry, and the undersides pale brown; greenish-brown pores are a sign of age, but if that is what you have, you can simply trim off the discolored part, which can be bitter. The thick, bulbous stems also should be firm—if they feel soft or hollow, they may harbor insects or other animal life. In good European markets, and some specialty markets here, the mushrooms will be displayed with a few of them sliced lengthwise in half to show that the stems are in good condition. The stems are tasty and only need marginal trimming to remove any tough bottom parts. Clean porcini with a soft brush; rinse briefly under cold water only if they are very dirty, and then pat dry with paper towels.

Whole porcini or large caps can be grilled or roasted. They are also good sliced and sautéed in olive oil or butter. Porcini should always be thoroughly cooked, because raw ones have been known to cause indigestion.

DRIED MORELS AND PORCINI Both morels and porcini are excellent when dried, and that is the way you are most likely to find them. Morels are dried whole, while porcini are sliced and then dried. The morels imported from Europe have often been dried over a wood fire and thus will have a smoky flavor, desirable or not, depending on your preference (avoid those that smell strongly of smoke, however, since it will overwhelm the mushroom flavor). Dried morels and porcini are intensely aromatic, and they will stay fragrant for months (or even years) if stored in an airtight container.

To use dried mushrooms, soak them in hot water to cover by an inch or so for about 30 minutes, until softened. "Reconstituted" morels are very close in flavor and texture to the fresh; after soaking, dried porcini can be slightly chewy. In either case, the flavorful soaking liquid should be strained through a sieve lined with a paper towel or a coffee filter and saved, to be used in a soup or sauce if not in the particular recipe.

Porcini, unlike morels, also freeze well, and flash-frozen porcini can be substituted for the fresh in most recipes. Porcini powder, ground from dried mushrooms, is also available, and many chefs like to dredge lamb chops and other meats or fish with the flavorful powder. If you buy the dried mushrooms in bulk, you can make your own porcini powder by grinding the broken bits of mushrooms in a spice or coffee grinder.

RISOTTO WITH ASPARAGUS, BLACK TRUFFLES, AND PROSECCO

RATHER THAN ADDING WINE at the start of cooking, as is standard practice, this risotto is lightened at the last minute with a generous splash of Prosecco, an Italian sparkling wine from the region around Venice. There's a whole black truffle in this dish, but the recipe will also work with just a drizzle of black truffle oil over the finished risotto. SERVES 4 AS A FIRST COURSE

1 pound asparagus [500 grams]

4 cups chicken stock, or 2 cans (14½ ounces each) low-sodium chicken broth plus enough water to make 4 cups [1 liter/can is about 400 grams]

1 tablespoon olive oil

1 garlic clove, minced

2 tablespoons unsalted butter [30 grams]

1 small onion, finely chopped

1 cup Arborio, Carnaroli, or Vialone Nano rice [200 grams]

½ cup Prosecco or other semi-dry sparkling wine [125 ml]

1 fresh or flash-frozen black truffle, cut into thin julienne strips

½ cup freshly grated aged Asiago or Parmigiano-Reggiano, plus a small chunk of cheese for shaving [25 grams]

1. Trim the tough ends off the bottom of the asparagus. Cut the stalks diagonally into 1-inch [2.5-cm] pieces, leaving the tips intact.

2. Bring the stock to a simmer in a medium saucepan over moderately high heat. Reduce the heat to keep the stock at the barest simmer.

3. Heat the oil in a large saucepan or large deep skillet over moderate heat. Add the garlic and cook, stirring, until fragrant, about 30 seconds. Add the asparagus and cook, stirring often, until crisp-tender, 2 to 3 minutes. Remove the asparagus and set aside.

4. Add the butter to the pan and heat until melted. Add the onion and cook, stirring occasionally, until softened, 3 to 5 minutes. Add the rice and cook, stirring to coat it with butter, until opaque, about 2 minutes.

5. Add about ½ cup [125 ml] of the hot chicken stock and cook, stirring often, until it has been absorbed by the rice. The stock should bubble gently as you stir; adjust the heat as necessary. Add another ½ cup [125 ml] of the stock and cook, stirring often, until it has been absorbed.

Continue to cook, adding stock about ½ cup [125 ml] at a time once the previous addition has been absorbed, until you have added all the stock. Add the Prosecco and cook, stirring, until it has been absorbed, the rice is al dente, and the risotto is creamy, about 20 minutes from the time you first added stock.

6. Stir in the asparagus and black truffle and cook until heated through, 1 to 2 minutes. Remove from the heat and stir in the grated cheese. Spoon the risotto into 4 warm shallow bowls. Using a vegetable peeler, shave cheese over each serving. Serve at once.

SOMMELIER WINE SUGGESTION   Giustino B., Prosecco de Valdobbiadene 1996; Veneto, Italy

TRU'S BLACK TRUFFLE RISOTTO WITH LOBSTER AND TRUFFLE BUTTER FROTH

CHEF RICK TRAMONTO serves this wonderfully indulgent dish at his restaurant, Tru, in Chicago, where the risotto is presented in individual copper pots. At home, shallow serving bowls will do just fine. The risotto is finished with a foamy truffle butter sauce—the recipe makes more of the sauce than you need for this dish, as just the "froth" is spooned over the risotto; use the leftover sauce on steamed asparagus or other vegetables, or stir it into mashed potatoes. SERVES 4 AS A FIRST COURSE

Two 1½-pound lobsters [750 grams]

TRUFFLE BUTTER SAUCE

1 teaspoon unsalted butter

1 small shallot, finely minced

½ cup dry white wine [125 ml]

1 cup heavy cream [225 grams]

2 tablespoons truffle butter

Pinch of freshly grated nutmeg

Salt and freshly ground white pepper

6 cups vegetable or chicken stock, or 2 cans (14½ ounces each) low-sodium broth plus enough water to make 6 cups [1.5 liters/can is about 400 grams]

2 tablespoons olive oil

1 large shallot, minced

1½ cups Arborio, Carnaroli, or Vialone Nano rice [300 grams]

½ cup dry white wine [125 ml]

Salt and freshly ground black pepper

⅓ cup heavy cream [75 ml]

2½ tablespoons unsalted butter, at room temperature [40 grams]

⅓ cup shelled fava beans, blanched in boiling water for 1 minute, cooled in an ice water bath, and peeled [45 grams]

2 tomatoes, peeled, seeded, and cut into small dice

1 fresh or flash-frozen black truffle, minced

2 tablespoons freshly grated Parmigiano-Reggiano

4 chervil sprigs

A few edible flowers, such as nasturtiums, Johnny-jump-ups, and/or chive blossoms for garnish (optional)

1. To prepare the lobsters, bring a large pot of water to a boil. Plunge the lobsters headfirst into the pot, cover, return to a boil, and cook for 12 minutes. Remove the lobsters and let cool.

2. Twist off the lobster tails. Using kitchen shears, split the tails open down the bottom (or just crack the tails with your hands). Remove the meat and cut into ½-inch [1-mm] slices; set

aside. Crack the lobster claws (and knuckles) and remove the meat. Cut the meat into bite-size pieces. Transfer all the lobster meat to a plate, cover, and refrigerate.

3. For the sauce, melt the unsalted butter in a small saucepan over moderate heat. Add the shallots and cook, stirring, until translucent, about 2 minutes. Add the wine, increase the heat to moderately high, and bring to a boil. Boil until reduced by half. Add the cream, reduce the heat slightly, and bring to a simmer. Simmer until the liquid is reduced to about 1 cup. Remove from the heat and set aside.

4. Meanwhile, bring the stock to a simmer in a large saucepan over moderately high heat. Reduce the heat to keep the stock at the barest simmer.

5. Heat the oil in a large saucepan or large deep skillet over moderate heat. Add the shallot and cook, stirring, until translucent, about 3 minutes. Add the rice and cook, stirring to coat it with oil, until opaque, about 2 minutes.

6. Add the wine and cook, stirring frequently, until it has evaportated. Add about ½ cup [125 ml] of the stock and cook, stirring, until the stock has been absorbed by the rice. The stock should bubble gently as you stir; adjust the heat as necessary. Add another ½ cup [125 ml] stock and cook, stirring, until it has been absorbed. Continue to cook, adding stock ½ cup [125 ml] at a time once the previous addition has been absorbed, until the rice is al dente and the risotto is creamy, about 20 minutes from the time you first added stock. (You may not need all the stock.) Season with salt and pepper to taste.

7. Meanwhile, to finish the sauce, bring the reduced cream mixture just to a simmer over moderate heat. Stir in the truffle butter. Season with the nutmeg and salt and pepper to taste. Set the saucepan aside in a warm place.

8. Stir the ⅓ cup [75 ml] cream and the butter into the risotto, then add the lobster, fava beans, tomatoes, and truffle. Cook, stirring, until heated through. Stir in the Parmesan, and season with additional salt and pepper to taste. Remove from the heat.

9. Reheat the truffle butter mixture just until hot. Using an immersion blender, blend until very foamy. (Or transfer to a standard blender and blend on high speed until foamy.) Spoon the risotto into 4 warm shallow serving bowls. Spoon about 2 tablespoons of the truffle "froth" over each serving and garnish with the chervil, and flowers, if using. Serve immediately.

SOMMELIER WINE SUGGESTION | Corton Domaine Chandon de Briarille 1997 Grand Cru; Côte de Nuit, France

PEELING AND SEEDING TOMATOES

TOMATOES can be peeled easily if they are first blanched briefly in boiling water. Remove the cores, without cutting too deep. Cut a shallow X in the bottom of each tomato and plunge them into a large saucepan of boiling water for about 15 seconds, or until the skin at the X is beginning to loosen. Carefully remove them with tongs or a slotted spoon and immediately transfer them to a bowl of ice water to cool. Drain well, then pull off the skin with your fingers; use a sharp paring knife for any stubborn bits.

To seed tomatoes, cut them crosswise in half and scoop out the seeds with a fingertip. Professional cooks sometimes prepare tomatoes by slicing off the top and bottom of each peeled tomato, halving or quartering it, and slicing off the inner "membranes," thereby removing the seeds and pulp as well; this leaves only the tomato flesh, to be sliced or diced. An alternative method is to slice the flesh off the seedy center portion, rather than vice versa.

RISOTTO WITH FRESH WHITE TRUFFLES

ONE OF THE BEST—and best-loved—ways of celebrating white truffle season is in a simple risotto, which allows the intoxicating flavor and aroma of the truffles to star. When it's not truffle season, you may want to get some of the same effect by making the risotto as directed—stir in some sautéed mushrooms at the end, if you like—and finishing the dish with about a tablespoon of truffle butter or a few teaspoons of white truffle oil. SERVES 4 TO 6 AS A FIRST COURSE

6 cups chicken stock, or 2 cans (14½ ounces each) low-sodium chicken broth plus enough water to make 6 cups [1.5 liters/can is about 400 grams]

1 tablespoon olive oil

1 small onion, minced

1 small garlic clove, finely minced

1½ cups Arborio, Carnaroli, or Vialone Nano rice [300 grams]

¼ cup dry white wine [60 ml]

3 tablespoons unsalted butter, at room temperature [45 grams]

½ to ¾ cup freshly grated Parmigiano-Reggiano [25 to 40 grams]

1 to 1½ ounces fresh white truffle [30 to 45 grams]

1. Bring the stock to a simmer in a medium saucepan over moderately high heat. Reduce the heat to keep the stock at the barest simmer.

2. Heat the oil in a large saucepan or large deep skillet over moderate heat. Add the onion and cook, stirring, until softened, about 3 minutes. Add the garlic and cook just until fragrant, about 30 seconds. Add the rice and cook, stirring to coat it with oil, until opaque, about 2 minutes.

3. Add the wine and cook, stirring frequently, until it evaporates. Add about ½ cup [125 ml] of the stock and cook, stirring, until it has been absorbed by the rice. The stock should bubble gently as you stir; adjust the heat as necessary. Add another ½ cup [125 ml] stock and cook, stirring, until it has been absorbed. Continue to cook, adding stock ½ cup [125 ml] at a time once the previous addition has been absorbed, until the rice is al dente and the risotto is creamy, about 20 minutes from the time you first added stock. (You may not need all the stock.)

4. Remove from the heat. Stirring vigorously with a wooden spoon, add the butter and Parmesan. Spoon the risotto into warm shallow bowls and shave the truffle over the top. Serve immediately.

SOMMELIER WINE SUGGESTION Chassagne-Montrachet, Domaine Morey "Les Vergers" 1998; Côte de Beaune, France

NO. 9 PARK'S WHITE-TRUFFLE GNOCCHI WITH LOBSTER, CHANTERELLES, AND PEAS

BARBARA LYNCH, chef of Boston's renowned No. 9 Park, is known for her ethereal gnocchi. Truffle flour is the secret ingredient here; just a few tablespoons give the pasta an amazingly intense flavor. This dish is so extravagant you could serve the gnocchi in the rich cream sauce without the lobster and/or fresh truffle, and they would still be sublime. In fact, they are even delicious on their own, sauced simply with brown butter and finished with a grating of fresh Parmesan. If chanterelles are not in season, use other wild mushrooms, such as oyster mushrooms, or even morels.

SERVES 4 TO 6 AS A FIRST COURSE

Two 1½- to 2-pound lobsters [675 grams]

WHITE-TRUFFLE GNOCCHI

1½ pounds Yukon Gold potatoes, peeled [675 grams]

¾ cup all-purpose flour, or more as needed [95 grams]

¼ cup truffle flour [35 grams]

1¼ teaspoons salt

2 large eggs, lightly beaten

2 teaspoons olive oil

4 ounces chanterelle mushrooms, trimmed, cleaned, and halved or quartered if large [115 grams]

⅛ teaspoon freshly ground black pepper

¼ cup fresh or thawed frozen peas

2 cups heavy cream [500 ml]

¼ teaspoon chopped thyme

1 tablespoon minced fresh chives

1 small to medium white truffle

1. To prepare the lobsters, bring a large pot of water to a boil. Plunge the lobsters headfirst into the pot, cover, return to a boil, and cook for 12 minutes. Remove the lobsters and let cool.

2. Twist off the lobster tails. Using kitchen shears, split the tail open down the bottom (or just crack the tail with your hands). Remove the meat and cut into bite-size pieces; set aside. Crack the lobster claws (and knuckles) and remove the meat. Cut the meat into bite-size pieces. Transfer all the lobster meat to a plate, cover, and refrigerate.

3. To make the gnocchi, put the potatoes in a large saucepan, add salted water to cover, and bring to a boil. Boil gently until the potatoes are tender when pierced with the tip of a sharp knife, 15 to 20 minutes for medium potatoes, 25 to 30 minutes for larger ones. Drain thoroughly. Immediately pass the potatoes through a ricer or a food mill into a large bowl. Let cool completely.

4. Sprinkle the all-purpose flour, truffle flour, and salt over the potatoes. Add the eggs and stir with a fork just until the potatoes and flour are evenly moistened. Turn out onto a very lightly floured surface and knead gently, adding no more than a teaspoon or so additional flour as necessary, until a soft dough forms.

5. Divide the dough into 8 pieces. One at a time, on an unfloured work surface, roll each piece under the palms of your hands into a ½-inch [1-cm]-thick rope. Using a pastry scraper or a sharp knife, cut the rope into ½-inch [1-cm] lengths. To give the gnocchi their characteristic ridged shape, roll each one down the back of the tines of a fork, or simply leave them in the "pillow" shape formed by cutting them, and place them on a flour-dusted baking sheet. Cover loosely with plastic wrap and set aside. (The gnocchi are best cooked soon after they are formed, but they can be shaped in advance and refrigerated for up to 4 hours.)

6. Heat the oil in a large skillet over medium-high heat. Add the mushrooms, season with ¼ teaspoon salt and pepper, and sauté, stirring frequently, until the liquid the mushrooms release has been absorbed and they just begin to brown, 8 to 10 minutes. Remove from the heat and set aside.

7. Bring a large pot of salted water to a boil. Meanwhile, bring a medium saucepan of salted water to a boil. Add the peas and cook just until tender, about 5 to 7 minutes for fresh peas, 3 to 5 minutes for frozen; drain well.

8. In a large deep skillet, bring the cream just to a boil over medium heat and boil gently until reduced by half. Remove from the heat.

9. Add the gnocchi to the large pot of boiling water, in 2 or 3 batches, and return to a boil, then reduce the heat slightly and boil gently until just cooked through, about 3 minutes after they float to the surface (taste one to make sure). Remove with a wire skimmer and drain briefly in a colander.

10. Meanwhile, bring the reduced cream to a simmer over moderate heat. Add the lobster, mushrooms, peas, thyme, ½ teaspoon salt, and pepper to taste and heat just until warmed through, 2 to 3 minutes.

11. Add the gnocchi to the skillet, stirring and tossing gently to coat. Transfer to warm shallow bowls and sprinkle the chives over the top. Shave the truffle over the top and serve immediately.

SOMMELIER WINE SUGGESTION | Domaine Jean-Marc Morey Meursault 1999; Burgundy, France

TRUFFLED RICE TORTA

TRIANGLES OF THIS UNUSUAL TORTA, accompanied by a simple green salad and a crisp white wine, make a very chic lunch. Cut into bite-size squares (see the Note below), it makes an unusual and irresistible hors d'oeuvre. SERVES 4 AS A FIRST COURSE OR LIGHT LUNCH

¼ cup plus 1 tablespoon extra-virgin olive oil

1 tablespoon yellow cornmeal

3 large eggs, lightly beaten

¼ teaspoon salt

2 cups cooked short-grain white rice, such as Arborio (about ⅔ cup raw rice) [300 grams/135 grams]

½ cup freshly grated Parmigiano-Reggiano [25 grams]

1½ teaspoons minced fresh, flash-frozen, or canned black truffle

⅛ teaspoon freshly ground black pepper

1. Preheat the oven to 350°F [175°C]. Use 1 tablespoon of the oil to generously grease an 8-inch [20-cm] square baking dish. Coat the bottom and sides of the dish with the cornmeal.

2. With a whisk, lightly beat the eggs in a medium bowl. Whisk in the salt. Stir the rice with a fork to separate the grains, then add to the eggs, along with the Parmesan, the remaining ¼ cup [60 ml] olive oil, the truffle, and pepper. Mix well to blend. Scrape into the prepared dish and smooth the top with a spatula.

3. Bake the torta for 40 to 45 minutes, until it is lightly browned at the edges and a knife inserted into the center shows no evidence of uncooked egg. Let cool on a rack for at least 10 minutes. (The torta can be made in advance, cooled, covered, and refrigerated for up to 2 days. Let return to room temperature before serving, or reheat in a preheated 325°F [160°C] oven, loosely covered with foil, for about 20 minutes.)

4. Cut the torta into 4 squares, then slice each square diagonally in half to make 2 triangles. Serve warm or at room temperature.

NOTE: To serve the torta as an hors d'oeuvre, cut into 1 by 2-inch [2.5 by 5-cm] rectangles, and arrange on a platter. (Makes 32 pieces.)

SOMMELIER WINE SUGGESTION | Ken Wright Cellars Pinot Gris 1999; Eugene, Oregon

CREAMY POLENTA WITH TALEGGIO CHEESE AND WHITE TRUFFLE

TALEGGIO, A SILKY, RICH CHEESE made from cow's milk, can be found at most cheese shops and at Italian markets. Choose a young cheese, one that's pale yellow with a semi-soft texture, as the flavor tends to become quite strong with age. SERVES 4 TO 6 AS A FIRST COURSE

1 cup polenta or coarse yellow cornmeal [130 grams]

3 cups chicken stock or canned low-sodium broth [750 ml]

1 cup milk [250 ml]

½ teaspoon salt

2½ ounces Taleggio cheese, rind trimmed, cut into small pieces

3 tablespoons unsalted butter, at room temperature

Freshly ground black pepper

1 fresh white truffle or 1½ to 2 teaspoons white truffle oil

1. Combine the polenta and 1 cup [250 ml] water in a medium bowl and whisk until smooth.

2. Combine the chicken stock, milk, and salt in a large heavy saucepan and heat over moderately high heat until hot. Whisk in the polenta and bring to a boil, whisking often. Reduce the heat to low and cook, stirring often with a wooden spoon, until the polenta is tender and the consistency of cooked hot cereal, 20 to 25 minutes.

3. Remove the pan from the heat. Add the cheese, butter, and pepper to taste, and stir until the butter has melted. Spoon into warm shallow bowls or plates and shave the fresh truffle over the top (or drizzle with the truffle oil). Serve at once.

NOTE: For a quick variation, substitute instant polenta or finely ground yellow cornmeal for the polenta or coarse cornmeal. Reduce the cooking time to 5 to 7 minutes, or until the polenta is tender.

> SOMMELIER WINE SUGGESTION Logan Chardonnay 1998; Monterey, California

FISH, POULTRY, AND MEAT

SCALLOP-TRUFFLE "NAPOLEONS" WITH CREAMED LEEKS

SHRIMP AND CANNELLINI BEANS WITH TRUFFLE OIL

GRILLED SEA BASS WITH WHITE TRUFFLE-GARLIC OIL

POACHED HALIBUT WITH BLACK TRUFFLE SABAYON

RM'S SEARED WILD STRIPED BASS ON CHIVE MASHED POTATOES WITH TRUFFLE VINAIGRETTE

CAFE BOULUD'S STEAMED TRUFFLED STRIPED BASS WITH ARTICHOKE AND BACON RAGOUT

PAN-SEARED SALMON WITH TRUFFLED FRENCH LENTILS

RED SNAPPER WITH TRUFFLE BEURRE BLANC

ROASTED WHOLE TROUT WITH PANCETTA AND BLACK TRUFFLES

ROASTED WHOLE FISH WITH TRUFFLE BUTTER

CHICKEN BREASTS STUFFED WITH HERBED TRUFFLE BUTTER

POUSSIN EN DEMI-DEUIL

GRILLED DUCK BREASTS WITH TRUFFLE HONEY

PICHOLINE'S ROASTED WILD PARTRIDGE WITH TRUFFLE FLANS

PORTERHOUSE STEAK WITH BLACK TRUFFLE SAUCE

BEEF TAGLIATA WITH BLACK TRUFFLES

INDIVIDUAL BEEF WELLINGTONS WITH SAUCE PERIGUEUX

BRAISED SHORT RIBS WITH BLACK TRUFFLE SAUCE

ROAST VEAL CHOPS WITH TRUFFLES AND FOIE GRAS

TRUFFLED OSSO BUCO

BABBO'S GRILLED VENISON WITH SALSIFY AND WHITE TRUFFLES

SCALLOP-TRUFFLE "NAPOLEONS" WITH CREAMED LEEKS

INSPIRED IN PART BY Daniel Boulud's famous "scallops in black tie," these truffle-stuffed scallops, served on a bed of creamy leeks, are a showstopper—and surprisingly easy to prepare. The white and black "napoleons" look stunning again the pale green leeks, and a garnish of minced black truffles adds a final elegant flourish. SERVES 4

1 large fresh or flash-frozen black truffle
(1½ to 2 ounces) [45 to 60 grams]

20 large diver's ("dry") sea scallops
(1¼ to 1½ pounds) [600 to 700 grams]

3 pounds leeks [1.4 kg]

2 tablespoons unsalted butter [30 grams]

Salt

½ cup chicken stock or canned low-sodium chicken broth [125 ml]

½ cup heavy cream [125 ml]

Freshly ground black pepper

2 tablespoons olive oil

1. Using a Japanese vegetable slicer or a mandoline, cut 20 paper-thin slices from the truffle. Finely mince the remaining truffle, wrap well, and set aside for garnish.

2. Pull off the tough side muscles from the scallops. With a sharp paring knife, slice each one horizontally almost in half, leaving it attached at one side. Insert a truffle slice into each scallop and press down gently on the top of the scallop so it holds together. Place the scallops on a plate, cover with plastic wrap, and refrigerate for 1 to 2 hours. (The flavor of the truffle will permeate the scallops.)

3. Meanwhile, trim the roots off the leeks and cut off all but the palest green tops. Split the leeks lengthwise in half and thinly slice them. Rinse well in a bowl of water, swishing them around to remove any grit; lift out the leeks with your hands, and repeat if necessary.

4. Melt the butter in a Dutch oven over moderately high heat. Add the leeks, season with salt, and cook, stirring frequently, until soft and translucent, 8 to 10 minutes. Do not let the leeks brown; reduce the heat slightly if necessary. Add the stock, reduce the heat, cover, and simmer very gently, stirring occasionally, until the leeks are tender, 7 to 9 minutes.

5. Add the cream and bring just to a boil over moderately high heat. Reduce the heat slightly and simmer gently until the cream is slightly reduced and thickened, about 2 minutes. Season with pepper and additional salt if necessary, remove from the heat, and set aside, covered. (The leeks can be made up to 6 hours in advance, covered, and refrigerated; add a little water or more stock when reheating if necessary.)

6. Heat 2 large heavy skillets, preferably nonstick, over moderately high heat until hot. Divide the olive oil between the skillets and heat until very hot but not smoking. Season the scallops on both sides with salt and pepper and carefully add to the pans. Cook until golden brown on the bottom, about 2 minutes. Turn the scallops and cook until browned on the second side and just cooked through, 1 to 2 minutes longer.

7. Meanwhile, reheat the leeks over moderately low heat, stirring frequently.

8. Spoon a bed of leeks onto each of 4 dinner plates. Arrange the scallops on top, scatter the minced truffle around the leeks, and serve immediately.

| SOMMELIER WINE SUGGESTION | Bollinger Special Cuvée NV; Champagne, France

SHRIMP AND CANNELLINI BEANS
WITH TRUFFLE OIL

SHRIMP AND CANNELLINI BEANS are a natural combination, often served as an appetizer in Italy; good-quality canned tuna is sometimes substituted for the shrimp. This recipe makes enough for a main course, perfect for a hot summer's evening. You could grill the shrimp instead of pan-searing them; thread them on wooden skewers to make turning easy. The salad could also be served on a bed of arugula or mâche. SERVES 4

2½ cups cooked cannellini beans (see Note) [400 grams]

¼ cup finely chopped Vidalia or other sweet onion [35 grams]

2½ tablespoons extra-virgin olive oil

About 1 teaspoon fresh lemon juice, or to taste

2 tablespoons minced flat-leaf parsley

Salt and freshly ground black pepper

1 pound medium shrimp, peeled and deveined [500 grams]

1½ tablespoons white truffle oil

1. Combine the beans and onion in a medium bowl; toss to mix well. Add 1 tablespoon of the olive oil and stir to coat. Add the lemon juice and parsley and toss to mix. Season with salt and pepper to taste. (The beans can be prepared several hours ahead, covered, and refrigerated; return to room temperature before proceeding.)

2. In a medium bowl, toss the shrimp with 1½ teaspoons of the olive oil. Season generously with salt and pepper.

3. Heat a large heavy skillet over moderate heat until hot. Add the remaining 1 tablespoon olive oil and heat until very hot but not smoking. Add the shrimp to the pan in a single layer and cook, turning once, until pink and just opaque throughout, 1 to 2 minutes per side. Remove from the heat.

4. Add the warm shrimp and 1 tablespoon of the truffle oil to the beans and toss gently to mix. Arrange the shrimp and beans on a serving platter or on individual plates and drizzle with the remaining 1½ teaspoons truffle oil. Serve immediately.

NOTE: You can substitute good-quality canned beans, rinsed and drained, for the cooked cannellini beans. If high-quality canned cannellini beans are not available, substitute smaller white beans; inferior canned cannellini can be mushy.

SOMMELIER WINE SUGGESTION Marc Deschamps "Les Champs de Cri" Pouilly Fumé 1998; Loire, France

GRILLED SEA BASS WITH WHITE TRUFFLE-GARLIC OIL

GRILLED SEA BASS or, more often, hake, with garlic oil is a specialty of the Basque region of Spain, and it is a favorite dish throughout much of the rest of the country as well. Here white truffle oil adds an unexpected, subtle nuance to the lusty, garlicky fish. SERVES 4

3 tablespoons olive oil

4 to 6 garlic cloves, thinly sliced lengthwise

4 skinless sea bass fillets (about 6 ounces each) [180 grams]

Salt and freshly ground black pepper

Vegetable or olive oil for grilling

1½ tablespoons minced flat-leaf parsley (optional)

1 tablespoon white truffle oil

1. Prepare a hot fire in a grill or preheat a cast-iron stove-top grill over moderately high heat.

2. Combine the olive oil and garlic in a small heavy skillet and cook over low heat, stirring occasionally, until the oil is fragrant and the garlic is barely golden, about 3 minutes. Do not overcook; the garlic will continue to brown in the hot oil as it stands. Remove from the heat.

3. Lightly brush the fish on both sides with some of the garlic oil and season generously with salt and pepper.

4. Brush the grill or grill pan lightly with oil (or, if you have a fish basket for grilling, brush it with oil and grill the fish in it). Place the fish skinned side up on the grill or in the grill pan and grill for 4 to 5 minutes, or until lightly golden on the bottom. Carefully turn the fillets and grill for 3 to 4 minutes longer, or until just cooked through.

5. Meanwhile, reheat the garlic oil over low heat just until warm. Add the parsley, if using, and remove from the heat. Stir in the truffle oil.

6. Place the fillets on serving plates, spoon the garlic and oil over them, and serve at once.

SOMMELIER WINE SUGGESTION Lagar de Cevera Albariño 2000; Rias Baixas, Spain

POACHED HALIBUT WITH BLACK TRUFFLE SABAYON

MOIST THYME-SCENTED HALIBUT FILLETS get the royal treatment with an ethereal cloud of truffle-infused sabayon. Sabayon is a foamy egg yolk sauce usually made with wine; here some of the aromatic wine-and-stock poaching liquid used for the delicate fish serves as its base. This is a most elegant dish. Serve it with buttered steamed or boiled new potatoes. SERVES 4

1 tablespoon unsalted butter, at room temperature

4 skinless halibut fillets (about 6 ounces each), about 1 inch thick [18 grams/2.5 cm]

1 tablespoon fresh lemon juice

2 teaspoons minced thyme, preferably lemon thyme

Salt and freshly ground black pepper

1 fresh or flash-frozen black truffle, cut into thin julienne strips

1 cup fish stock (see Note) [250 ml]

½ cup dry white wine [125 ml]

1 small tomato, peeled, seeded, and cut into ¼-inch dice [.5 cm]

1 medium shallot, minced

3 large egg yolks

1. Preheat the oven to 375°F [190°C]. Use the softened butter to generously butter a 2- to 2½-quart [2- to 2.5-liters] gratin or other baking dish large enough to hold the halibut comfortably.

2. Arrange the halibut fillets about ¼ inch [.5 cm] apart in the gratin dish. Drizzle the lemon juice over the fish, sprinkle with the thyme, and season generously with salt and pepper. Scatter half the truffle strips over the fish. Add the fish stock and wine, pouring them down the side of the dish, not over the fillets. Scatter the tomato and shallot around and between the fillets.

3. Cut a piece of parchment paper to fit inside the gratin dish. Lightly grease one side of the parchment and place the paper buttered side down on top of the fillets. Bake for about 10 minutes, or until the fillets are just opaque throughout. Transfer the fish to a warm platter and cover loosely with foil to keep warm.

4. Carefully tilt the gratin dish and pour the cooking juices into a small saucepan. Bring the liquid to a boil over moderate heat and cook until reduced to about ¾ cup [185 ml]. Taste and season with additional salt and pepper if necessary. Set a small sieve over a glass measuring cup and strain ¼ cup [60 ml] of the poaching liquid into the cup; let cool slightly. Pour the remaining poaching liquid over the fish in the gratin dish and cover to keep warm.

5. To make the sabayon, combine the egg yolks and the reserved ¼ cup [60 ml] poaching liquid in a large heatproof bowl. Set the bowl over a pot of simmering water and whisk constantly until the mixture is foamy and holds its shape when dropped from the whisk, 7 to 10 minutes. Season with salt and pepper if needed. Fold in the remaining truffle.

6. Transfer the halibut fillets to 4 shallow bowls or plates. Spoon the reserved poaching liquid, with the tomato, over the top. Top each fillet with a few tablespoons of the truffle sabayon and serve at once.

NOTE: Good-quality frozen fish stock can be found at many fish markets and some supermarkets. If it is unavailable, substitute ½ cup [125 ml] bottled clam juice mixed with ½ cup [125 ml] water.

| SOMMELIER WINE SUGGESTION | Domaine S. Maroslavac Puligny-Montrachet 1998; Côte de Beaune, France |

RM'S SEARED WILD STRIPED BASS ON CHIVE MASHED POTATOES WITH TRUFFLE VINAIGRETTE

KNOWN FOR HIS SOPHISTICATED, flavorful seafood cuisine, Chef Rick Moonen recently opened his own restaurant in New York City, called, appropriately enough, rm. This is one of his signature dishes. Brushing the fish with butter before serving it is a chef's trick that results in crispy browned skin. The recipe makes a bit more truffle vinaigrette than you will need, but any extra can be drizzled over steamed vegetables or used to dress a salad of arugula or another pungent green and fresh herbs.

SERVES 6

TRUFFLE VINAIGRETTE

½ cup chicken stock or canned low-sodium chicken broth [120 ml]

1 tablespoon minced shallot

1 tablespoon sherry vinegar

Generous pinch of salt

Pinch of freshly ground black pepper

¼ cup grapeseed or canola oil [60 ml]

3 tablespoon white truffle oil

1½ tablespoons minced truffle peelings (reserved from fresh truffles, or use canned truffle peelings)

Chive Mashed Potatoes (recipe follows)

4 ounces haricots verts [120 grams]

2 tablespoons olive oil

1 tablespoon unsalted butter, at room temperature, **plus 2 teaspoons butter**

8 ounces shiitake mushrooms, stems removed and caps thinly sliced [225 grams]

3 tablespoons finely chopped shallots

1 tablespoon minced garlic

1 teaspoon thyme leaves

Salt and freshly ground black pepper

6 striped bass fillets (6 to 8 ounces each), **preferably wild,** skin left on

2 teaspoons vegetable oil

1 large tomato, peeled, seeded, and diced

1. To make the vinaigrette, bring the chicken stock to a boil in a small saucepan over high heat. Boil until reduced to 2 tablespoons. Remove from the heat.

2. Put the shallots in a small bowl, pour the hot stock over them, and let steep for 10 minutes

3. Add the vinegar, salt, and pepper to the shallots, whisking to mix. Whisking constantly, add the grapeseed oil and then the truffle oil in a thin, steady stream until well blended and emulsified. Add the truffle peelings. (The vinaigrette can be made early in the day, covered, and refrigerated. Bring to room temperature before using.)

4. Make the chive mashed potatoes; keep warm.

5. Meanwhile, preheat the oven to 375°F [190°C].

6. Bring a medium saucepan of salted water to a boil. Add the haricots verts and cook until just tender, 5 to 7 minutes. Drain, transfer to an ice bath to cool, and drain again.

7. Heat the olive oil with the 2 teaspoons butter in a large skillet, preferably nonstick, over moderately high heat until hot. Add the shiitakes and sauté, stirring frequently, until tender and lightly browned, 7 to 10 minutes. Add the shallots, garlic, thyme, ¼ teaspoon salt, and ⅛ teaspoon pepper. Cook, stirring frequently, until the garlic and shallots are softened, about 3 minutes. Remove from the heat and set aside.

8. Season the bass fillets on both sides with salt and pepper. Rub the remaining 1 tablespoon butter over the skin side of the fillets. Heat 2 large ovenproof skillets, preferably nonstick, over high heat until hot. Add half the vegetable oil to each pan and heat until very hot but not smoking. Add the fillets to the pans, skin side down, and cook until the skin is browned, about 2 minutes. Carefully turn the fillets over, transfer the pans to the oven, and roast until the fillets are just cooked through, 3 to 5 minutes.

9. Meanwhile, add the haricots verts to the shiitake mixture and reheat over moderate heat, stirring occasionally. Stir in the tomato and remove from the heat.

10. Spoon a mound of potatoes onto the center of each of 6 plates. Place the fillets on the potatoes and arrange the shiitake mixture around them. Drizzle the vinaigrette over the shiitakes and serve at once.

SOMMELIER WINE SUGGESTION Qupe "Ibarra Young Vineyards" Marsanne 2000; Santa Barbara, California

CHIVE MASHED POTATOES

SERVES 6

¼ cup canola or other flavorless vegetable oil [60 ml]

¼ cup [60 ml] plus 1 tablespoon minced chives (2 to 3 bunches)

Salt

2 pounds baking potatoes, peeled and quartered lengthwise [900 grams]

3 tablespoons unsalted butter, at room temperature [45 grams]

¾ cup heavy cream [180 ml]

Freshly ground black pepper

1. Combine the oil and 1 tablespoon of the chives in a mini processor and process until well blended. Pour into a small bowl and stir in a pinch of salt. Cover and set aside. (The oil can be made early in the day and refrigerated. Bring to room temperature before using.)

2. Put the potatoes in a large pot and add salted water to cover by about 1 inch. Bring to a boil and cook until the potatoes are tender, 12 to 15 minutes. Drain.

3. Put the potatoes through a food mill or potato ricer back into the pot. Set the pot over low heat and beat in the butter. Beat in the cream, then beat in the chive oil. Season with salt and pepper to taste. (The potatoes can be prepared to this point and set aside, partially covered, at room temperature for up to 30 minutes. Reheat gently over low heat, stirring frequently.)

4. Stir the remaining ¼ cup [60 ml] minced chives into the potatoes and serve.

CAFE BOULUD'S STEAMED TRUFFLED STRIPED BASS WITH ARTICHOKE AND BACON RAGOUT

FOR THIS EARTHY BUT SOPHISTICATED DISH, Chef Andrew Carmellini of Café Boulud in New York City covers fillets of striped bass with thin slices of truffle, echoing the shimmering scales of the whole fish in the wild, then serves them on a flavorful bed of artichokes and vegetables with a fragrant truffle-infused sauce made with the artichoke braising liquid. Finished in a blender, the sauce looks creamy but contains no cream. SERVES 4

Artichoke and Bacon Ragout (recipe follows)

1 large fresh or flash-frozen black truffle (2 to 3 ounces) [60 to 90 grams]

2 tablespoons extra-virgin olive oil

3 tablespoons unsalted butter [45 grams]: 1 tablespoon melted, 2 tablespoons at room temperature

4 center-cut striped bass fillets (about 6 ounces each), preferably wild, skin left on [180 grams]

Salt and freshly ground black pepper

2 shallots, minced

⅔ cup artichoke cooking liquid (reserved from Artichoke and Bacon Ragout) [150 ml]

¾ to 1 teaspoon black truffle oil, or more to taste

Splash of sherry vinegar

Celery leaves and/or tiny chervil sprigs, for garnish

Fleur de sel

1. Prepare the artichoke and bacon ragout; reserve ⅔ cup [150 ml] of the cooking liquid for the sauce.

2. Using a Japanese vegetable slicer or a mandoline, slice the truffle across the widest diameter into ¹⁄₁₆-inch [2-mm]-thick slices. Reserve the scraps for the sauce.

3. Combine 1 tablespoon of the olive oil with the melted butter and brush over both sides of the bass fillets. Season the fish on both sides with salt and pepper and set skin side down. Using one-quarter of the truffle slices for each fillet, cover the top of each fillet with truffle slices, arranging the slices in overlapping horizontal rows. Place the fillets truffled side up on a buttered heatproof plate; set aside.

4. To make the sauce, heat the remaining 1 tablespoon olive oil in a small saucepan over moderately high heat until hot. Add the shallots and cook, stirring constantly, until softened, about

1 minute. Add the reserved truffle scraps and cook, stirring, until fragrant, about 30 seconds. Add the reserved ⅔ cup [150 ml] artichoke cooking liquid, bring to a simmer, and simmer for 1 to 2 minutes to blend the flavors. Remove from the heat and set aside.

5. If you do not have a stove-top steamer, you can use a deep skillet large enough to hold the plate of fish with some space around it for heat circulation: Fit the skillet with a wire cake rack, or use crumpled aluminum foil to construct a rack that will support the plate. Fill the steamer or skillet with an inch [2.5 cm] or so of water and bring to a boil. Place the plate of fish in the steamer, cover tightly (if you do not have a domed lid to cover the skillet, tent it with foil—the lid or foil should not touch the truffled tops of the fish), and steam for 6 to 8 minutes, or until the fish is just opaque throughout.

6. Meanwhile, reheat the artichoke and bacon ragout over low heat, stirring occasionally.

7. Bring the sauce just a simmer over low heat. Using an immersion blender, blend in the 2 tablespoons [30 grams] softened butter and the truffle oil. Alternatively, transfer the warm sauce to a regular blender, immediately add the butter and oil, and blend until emulsified and foamy. Season with the vinegar and salt and pepper to taste.

8. Arrange the ragout in the centers of 4 large shallow bowls. Place the bass on top and spoon the sauce around the fish. Garnish with the celery leaves and/or chervil, and sprinkle a few grains of fleur de sel on top of each fillet. Serve immediately.

| SOMMELIER WINE SUGGESTION | Palliser Sauvignon Blanc 2000; Marlborough, New Zealand |

ARTICHOKE AND BACON RAGOUT

SERVES 4

1 lemon, halved

4 large artichokes

½ cup pearl onions [70 grams]

3 tablespoons light, fruity extra-virgin olive oil

3 carrots, peeled and cut on the diagonal into ¼-inch-thick slices [.5 cm]

3 celery stalks, peeled and cut on the diagonal into ¼-inch-thick slices [.5 cm]

2 ounces smoky slab bacon, in one piece [60 grams]

Bouquet garni: 1 small bunch of parsley, 1 small bunch of basil, 3 thyme sprigs, ½ rosemary sprig, 2 garlic cloves (peeled), 15 coriander seeds, 15 fennel seeds, 8 peppercorns, and 2 bay leaves, tied in a square of cheesecloth

½ cup dry white wine [125 ml]

4 cups chicken stock, or 2 cans (14½-ounces each) low-sodium chicken broth plus enough water to make 4 cups [1 liter/400 grams]

1. To prepare the artichokes, fill a medium bowl with water, squeeze the juice of the lemon into it, and add the lemon halves. One at a time, using a sharp knife, cut off the stem of each artichoke. Starting at the bottom of the artichoke and working your way around it, bend back and snap off the green leaves until you reach the pale inner cone of leaves. Discard the green leaves (or reserve them; see Note on page 212). Cut off the inner cone of leaves. Using a sharp-edged tea-spoon or a grapefruit spoon, scrape out the hairy choke from the center of the artichoke. Trim off all the green or tough parts from the bottom. As you finish each artichoke, cut it in half, then cut crosswise into thick slices, and place in the bowl of lemon water to prevent discoloration. Set the artichokes aside in the lemon water.

2. Blanch the onions in a saucepan of boiling water for 30 seconds, then transfer to an ice bath to cool (blanching the onions makes it easy to peel them). Drain, trim, and peel the onions.

3. Heat the olive oil in a Dutch oven or large deep skillet over moderately high heat until hot. Add the pearl onions, carrots, celery, and bacon, stir to coat with oil, and reduce the heat to moderate. Cook, stirring occasionally, until the carrots and celery are crisp-tender and the bacon has begun to render its fat, 8 to 10 minutes.

4. Add the artichokes and bouquet garni, then stir in the wine, increase the heat to moderately high, and bring to a simmer. Simmer until the wine has reduced by two-thirds. Add the stock and bring to a simmer, then reduce the heat and simmer gently until the artichokes are just tender, 15 to 20 minutes.

5. Drain the vegetables in a large sieve set over a bowl, reserving the liquid. Discard the bouquet garni. Cut the bacon into ⅜-inch [1-cm] cubes. Transfer the vegetables and bacon to a saucepan and set aside. Set aside ⅔ cup [150 ml] of the reserved cooking liquid for the sauce; discard the rest or reserve it for another use. (The ragout can be made ahead and set aside at room temperature for up to 1 hour or covered and refrigerated for up to 8 hours.)

PAN-SEARED SALMON WITH TRUFFLED FRENCH LENTILS

LENTILS ARE A CLASSIC ACCOMPANIMENT TO SALMON; their earthiness contrasts with the silky sweetness of the unctuous fish. Here the delicate French lentils known as *lentilles de Puy* are finished with bacon, tiny-diced carrots and onion, and julienned black truffles. The lentils would also make a delicious accompaniment for an appetizer of seared foie gras. SERVES 4

---

8 ounces (generous 1 cup) French lentils (lentilles de Puy), picked over and rinsed [225 grams]

2 cups chicken stock or canned low-sodium chicken broth [500 ml]

3 slices of bacon, cut into ⅛-inch strips [3 mm]

½ cup diced (⅛-inch) onion [70 grams/3 mm]

¼ cup diced (⅛-inch) carrot [35 grams/3 mm]

Salt

About 2½ teaspoons olive oil

4 skinless center-cut salmon fillets (about 6 ounces each), any pinbones removed [180 grams]

Coarse sea salt or kosher salt

Freshly ground black pepper

1 to 1½ ounces fresh or flash-frozen black truffle, cut into thin julienne strips [30 to 34 grams]

---

1. Put the lentils in a large saucepan with the stock and enough water to cover by about 2 inches [5 cm]. Bring to a boil, reduce the heat, and simmer gently, stirring occasionally, until the lentils are tender, 15 to 20 minutes. Drain the lentils, reserving the cooking liquid.

2. Cook the bacon in a large skillet over moderate heat, stirring occasionally, until lightly browned and crisp, about 5 minutes. Using a slotted spoon, transfer the bacon to paper towels to drain, leaving the bacon fat in the skillet.

3. Add the onion to the drippings in the skillet and cook, stirring frequently, until slightly softened, about 3 minutes. Add the carrots and a generous pinch of salt, reduce the heat to moderately low, and cook, stirring, until the carrots are beginning to soften, about 5 minutes. Remove from the heat and set aside.

4. Heat another large heavy skillet over moderately high heat until hot, 2 to 3 minutes. Add 1½ tea-spoons of the olive oil and heat until very hot but not smoking. Meanwhile, brush the salmon lightly on both sides with the remaining oil and season generously with coarse salt and pepper.

5. Add the salmon skinned side up to the pan and cook until golden brown on the bottom, about 4 minutes. Turn the salmon over, reduce the heat to moderate, and cook until the salmon is just barely translucent in the center, 3 to 5 minutes longer.

6. Meanwhile, add the lentils, ½ cup [125 ml] of the reserved cooking liquid, ½ teaspoon salt, and ⅛ teaspoon pepper to the skillet with the onion and carrots. Bring to a simmer gently over moderately low heat, stirring occasionally, and simmer until the lentils are heated through, about 2 minutes. Stir in the truffles and bacon and season with additional salt and/or pepper to taste. The lentils should be very moist; if necessary, stir in a few more tablespoons or so of the reserved cooking liquid.

7. Spoon a bed of lentils onto each serving plate. Top each with a salmon fillet and serve immediately.

VARIATION

SUBSTITUTE 1 to 1½ tablespoons black or white truffle oil for the black truffle.

SOMMELIER WINE SUGGESTION Rutz Cellas "Dutton" Ranch Pinot Noir 1998; Russian River Valley, California

RED SNAPPER WITH TRUFFLE BEURRE BLANC

THE FASHION FOR BEURRE BLANC, a silky white wine butter sauce that was the shining star of nouvelle cuisine, may have come and gone, but it is still a classic and sumptuous accompaniment to simply cooked fish—especially when it's made with truffle butter. If you happen to have a black truffle on hand, make the sauce with 6 tablespoons unsalted butter, omitting the truffle butter, then whisk in a few teaspoons finely minced or grated truffle. SERVES 4

1 tablespoon white wine vinegar

1 tablespoon dry white wine

½ small shallot, finely minced

4 tablespoons cold unsalted butter, cut into small cubes [60 grams]

2 tablespoons cold truffle butter, cut into small cubes [30 grams]

Salt and freshly ground black pepper

4 red snapper fillets (about 6 ounces each), skin left on [180 grams]

1 tablespoon olive oil

Chervil or parsley sprigs, for garnish

1. To make the beurre blanc, combine the vinegar, wine, and shallot in a small heavy nonreactive saucepan. Bring to a simmer over moderate heat and cook until the liquid is reduced to about 2 teaspoons. Remove from the heat and immediately add about 1 tablespoon [15 grams] of the unsalted butter, whisking until the butter softens but does not completely melt. Add another tablespoon [15 grams] or so of the butter, whisking until the mixture starts to become creamy. Continue to add the remaining unsalted butter and then the truffle butter in this fashion, whisking constantly and not allowing the butter to melt entirely; if the mixture becomes too cold to soften, return the pan to low heat briefly as necessary. Season with salt and pepper to taste. Transfer the beurre blanc to the top of a double boiler and set over warm-to-hot—not simmering—water to keep warm. (Or set the saucepan in a warm—not hot—spot on the stove.)

2. Season the snapper on both sides with salt and pepper. Heat a large heavy skillet over moderately high heat until hot, then add the oil and heat until it is very hot. Add the snapper skin side down and cook until lightly golden brown on the bottom, about 4 minutes. Turn the fillets over and cook until just opaque throughout, about 4 minutes longer.

3. Transfer the fish to serving plates and spoon the beurre blanc over them. Garnish with chervil sprigs, and serve at once.

NOTE: Because of the acid of the vinegar and white wine in the sauce, be sure to use a nonreactive saucepan; enameled cast-iron or stainless steel is ideal. It's best to make the sauce just before cooking the fish, so that it maintains its creamy consistency.

| SOMMELIER WINE SUGGESTION | Rutz Meursault Jobard-Meursault "Poruzot" 1998; Côte de Beaune, France |

Black Truffles

ROASTED WHOLE TROUT WITH PANCETTA AND BLACK TRUFFLES

BECAUSE TROUT IS SUCH A LEAN FISH, wrapping it in pancetta—not to speak of the enclosed truffles that impart their heady perfume—makes perfect sense. The flavorful salty pancetta brings out both the earthy truffle fragrance and the sweetness of the trout for a truly inspired dish. SERVES 4

4 trout (12 ounces each), cleaned and scaled [350 grams] (see Note)

Salt and freshly ground black pepper

8 small thyme sprigs

16 thin slices of pancetta (about 4 ounces) [120 grams]

1 small fresh or flash-frozen black truffle (about 1 ounce), thinly sliced [30 grams]

1. Preheat the oven to 425°F [220°C]. Grease a large heavy rimmed baking sheet.

2. Rinse the trout and pat dry. With kitchen shears, cut off the fins. Season the trout inside and out with salt and pepper, rubbing the seasonings into the skin. Stuff 2 thyme sprigs into the cavity of each fish.

3. Arrange 4 slices of the pancetta on a work surface, overlapping them slightly so they form a square about 5½ inches [14 cm] across. Using one-quarter of the truffle slices, arrange a line of truffle slices lengthwise down the center of one trout; then place the remaining slices inside the cavity of the fish. Carefully lift up the pancetta square (the slices will stick together) and lay it over the center of the fish, leaving the head and tail exposed. Tuck the edges of the slices under the fish and secure the pancetta with a length of kitchen twine. Place the trout on the prepared baking sheet, and repeat with the remaining fish.

4. Roast for 14 to 17 minutes, or until the pancetta is beginning to turn golden brown and the fish is opaque throughout (test with a small sharp knife inserted into the thickest part of one fish). Cut off the strings, transfer the trout to plates, and serve, with a fish knife for each guest if you have them. To eat the trout, pull open the pancetta slices to uncover the fish. Run a knife down the back of the fish to split the skin, then lift off the top fillet, skin and all, and set to one side. To reach the bottom fillet, cut through the backbone just behind the head and just in front of the tail, and lift out and discard the backbone and ribs.

NOTE: Fish always tastes better cooked on the bone. However, if you are not sure about your guests' filleting techniques, ask the fishmonger to bone the trout (through the stomach, not the back). Prepare as directed above, but reduce the roasting time to 12 to 14 minutes.

SOMMELIER WINE SUGGESTION Bodegas Reyes "Teofilo Reyes" 1998; Ribera del Duero, Spain

ROASTED WHOLE FISH WITH TRUFFLE BUTTER

NOTHING COULD BE EASIER than roasting a whole fish. Simply ask your fishmonger for the finest catch of the day—the truffle butter does the rest. You can roast fish of any size this way, adjusting the cooking time as necessary. Count on about one pound of fish on the bone per serving. Traditionally, a fine fish is presented intact in all its glory (often with a lemon slice or parsley sprig covering the eye), but if your guests are squeamish, you can carefully remove the head after cooking. SERVES 4 TO 6

About 1 tablespoon unsalted butter, softened [15 grams]

One 5½- to 6-pound whole fish, such as bluefish, Pacific cod, flounder, sea bass, or halibut, cleaned and scaled [2.5 to 2.75 kg]

Salt and freshly ground black pepper

1 small lemon, cut into thin slices

2 tarragon or flat-leaf parsley sprigs

3 to 4 tablespoons cold truffle butter [45 to 60 grams]

1. Preheat the oven to 375°F [190°C]. Use the softened butter to generously butter a shallow baking dish large enough to hold the fish.

2. Rinse the fish and pat dry. Using kitchen shears, cut off the fins. Season the fish inside and out with salt and pepper. Stuff the lemon slices and tarragon inside the cavity. Using 2 tablespoons [30 grams] in all, distribute heaping teaspoonfuls of cold truffle butter throughout the cavity of the fish. Place the fish in the prepared baking dish.

3. Melt the remaining 1 to 2 tablespoons [15 to 30 grams] truffle butter in a small saucepan over low heat. Drizzle the melted butter over the fish. Bake for 12 to 15 minutes per inch [2.5 cm] of thickness (measured at the thickest part of the fish), or until the flesh is opaque throughout (an instant-read thermometer inserted into the thickest part of the flesh should register about 140°F [60°C]).

4. Spoon a little of the melted butter in the bottom of the baking dish over the fish, then carefully transfer the fish to a warm platter; set the baking dish aside. With a sharp knife, slit the skin down the back of the fish. Slide the knife under the top fillet to separate it from the backbone; then cut the fillet into serving pieces and, using a wide metal spatula, transfer to warmed serving plates or a platter. Cut through the backbone at the head and tail, and lift out and discard the backbone and ribs. Cut the bottom fillet into serving pieces and transfer to plates or the platter. Spoon the melted truffle butter remaining in the baking dish over the fish and serve at once.

SOMMELIER WINE SUGGESTION Lucien Crochet "Le Chene" Sancerre 1996; Loire, France

CHICKEN BREASTS STUFFED WITH HERBED TRUFFLE BUTTER

IF YOU LOOK CLOSELY, you'll see that this is actually a refined version of chicken Kiev. Little bundles of herbed boneless chicken breasts are stuffed with truffle butter and fried until crisp and light. The crust seals in all the flavors, but once the chicken is cut open, the truffle butter oozes out, releasing its intoxicating aroma. Serve with orzo and perhaps a cucumber salad, as well as some excellent French bread to absorb the sauce. SERVES 4

6 tablespoons truffle butter, at room temperature [90 grams]

1 tablespoon minced chives

½ teaspoon fresh lemon juice

4 large skinless, boneless chicken breast halves (7 to 8 ounces each) [200 to 225 grams]

Salt and freshly ground black pepper

⅓ cup all-purpose flour [45 grams]

2 large eggs

1½ cups fine bread crumbs, preferably fresh [70 grams]

Peanut or vegetable oil, for deep-frying

1. Combine the truffle butter, chives, and lemon juice in a small bowl; mix with a wooden spoon or rubber spatula until well blended. Divide the butter into 4 equal portions and shape each one into a narrow cylinder about 3 inches [8 cm] long. Wrap tightly in plastic wrap and refrigerate or freeze until firm, at least 1 hour.

2. One at a time, place each chicken breast between 2 sheets of parchment or waxed paper and using the smooth side of a meat mallet or a rolling pin, pound the chicken until it is almost doubled in size and flattened to a ¼-inch [.5-cm] thickness. Season both sides lightly with salt and pepper.

3. Place a flattened chicken breast smooth side down on the work surface. Lay a truffle butter cylinder across the larger of the 2 long sides of the breast. Fold the edge of the breast over the cylinder, tuck in the ends to enclose the cylinder, and roll up, pressing gently to form a sealed packet. (If necessary, thread a toothpick through the breast meat to secure it.) Transfer to a plate and refrigerate while you prepare the remaining chicken.

4. Spread the flour on a small plate. Lightly beat the eggs in a shallow bowl. Spread the bread crumbs on a larger plate. One at a time, dredge each chicken packet in the flour to coat lightly, then roll it in the beaten egg to coat thoroughly and lay it in the crumbs; toss them over the top and sides to coat the entire surface, and pat gently to help the crumbs adhere. Transfer the chicken to a wire rack set in a baking pan, cover the pan with plastic wrap (without touching the chicken), and refrigerate for at least 1 hour to set the crumbs and firm the truffle butter.

5. Pour about 3 inches [8 cm] of oil into a deep fryer or a large heavy saucepan and heat to 375°F [190°C]. Carefully add the chicken to the hot oil and cook until golden brown all over, about 5 minutes. Drain briefly on paper towels, and remove any toothpicks before serving.

NOTE: If necessary, the cooked chicken can be held on a small baking sheet in a preheated 200°F [100°C] oven for up to 30 minutes.

SOMMELIER WINE SUGGESTION | Rudd Chardonnay 1998; Carneros, California

POUSSIN EN DEMI-DEUIL

POULARDE EN DEMI-DEUIL is a classic French dish from the Lyonnais region, home of the renowned Bresse chicken. *Demi-deuil* means "half-mourning," which refers to the fact that the breast of the bird is swathed in black—sliced black truffles, that is. This variation allows you to present each guest with his or her own roasted bird. You can prepare the dish with small Cornish hens, if necessary, but poussins (young chickens), available at specialty butchers and some supermarkets, are smaller, more delicate, and more flavorful.

Serve these with scalloped or roasted potatoes and fresh peas. The truffled birds really need no other adornment, but if you want to accompany them with an easy pan sauce, see the Note below. SERVES 4

4 poussins (baby chickens) (about 1¼ pounds each) [600 grams]

1 small fresh or flash-frozen black truffle (about 1 ounce), cut into ¹⁄₁₆-inch or slightly thinner slices [30 grams/2 mm]

Salt and freshly ground black pepper

6 tablespoons unsalted butter: 4 tablespoons at room temperature, 2 tablespoons melted [90 grams/60 grams/30 grams]

Fleur de sel

1. Preheat the oven to 400°F [200°C]. Grease a large shallow roasting pan.

2. Rinse the poussins under cold running water; dry thoroughly inside and out with paper towels. Using your fingertips, carefully loosen the flesh over the breast of each chicken, working first from the tail end and then from the neck; be careful not to tear the skin. Using one-quarter of the truffle slices for each bird, lift up the skin and carefully arrange the slices over the breast meat. Season the chickens inside and out with salt and pepper, rubbing the seasonings into the skin. Rub 1 tablespoon [15 grams] of the softened butter generously over each bird. Tie the legs of each chicken together with kitchen twine.

3. Arrange the poussins in the prepared roasting pan and roast for 20 minutes. Baste with the melted butter and roast for about 5 minutes longer. Baste the birds with the pan juices. Roast

for about 10 minutes longer, basting once more, until the internal temperature of the thickest part of the thigh registers 175°F [80°C] on an instant-read thermometer. Cover the poussins loosely with foil and let rest in a warm place for 5 to 10 minutes.

4. Transfer the poussins to plates and set out a small bowl of fleur de sel for individual sprinkling.

NOTE: To make a pan sauce for the poussin, transfer the birds to a platter, cover with foil, and set aside in a warm place. Spoon off most of the fat from the juices in the roasting pan. Set the pan over low heat and add ⅓ cup [75 ml] dry white wine, stirring to release the browned bits on the bottom of the pan. Bring to a boil and boil, stirring once or twice, just to cook off the alcohol. Add 2 tablespoons [30 grams] unsalted butter and 1 teaspoon thyme leaves and stir until the butter is melted. Pour into a small pitcher and serve.

| SOMMELIER WINE SUGGESTION | Alban Vineyards "Lorraine" Syrah 1997; Edna Valley, California |

SALT FROM THE SEA

Plain old table salt, iodized or not, is far from the only choice when it comes to seasoning. Table salt is mined from rock salt deposits and treated with additives to prevent clumping, among other things. Most chefs and many cooks prefer to use kosher salt or sea salt of various types.

KOSHER SALT is also mined, but it does not contain additives. It is coarse and flaky, and because of its texture, is less salty per volume measure (i.e., teaspoon per teaspoon) than table salt.

MOST SEA SALT comes from France, where it is called *sel gris*, or gray salt. Sea salt comes from evaporation rather than mining, and it is harvested from salt marshes or flats off the country's Atlantic and Mediterranean coasts. The best French sea salt comes from towns along the coast of Brittany, most notably Guérande, and from the small offshore islands of Ré and Noirmoutier. Here the sea salt is harvested by hand as the saltwater evaporates from the shallow pools and beds, using tools that look like long-handled rakes, and it is not treated at all, or even washed—leaving the salt perfumed with "essence of the sea." What is called Celtic sea salt also comes from Brittany's coast. Sea salt may be left in large crystals or ground finer. There are three types—fine, medium-flake, and coarse—but fine and coarse are the most common. Coarse sea salt can be sprinkled on fish such as salmon or sometimes on meat before cooking, or added as a finishing touch. It can also be finely ground before using, with a salt mill.

Good sea salt has its own flavor, not just a salty taste. But the "caviar" of salts is what is called *fleur de sel*, "the flower of salt." Like the best French sea salt, fleur de sel comes from Brittany and the offshore islands, but it is much rarer than ordinary sea salt. It is a delicate salt that floats to the surface of the salt flats; to harvest it, it must be removed each day with small wooden shovels rather than rakes. All sea salt is seasonal, the harvest running throughout the warm summer months, but the formation of fleur de sel depends even more so on specific climatic conditions, and so the harvest is not always reliable. Even in a good year, fleur de sel represents only a tiny fraction of the sea salt harvest (which, in turn, is minuscule compared to that of mined salts).

FLEUR DE SEL, not surprisingly, is expensive, but a little—just a few grains—goes a long way. It is used for finishing a dish, not for cooking, and it has a real depth of flavor. Some detect violets, but it always has a clean, pure scent of the sea. Le Paludier is a particularly fragrant brand; Esprit du Sel, from the Ile de Ré, is also good and more widely available. Fleur de sel can be sprinkled over hot foods, such as sliced rare duck breast or steak, or cold dishes such as carpaccio or raw tuna. A favorite French snack is a slice of a country loaf spread with sweet butter and sprinkled with fleur de sel.

Note that the French sea salt that comes from the Mediterranean coast, along Provence and the Camargue, is usually commercially harvested and washed, and it often contain additives. England produces a high-quality sea salt called Maldon, and Japan also produces sea salt.

NOTE: Although we generally prefer to use sea salt and kosher salt, for the sake of convenience, the specified measurements in the recipes in this book are for table salt, since that is the type most commonly available. If substituting kosher salt, you will probably need to use a bit more; if using fine sea salt, you may need to add less, since, depending on the type, it can taste saltier than table salt.

GRILLED DUCK BREASTS WITH TRUFFLE HONEY

ALTHOUGH TRUFFLE HONEY IS INFUSED with the scent of Italian white truffles, fragrant honey is a favorite ingredient in the South of France. Here the duck breasts are first marinated in a typical Provençal combination of garlic, rosemary, and thyme, then glazed with the honey as they cook on the grill.

Magrets are the breasts of moulard ducks, the ones that are raised for foie gras. Large and meaty (one half-breast will serve two people), they are usually treated more like steak—they are best cooked only to rare or medium-rare. Magrets are available from specially butchers and mail-order sources; if they are unavailable, substitute 4 Pekin (Long Island) duck breasts, and reduce the cooking time accordingly (see Note). Grilled fennel and wild rice would make fine accompaniments. SERVES 4

1 tablespoon coarsely chopped rosemary	**Salt and freshly ground black pepper**
1 teaspoon thyme leaves	**3 to 4 tablespoons truffle honey**
4 garlic cloves, thinly sliced	**Fleur de sel or coarse sea salt**
2 large boneless magrets (duck half-breasts; about 1 pound each), skin on [500 grams]	

1. Combine the rosemary, thyme, and garlic on a cutting board and use a large sharp heavy knife to chop them together a few times. Put the duck breasts in a baking dish or other container and rub about two-thirds of the herb mixture over the meaty side. Rub the remaining garlic and herbs over the skin. Cover and refrigerate for about 2 hours.

2. Prepare a hot fire in a grill (alternately, the duck can be cooked in a stove-top grill pan; preheat it over moderately high heat while you are searing the duck breasts in step 3 below).

3. Meanwhile, brush the garlic-herb mixture off the duck breasts. Using a sharp knife, score the skin of each breast in a crisscross pattern, cutting almost but not quite down to the meat. Heat a large heavy skillet over moderately high heat until hot. Add the duck breasts skin side down and cook until the skin is lightly golden brown and the duck has released a lot of its fat, 5 to 7 minutes. Transfer to a plate. Reserve the melted duck fat for another use, such as pan frying potatoes, or discard it.

4. Season the duck on both sides with salt and pepper. Place skin side down on the grill (or in the grill pan) and cook for 4 to 5 minutes, or until the skin is deep golden brown. Turn the breasts over and grill for about 5 minutes longer, or until cooked to rare. Brush the duck skin generously with honey, turn over, and grill until the honey begins to caramelize, 1½ to 2 minutes. Brush the meaty side of the breasts generously with the remaining honey, turn over, and grill for 1 to 1½ minutes longer. Transfer the duck to a platter, cover loosely with foil, and let rest for 5 minutes.

5. Transfer the duck breasts to a cutting board, preferably one with a moat to catch juices, and cut the meat on the diagonal into thin slices. Arrange the slices on serving plates or a platter, spoon the juices from the platter and cutting board over them, and sprinkle lightly with fleur de sel. Serve at once.

NOTE: If magrets are unavailable, substitute 4 Pekin (Long Island) duck breasts, which generally weigh 5 to 6 ounces. Marinate the breasts as directed, but omit the pan-searing in step 3. Brush the garlic-herb mixture off the breasts, score the skin as described above, and season with salt and pepper. Grill the duck for 3 to 4 minutes on each side, or until rare, before brushing with the honey and continuing as directed.

| SOMMELIER WINE SUGGESTION | Château de Musset 1998; Montagne-St. Emilion, France |

PICHOLINE'S ROASTED WILD PARTRIDGE WITH TRUFFLE FLANS

AT PICHOLINE, TERRY BRENNAN'S LOVELY MANHATTAN RESTAURANT, this dish is prepared with wild Scottish red-legged partridge, which is in season only from early fall through December; farm-raised partridge, however, which are also tasty, are available all year round, from specialty butchers and mail-order sources (see Sources, page 234). Browning the bird on the stovetop and then finishing it briefly in the oven leaves the meat succulent and moist.

Here we include the recipes for the two sauces served with the pheasant at the restaurant, an unusual and delicious "chocolate sauce" and a port vinaigrette, but the dish is impressive even with just the easy vinaigrette. Serve the pheasant on a bed of garlicky braised greens, such as chard, with sautéed porcini or other flavorful mushrooms. SERVES 6

Chocolate Madeira Sauce (recipe follows)

Truffle Flans (recipe follows)

3 partridges

Salt and freshly ground black pepper

1 tablespoon unsalted butter [15 grams]

3 sage leaves

1½ tablespoons grapeseed or other flavorless vegetable oil

1 cup port [250 ml]

3½ tablespoons truffle juice

1 ounce truffle peelings (reserved from fresh truffles, or use canned truffle peelings) [30 grams]

¾ teaspoon lemon juice

1 to 2 ounces fresh or flash-frozen black truffles [30 to 60 grams]

1. Make the madeira sauce and the truffle flans.

2. Preheat the oven to 400°F [200°C]. Lightly oil a large roasting pan. Season the partridges inside and out with salt and pepper. Put 1 teaspoon of the butter and 1 sage leaf in the cavity of each partridge. Heat 1 tablespoon of the oil in a large flameproof casserole (or use 2 large heavy skillets) over moderately high heat until very hot. Add the partridges breast side down and cook until golden brown, 5 to 7 minutes; reduce the heat slightly if necessary. Using tongs, turn the partridges on their sides and cook until golden brown, about 7 minutes. Turn the birds onto their other sides and cook until golden brown, about 7 minutes. Turn the partridges breast side up and cook just to brown the backs lightly, 2 to 3 minutes. Transfer the birds to the prepared

roasting pan and roast for 12 to 14 minutes, until the juices run clear when the thigh is pierced; an instant-read thermometer inserted into the thickest part of the thigh should register 175°F [80°C]. Transfer to a platter, cover loosely with foil, and let rest in a warm spot for 10 minutes.

3. Meanwhile, to make the vinaigrette: Combine the port, truffle juice, and truffle peelings in a small heavy saucepan. Bring to a simmer over moderate heat and simmer until thick and syrupy; you should have about 2½ tablespoons liquid. Remove from the heat and let cool, then whisk in the lemon juice, the remaining 1½ tablespoons of oil, and a pinch of salt. Set aside.

4. If necessary, rewarm the flans in the turned-off oven for about 10 minutes (a knife inserted in the center of a flan should emerge hot). Reheat the sauce over low heat.

5. Carve the partridges. Drizzle the vinaigrette around the plates. Invert a truffle flan onto one side of each plate. Arrange a partridge leg and breast in the center of each plate. Spoon the chocolate sauce over the partridge. Shave the truffles over and around the flans, and serve immediately.

SOMMELIER WINE SUGGESTION Domaine Serene "Evenstad Reserve" Pinot Noir 1999; Willamette Valley, Oregon

CHOCOLATE MADEIRA SAUCE

Carcasses of 3 partridges or 1 chicken, chopped with a cleaver, **or 1½ pounds chicken backs, necks, and/or wings,** chopped [750 grams]

1 teaspoon olive oil

1 small onion, chopped

1 celery stalk, chopped

1 small carrot, chopped

1 garlic clove, crushed

Salt

½ cup Madeira [125 ml]

2 thyme sprigs

1 bay leaf

4 white peppercorns

2 cups unsalted chicken stock or canned chicken broth (see Note) [500 ml]

2 cups unsalted veal stock (or additional chicken stock) (see Note) [500 ml]

1 ounce bittersweet chocolate, finely chopped [30 grams]

Freshly ground black pepper

1. Preheat the oven to 400°F [200°C]. Put the bones in a roasting pan and roast, stirring once or twice, for about 45 minutes, until well browned.

2. Meanwhile, heat the olive oil in a large saucepan over moderately high heat. Add the onion, celery, carrot, garlic, and a generous pinch of salt. Reduce the heat to moderate and cook, stirring frequently, until the vegetables are softened and golden brown, about 5 minutes. Add the

Madeira and bring to a simmer, scraping up any browned bits from the bottom of the pan. Add the thyme sprigs, bay leaf, and peppercorns and simmer until the liquid is reduced by half.

3. Add the roasted bones to the saucepan. Pour off the fat from the roasting pan, set the pan over moderately low heat, and add 1 cup [250 ml] of the chicken stock, stirring to deglaze the pan. Pour the stock into the saucepan, add the remaining 1 cup [250 ml] chicken stock and the veal stock, and bring to a simmer. Reduce the heat to low and simmer, skimming off the fat and foam frequently, until the liquid is reduced by one-quarter, about 20 minutes.

4. Strain the sauce through a fine sieve into a medium saucepan. Bring to a simmer and simmer, skimming frequently, until reduced to ½ cup. Remove from the heat, add the chocolate, and let stand for 30 seconds, then whisk until smooth. Season with salt and pepper to taste. (The sauce can be made up to 1 day ahead, covered, and refrigerated. Reheat gently before serving.)

NOTE: Because the stock is reduced by so much to make the sauce, it is best to use unsalted stock, so that the final result is not overly salty. Prepared chicken and veal stocks are available at many gourmet shops.

TRUFFLE FLANS

SERVES 6

⅓ cup peeled garlic cloves (about 1 large head) [55 grams]

About ¾ cup olive oil [185 ml]

1 to 2 ounces fresh or flash-frozen black truffles [30 to 60 grams]

½ cup chicken stock or canned low-sodium chicken broth [125 ml]

1 cup heavy cream [250 ml]

1 cup milk [250 ml]

½ cup freshly grated Parmigiano-Reggiano [35 grams]

3 large eggs

2 large egg yolks

½ teaspoon salt

1. Combine the garlic and enough oil to just cover in a small heavy saucepan and bring to a simmer over moderate heat. Reduce the heat and simmer very gently until the garlic is soft, about 15 minutes. Let cool, then drain the garlic thoroughly (reserve the garlic oil for another use).

2. Meanwhile, combine the truffles and chicken stock in another small heavy saucepan and bring to a simmer over moderate heat. Reduce the heat and simmer gently until the truffles soften slightly, about 10 minutes. Transfer the truffles to a mini processor, reserving the chicken stock. Process to a coarse puree, adding a little of the chicken stock as necessary.

3. Combine the cream, milk, Parmesan, and garlic in a medium saucepan and bring to a simmer over moderate heat. Reduce the heat to very low (use a heat diffuser if you have one) and simmer very gently for 20 minutes to infuse the liquid.

4. Preheat the oven to 300°F [150°C]. Generously butter six 4-ounce [125-ml] ramekins.

5. Transfer the cream mixture to a blender and puree. Strain through a fine sieve into a bowl.

6. In a medium bowl, whisk the eggs and egg yolks until blended. Gradually whisk in the cream mixture. Whisk in the truffle puree and salt.

7. Pour the flan mixture into the prepared ramekins. Put the ramekins in a baking pan that will hold them comfortably, and add enough hot water to the pan to reach halfway up the sides of the ramekins.

8. Bake for 40 to 45 minutes, or until the flans are just set. Keep warm in the water bath until ready to serve. (The flans can be made up to 4 hours in advance. Remove from the water bath, let cool, and refrigerate; bring to room temperature, then reheat in a hot oven for about 10 minutes.)

PORTERHOUSE STEAK WITH BLACK TRUFFLE SAUCE

A VARIATION ON A CLASSIC FRENCH PAN SAUCE, this buttery truffle sauce is a sublime accompaniment to a medium-rare steak. You can substitute rib-eye steaks, T-bone, sirloin, or another favorite cut for the porterhouse. Serve with mashed potatoes or sliced potatoes sautéed with garlic and buttered sugar snap peas. SERVES 4

4 tablespoons unsalted butter, at room temperature [60 grams]

2 teaspoons olive oil

2 porterhouse steaks (about 1¼ pounds each), cut 1¼ inches thick [600 grams/3 cm]

Salt and freshly ground black pepper

1½ tablespoons minced shallots

⅓ cup beef stock, preferably homemade [75 ml]

¼ cup Cognac or other brandy [60 ml]

1 fresh or flash-frozen black truffle, sliced paper-thin

1. Put ½ tablespoon [10 grams] of the butter and 1 teaspoon of the olive oil in each of 2 large heavy skillets and heat over moderately high heat until the butter is melted and foaming. Season the steaks on both sides with salt and pepper, add to the pans, and cook, turning once, for 3 to 4 minutes on each side for medium-rare. Transfer the steaks to a warm platter and cover loosely with foil.

2. Pour off the fat from the skillets and set one pan aside. Add 1 tablespoon [15 grams] of the butter and the shallots to the other skillet and cook over moderate heat, stirring frequently, until the shallots are softened, about 2 minutes.

3. Meanwhile, add about 2 tablespoons [30 grams] of the stock to the reserved skillet, stirring and scraping the bottom of the pan to release the browned bits (the pan should still be hot enough for deglazing; set it over moderate heat briefly if necessary). Add these pan juices to the skillet with the shallots, along with the remaining stock, increase the heat to moderately high, and bring to a boil. Boil, stirring occasionally, until reduced almost to a glaze.

4. Add the Cognac and cook, stirring once or twice, until slightly reduced, about 2 minutes. Remove from the heat and add the truffle. Gradually add the remaining 2 tablespoons [30 grams] butter ½ tablespoon at a time, stirring with a wooden spoon until the butter is just incorporated and the sauce has thickened slightly.

5. Spoon the sauce over the steaks, and serve immediately. Be sure to serve some of the fillet portion of the steaks to each guest when you slice the steaks. (Porterhouse steaks are cut so they have meat from both the flavorful loin and, on the other side of their central bone, a smaller section from the more tender fillet.)

SOMMELIER WINE SUGGESTION	Tenuta San Guido Bolgheri-Sassicaia, Sassicaia 1995; Tuscany, Italy

Truffled Eggs

BEEF TAGLIATA WITH BLACK TRUFFLES

TAGLIATA MEANS "SLICED" IN ITALIAN, and the term usually refers to beef or veal. Here beef tenderloin is cut into medallions and pounded gently to thin the slices a bit, then quickly pan-seared just until rare and tossed with herbs, and, in a twist on the classic, truffle butter. The beef is served over arugula, wilted and dressed by the warm pan juices. The dish is simple to prepare (a sharp knife makes it easy to slice the meat, but ask the butcher to do this if you prefer) and deliciously aromatic. Serve with panfried potatoes. SERVES 4

1¼ pounds center-cut beef tenderloin
600 grams]

Salt and freshly ground black pepper

1 small bunch of arugula, trimmed and washed

About 2 tablespoons olive oil

3 tablespoons packed slivered basil leaves

2 tablespoons slivered sage leaves
(see Note)

2 tablespoons truffle butter [30 grams]

---

1. Cut the beef into 12 thin slices. One at a time, place each slice between 2 sheets of plastic wrap and, with the smooth side of a meat mallet or a rolling pin, pound gently to just slightly less than ¼-inch [.5-cm] thick. Season on both sides with salt and pepper.

2. Arrange a small mound of the arugula on each of 4 serving plates. Set aside.

3. Heat a large heavy skillet over high heat until hot. Add 2 teaspoons of the olive oil and heat until very hot but not smoking. Add 4 of the slices of beef and cook just until browned on the first side, about 1 minute. Turn the slices over, scatter one-third of the herbs over them, and cook just until lightly browned on the second side, about 30 seconds. Transfer to a platter. Repeat with the remaining beef, in 2 more batches, adding the remaining oil to the pan as necessary and heating it before adding the next batch of meat.

4. Reduce the heat to low and add the truffle butter to the pan. Working quickly so the meat doesn't overcook, return all the beef to the pan, along with any juices that have accumulated on the platter, and turn the slices once or twice in the sauce, just until heated through. Arrange the steak on top of the arugula and spoon the pan juices over the meat. Serve immediately.

NOTE: Use small sage leaves if possible; larger ones can sometimes be too pungent.

SOMMELIER WINE SUGGESTION Morgan François Pillet Domaine des Souchones 1999; Beaujolais, France

INDIVIDUAL BEEF WELLINGTONS WITH SAUCE PERIGUEUX

TRADITIONAL BEEF WELLINGTON is always a showstopper, but once the first slice is cut and removed, the magnificent structure usually deteriorates rapidly into a soggy pile of meat and crumbly pastry. The solution is to make tidy individual portions featuring the same luxurious combination of flavors, including intense mushroom duxelles, the sumptuous truffled brown sauce known as Périgueux, and a crisp puff pastry crust. We've done away with the layer of foie gras often included in classic recipes, because to our palates, it is a tad too rich. Serve with buttered asparagus or haricots verts. SERVES 4

4 center-cut beef tenderloin steaks (tournedos) (about 6 ounces each), 1½ inches thick, trimmed of fat [180 grams/4 cm]

1½ tablespoons olive oil

Salt and freshly ground black pepper

Mushroom Duxelles (recipe follows)

1 package (14 ounces) frozen all-butter puff pastry, thawed according to package directions [about 400 grams]

1 large egg

1 tablespoon heavy cream or milk

SAUCE PÉRIGUEUX

2 tablespoons unsalted butter [30 grams]

2 tablespoons all-purpose flour

1 tablespoon tomato paste

2 cups rich beef stock (see Note) [500 ml]

⅓ cup Madeira [75 ml]

1 fresh or flash-frozen black truffle, thinly sliced

1 tablespoon truffle juice (optional)

Salt and freshly ground black pepper

1. Rub the beef with the olive oil and season with salt and pepper. Heat a large cast-iron skillet or other heavy skillet over high heat until hot. Add the beef to the pan, without crowding, and cook, turning once or twice, until crusty brown outside but still very rare inside, 4 to 5 minutes. Transfer to a plate and let cool. Cover and refrigerate until well chilled, at least 4 hours. (The beef can be seared up to 1 day ahead.)

2. Arrange the tournedos 2 to 3 inches [5 to 8 cm] apart on a parchment-lined baking sheet. Top with the duxelles, spreading it evenly. Set the tournedos aside on the baking sheet.

3. Lay the pastry sheet on a lightly floured work surface. If necessary, roll out the dough so it is no more than ⅛ inch [3 mm] in thickness. Using a plate or pan lid as a guide, cut out four 5-inch [13-cm] rounds of pastry. If desired, cut out shapes from some of the dough scraps to use as decoration.

4. Beat the egg with the cream in a small bowl until well blended. Brush a pastry round with some of the egg wash, then invert it over a tournedo. Pinch the edges of the pastry together, pleating it as needed, to enclose the meat. Repeat with remaining pastry and meat. Brush the pastry all over with egg wash. Decorate with pastry scraps, if desired, and brush again. Cover and refrigerate the remaining egg wash. Cover the wrapped beef with plastic wrap, and refrigerate until the pastry is firm to the touch, at least 30 minutes (or as long as overnight).

5. Meanwhile, to make the sauce base, melt the butter in a medium saucepan over moderately low heat. Whisk in the flour and cook, whisking, until the mixture is well blended and just beginning to color, about 3 minutes. Whisk in the tomato paste until well blended. Gradually whisk in the beef stock and about ¼ cup [60 ml] of the Madeira. Bring to a boil over moderate heat, whisking, then reduce the heat to moderately low and simmer until the sauce is reduced to 1 cup [250 ml], about 30 minutes. Remove the pan from the heat and set aside.

6. When ready to cook the beef, preheat the oven to 425°F [220°C].

7. Brush the beef Wellingtons with the reserved egg wash. Bake until the pastry is puffed and golden, about 15 minutes for medium-rare beef.

8. Meanwhile, to finish the sauce, bring it just to a slow simmer over moderately low heat. Stir in the remaining Madiera, the truffle, and the truffle juice, if using, reduce the heat to low, and cook, stirring, for about 2 minutes to blend the flavors. Season with salt and pepper if necessary.

9. Transfer the beef to 4 dinner plates, spoon the sauce around it, and serve.

NOTE: If you have homemade beef stock stored in your freezer, you will want to use it for this recipe. If not, good-quality beef stock is available in the refrigerator or freezer section of many gourmet markets.

SOMMELIER WINE SUGGESTION | Jean Pierret Francois Perrin "Les Sinards" Châteauneuf-du-Pape 1998; Rhône, France

MUSHROOM DUXELLES

MAKES ABOUT ½ CUP [125 ML]

1½ tablespoons unsalted butter [25 grams]

1 shallot, minced

4 ounces wild or cultivated mushrooms,
trimmed, cleaned, and finely chopped
[125 grams]

2 teaspoons all-purpose flour

3 tablespoons heavy cream

1 tablespoon minced chives

1 tablespoon chopped flat-leaf parsley

¼ teaspoon fresh lemon juice

Salt

Dash of cayenne

1. Melt the butter in a large skillet over moderate heat. Add the shallot and cook, stirring, until softened, 1 to 2 minutes. Add the mushrooms and cook, stirring occasionally, until most of the liquid they release has evaporated, about 10 minutes.

2. Sprinkle the flour over the mushrooms and cook, stirring, until well blended, about 2 minutes. Increase the heat to high, add the cream, and bring to a boil, stirring frequently. Continue cooking until the liquid has evaporated and the mushrooms are almost dry. Remove from the heat and stir in the chives, parsley, lemon juice, salt to taste, and the cayenne. Let cool completely. (The duxelles can be made up to 2 days ahead, covered, and refrigerated.)

BRAISED SHORT RIBS WITH BLACK TRUFFLE SAUCE

IF YOU CONSIDER SHORT RIBS humble comfort food, think again. Most of today's star chefs have at least one signature recipe for succulent braised short ribs. The tantalizing cooking aromas that will fill your kitchen as the meat cooks are reason enough to make this truffled version—not to mention the rich, heady flavors. Serve with mashed potatoes and fresh peas. SERVES 4 TO 6

5½ to 6 pounds beef short ribs (bone-in), cut crosswise into 3- to 4-inch pieces (have the butcher do this) and trimmed of excess fat [2.5 to 2.75 kg/8 to 10 cm]

Salt and freshly ground black pepper

4 to 6 tablespoons olive oil

1 large onion, halved and thinly sliced

1 large carrot, chopped

1 celery stalk, chopped

½ cup dry red wine [125 ml]

1 can (28 ounces) diced tomatoes, drained [800 grams]

½ cup beef stock, preferably homemade [125 ml]

1 tablespoon balsamic vinegar

¼ cup chopped flat-leaf parsley [60 ml]

1 tablespoon chopped rosemary

4 garlic cloves, minced

⅛ teaspoon crushed hot red pepper

2 tablespoons truffle juice

1 fresh or flash-frozen black truffle, cut into thin julienne strips

1. Season the short ribs with salt and pepper. Heat ¼ cup [60 ml] of the oil in a large skillet over moderately high heat. Working in batches, add the meat to the pan, without crowding, and cook, turning occasionally, until browned on all sides, 5 to 7 minutes per batch; add more oil to the pan if necessary. As the ribs are cooked, transfer to paper towels to drain, then arrange in a shallow roasting pan.

2. Meanwhile, preheat the oven to 350°F [175°C].

3. When all the ribs have been browned, add the onion, carrot, and celery to the skillet and cook over moderate heat, stirring frequently, until softened, 5 to 7 minutes. Scatter the vegetables over the short ribs.

4. Discard the oil from the skillet. Add the wine to the pan and bring to a boil over moderate heat, scraping up the browned bits from the bottom with a wooden spoon. Pour over the short ribs.

5. Combine the tomatoes, stock, balsamic vinegar, 3 tablespoons of the parsley, the rosemary, garlic, and hot pepper in a medium bowl, stirring to mix well. Pour the mixture over the short ribs and cover the pan tightly with aluminum foil.

6. Bake the short ribs for about 2½ hours, carefully lifting the foil once or twice to baste them with the pan juices, until the meat is fork-tender. Remove the foil and bake for 15 minutes longer.

7. Using tongs or a slotted spoon, transfer the short ribs to a serving platter. Skim off the fat from the pan juices. Stir in the truffle juice and truffle (the heat from the pan will warm the truffle sufficiently). Spoon the sauce over the short ribs and sprinkle with the remaining 1 tablespoon parsley.

SOMMELIER WINE SUGGESTION Altesino Brunello di Montalcino 1994; Tuscany, Italy

ROAST VEAL CHOPS WITH TRUFFLES AND FOIE GRAS

FROM NEW YORK CHEF FRANK WHITTAKER, these luscious veal chops are garnished with seared foie gras and shaved white or black truffles. The rich sauce is made with Barolo, which some describe as tasting of truffles, making it a more than fitting companion. Here the chops are served atop golden polenta cakes, but for an easier version, substitute toasted 3-inch [8-cm] rounds of brioche (about ½ inch thick).

SERVES 4

3 tablespoons plus 1 teaspoon olive oil, plus more if necessary

1 shallot, minced

1 cup Barolo [250 ml]

½ cup demi-glace (see Note) [125 ml]

Salt and freshly ground black pepper

16 asparagus spears, trimmed to 4 inches long [10 cm]

6 ounces shiitake mushrooms, stems removed and caps quartered [180 grams]

Creamy Polenta (page 137), made with ¼ cup freshly grated Parmigiano-Reggiano instead of Taleggio and without the truffle, poured into a buttered 9 by 12-inch pan, and chilled until firm [20 grams/23x30 cm]

4 veal rib chops, about 1½ to 2 inches thick [4 to 5 cm]

2½ ounces fresh duck foie gras, cut into 4 slices [70 grams]

1 to 2 ounces black or white truffles [30 to 60 grams]

Chervil sprigs or basil leaves, for garnish

1. Heat 2 teaspoons of the olive oil in a medium saucepan over moderate heat. Add the shallot and cook, stirring occasionally, until translucent, 2 to 3 minutes. Add the wine, bring to a boil, and boil until reduced to ¼ cup [60 ml]. Add the demi-glace, bring to a simmer, and simmer until reduced to ½ cup [125 ml]. Remove from the heat and season with salt if necessary and pepper to taste. Set aside.

2. Preheat the oven to 350°F [175°C]. Lightly grease a large rimmed baking sheet.

3. Bring a large saucepan of salted water to a boil. Add the asparagus and cook until just tender, about 3 minutes. Drain, rinse under cold running water, and drain again. Spread the asparagus in a small baking pan and set aside at room temperature.

4. Heat 1 tablespoon of the oil in a large skillet, preferably nonstick, over moderately high heat. Add the shiitakes, season with ¼ teaspoon salt and a generous pinch of pepper, and cook, stirring occasionally, until golden brown and tender, 5 to 7 minutes. Set the pan aside.

5. To make the polenta cakes, use a 3½- to 4-inch [9- to 10-cm] round cutter to cut out 4 rounds from the chilled polenta (reserve the remaining polenta for another use). Heat 2 teaspoons of the oil in a large nonstick skillet over moderate heat. Add the polenta cakes and cook until golden brown on the first side, about 3 minutes. Turn and cook until golden brown on the second side, 2 to 3 minutes. Transfer to a small oiled baking sheet and set aside.

6. Heat the remaining 1 tablespoon olive oil in a large heavy skillet over moderately high heat. Season the veal chops on both sides with salt and pepper. Add 2 of the chops to the pan and cook until golden brown on the first side, 4 to 5 minutes. Turn and cook until golden brown on the second side, 4 to 5 minutes. Transfer to the prepared baking sheet and cook the remaining 2 chops, adding a little more oil to the pan if necessary.

7. Put the veal in the oven and cook until medium-rare, about 12 minutes for 1½-inch [4-cm]-thick chops, or about 15 minutes for 2-inch [5-cm]-thick chops (the chops should register 130° to 135°F [55° to 57°C] on an instant-read thermometer), or cook until desired doneness. Transfer the veal to a platter, cover with foil, and let rest for 5 minutes.

8. Meanwhile, put the polenta and the asparagus in the oven to heat through, about 3 minutes. Reheat the sauce over low heat. Reheat the mushrooms over moderate heat.

9. Just before serving, heat a large skillet, preferably nonstick, over moderately high heat. Season the foie gras on both sides with salt and pepper. Add the foie gras to the skillet and cook until golden brown on the first side, 1 to 2 minutes. Turn and cook until golden brown on the second side, 1 to 2 minutes longer. Remove from the heat.

10. Place a polenta cake on each plate. Set the veal chops on top of the polenta and place the foie gras on top of the veal. Arrange the asparagus around the veal, scatter the mushrooms around the plates, and spoon the sauce over all. Shave the truffle over the veal, garnish with the chervil, and serve immediately.

NOTE: Small containers of demi-glace are available at specialty shops and in some supermarkets.

SOMMELIER WINE SUGGESTION   Bricco Rocche Ceretto Barolo 1996; Piedmont, Italy

TRUFFLED OSSO BUCO

A SILKY VEAL STEW CAN WARM THE SOUL; add a bit of truffle and it can set it on fire. If it is important to you that the veal shanks hold their shape during cooking, tie each one securely with cotton kitchen twine, then remove it just before serving. Gremolata, a mixture of lemon zest, parsley, and garlic, is the traditional garnish for osso buco; our version adds orange zest as well. Serve with creamy polenta (see page 137 for a recipe) and broccoli rabe. SERVES 4 TO 6

4 veal shanks (preferably hind shanks; 10 to 12 ounces each), cut crosswise into 1½- to 2-inch pieces (have your butcher do this) [280 to 350 grams/4 to 5 cm]

½ cup all-purpose flour [60 grams]

Salt and freshly ground black pepper

⅓ to ½ cup olive oil [75 to 125 ml]

4 tablespoons unsalted butter [60 grams]

1 large onion, finely chopped

2 carrots, thinly sliced

1 celery stalk, finely chopped

2 garlic cloves, minced

1 cup dry white wine [250 ml]

2 cups chicken stock, or 1 can (14½ ounces) low-sodium chicken broth plus enough water to make 2 cups [500 ml/400 grams]

1 can (14½ ounces) diced tomatoes, drained [400 grams]

1 tablespoon chopped fresh marjoram or 1 teaspoon dried marjoram

3 tablespoons truffle juice

1 fresh or flash-frozen black truffle, cut into thin julienne strips

GREMOLATA

3 tablespoons finely chopped flat-leaf parsley

1 teaspoon grated lemon zest

½ teaspoon grated orange zest

1 garlic clove, minced

1. Trim any excess fat from the veal. Spread the flour on a plate. Season the veal well with salt and pepper and dredge in the flour, shaking off the excess.

2. Heat ⅓ cup [75 ml] of the olive oil in a large skillet over moderately high heat until hot. Working in batches, add the veal shanks, without crowding, and cook, turning occasionally, until browned on all sides, 8 to 10 minutes per batch; add more oil to the pan if necessary. Transfer the veal shanks to paper towels to drain.

3. Meanwhile, melt the butter in a large Dutch oven or other flameproof casserole over moderately low heat. Add the onion, carrots, celery, and garlic and cook, stirring occasionally, until soft and very lightly browned, 10 to 15 minutes.

4. When all the veal has been browned, pour off the fat from the skillet. Add the wine to the pan and bring to a boil over moderate heat, scraping up any browned bits from the bottom of the pan with a wooden spoon.

5. Arrange the browned veal shanks, marrow end up, in a single layer over the vegetables in the Dutch oven. (It's fine if they fit quite snugly.) Add the wine mixture from the skillet, the stock, tomatoes, and marjoram. Bring to a boil over moderately high heat. Reduce the heat to low, cover, and cook, until the veal is fork-tender, about 1½ hours. Transfer the veal shanks to a shallow serving bowl or platter; cover with foil, and set aside in a warm spot.

6. Skim off the fat from the cooking liquid. Bring to a boil over high heat and cook until the sauce has reduced to about 3 cups. Reduce the heat to low and season with additional salt and pepper if necessary. Stir in the truffle juice and truffle and heat for 2 minutes to blend the flavors.

7. Meanwhile, make the gremolata: Toss the parsley, lemon zest, orange zest, and garlic together in a small bowl.

8. Stir half the gremolata into the truffle sauce. Spoon the sauce over the veal shanks, sprinkle the remaining gremolata over the top, and serve.

SOMMELIER WINE SUGGESTION La Rioja Alta "904" Gran Reserva 1990; Rioja, Spain

BABBO'S GRILLED VENISON WITH SALSIFY AND WHITE TRUFFLES

BABBO, ONE OF CHEF MARIO BATALI'S several New York City restaurants, is known for an imaginative menu that highlights game and organ meats. Denver steaks are boneless venison leg steaks cut from the top round; they can be found at some specialty butchers and through mail-order sources (see Sources, page 234), but, if necessary, you can substitute the more readily available tenderloin (adjust the cooking time accordingly, depending on the thickness of the meat.) Sautéed salsify flavored with anisette and anchovy makes an unusual accompaniment to the grilled marinated venison, finished with a shower of fragarant, earthy white truffles. SERVES 4

1 teaspoon juniper berries

2 rosemary sprigs, bruised with the back of a heavy knife, plus 1 teaspoon minced rosemary

4 garlic cloves, thinly sliced

1½ cups [350 ml] plus 2 teaspoons extra-virgin olive oil

4 boneless venison leg steaks (Denver steaks) (about 8 ounces each), cut about ¾ inch thick [250 grams/2 cm]

Juice of 1 lemon

12 ounces salsify [350 grams]

2 cups full-bodied red wine [500 ml]

½ cup sugar [100 grams]

Pinch of ground cloves

Pinch of ground cinnamon

2 tablespoons anisette liqueur

1 teaspoon anchovy paste

Salt and freshly ground black pepper

1 small fresh white truffle

1. To make the marinade, combine the juniper berries, rosemary sprigs, half the garlic, and 1½ cups [350 ml] of the olive oil in a small bowl. Put the venison in a shallow baking dish and pour the marinade over the meat, turning to coat. Cover and refrigerate for 2 hours.

2. Fill a medium bowl with cold water and add the lemon juice. Peel the salsify. Cut it into 4-inch [10-cm] lengths and quarter each piece lengthwise; add the prepared salsify to the lemon water as you work, to keep it from darkening. Cover and refrigerate.

3. To make the sauce, combine the wine and sugar in a small nonreactive saucepan and bring to a boil over high heat. Reduce the heat to a simmer and simmer until the wine has reduced by about three-quarters and is syrupy. Add the cloves, cinnamon, and the minced rosemary and set aside.

4. Prepare a hot fire in a barbecue grill or preheat a cast-iron stove-top grill over moderately high heat.

5. Heat the remaining 2 tablespoons oil in a large skillet over high heat. Drain the salsify and pat dry. Add the salsify to the pan and cook, stirring occasionally, until browned and tender, 8 to 10 minutes; reduce the heat slightly if the salsify starts to brown too much. Add the remaining garlic and cook, stirring, until fragrant, about 1 minute. Add the anisette and anchovy paste and toss to coat. Remove from the heat and cover to keep warm.

6. Remove the venison from the marinade, draining it thoroughly; discard the marinade. Season on both sides with salt and pepper. Place the venison on the grill or in the grill pan and cook, turning once, for about 3 to 4 minutes per side for medium-rare (the meat should register about 125°F [50°C] on an instant-read thermometer). Transfer to a platter, cover with foil, and let rest for about 5 minutes.

7. Meanwhile, heat the salsify over low heat, stirring once or twice, until warmed through. Reheat the sauce over moderately low heat; if the sauce seems too syrupy, stir in a little water.

8. Slice the venison and arrange on serving plates. Place the salsify next to the venison. Drizzle the sauce over the meat, shave the truffle over the top, and serve immediately.

SOMMELIER WINE SUGGESTION Chateau de Beaucastel Chateauneuf-du-Pape 1986; Rhône, France

PIZZA, FOCACCIA, AND PANINI

MINI PIZZAS WITH ROBIOLA
CHEESE AND WHITE TRUFFLES

WHITE PIZZA WITH TRUFFLE OIL

FOCACCIA WITH ROBIOLA
CHEESE AND WHITE TRUFFLE OIL

PANINI WITH SMOKED TURKEY
AND TRUFFLE MAYONNAISE

PANINI WITH BRESAOLA,
ARUGULA, AND BLACK TRUFFLE
PUREE

PROSCIUTTO AND TRUFFLE
BUTTER PANINI

MINI PIZZAS WITH ROBIOLA CHEESE AND WHITE TRUFFLES

WHEN WHITE TRUFFLES ARE IN SEASON, serve these "gourmet" pizzas as the first course before a roast fillet of beef or other luxurious but simple entrée. Cut into wedges, they would also make an impressive hors d'oeuvre. Of course, if you don't have white truffles to spare, the pizzas are delicious simply with white truffle oil drizzled over the robiola just before serving.

Robiola, specifically *robiola Piemonte*, is a creamy, soft rindless Italian cheese that can be found at good cheese shops and specialty markets. There's also a version of robiola from the Lombardy region of Italy—rarely available here—that has a reddish-brown rind and is much stronger in flavor. The creamy type is the kind of robiola you want for this recipe. SERVES 4

½ **recipe Pizza Dough** (page 188), divided into 4 pieces, shaped into balls, and allowed to rise as directed

Cornmeal, for dusting

Extra-virgin olive oil

3 to 4 ounces creamy robiola cheese [90 to 120 grams]

1 medium fresh white truffle (about 1 ounce) [30 grams]

1. While the dough is rising, position one oven rack in the lowest part of the oven and the other in the upper part. Place a baking stone or quarry tiles (see page 188) on the lower oven rack, turn the oven on to 500°F [260°C], and preheat for at least 30 minutes.

2. Lightly dust a pizza peel or the back of a baking sheet with cornmeal. Prepare 2 pizzas at a time (unless you have a large baking stone or enough quarry tiles to accommodate 4). Using a rolling pin, on a very lightly floured surface, roll one piece of dough to a 6- to 7-inch [15- to 18-cm] round. Transfer to the prepared pizza peel, and roll out a second round of dough.

3. Lightly brush the dough on the pizza peel with olive oil, prick it all over with a fork, and slide it onto the hot baking stone. Transfer the second round of dough to the peel (dusting the peel with additional cornmeal if necessary), brush with oil, prick with the fork, and slide onto the stone.

4. Bake for 8 to 10 minutes, or until golden brown and crisp. Transfer to a large baking sheet, and prepare and bake the remaining pizza crusts.

5. While the second batch of pizzas is baking, spread one-quarter of the robiola over each baked crust. When you remove the second batch of crusts, place the first batch (still on the baking sheet) on the upper oven rack and bake for about 2 minutes to heat through and melt the robiola.

6. Meanwhile, spread the remaining robiola over the 2 hot crusts, return to the baking stone, and bake just until the robiola melts, 1 to 2 minutes.

7. Shave the truffle over the pizzas and drizzle a little olive oil over the top, if desired. Serve immediately.

VARIATION

To make 2 large pizzas, divide the dough in half instead of quarters and let rise as directed. Roll each piece of dough out to a 10- or 11-inch [25- to 28-cm] round (it's fine if they are slightly irregular), and proceed as directed. (The baking time will be the same.)

PIZZA DOUGH

Good pizza dough is really very easy to make—it takes only a few minutes to put together, and then it just needs a little time to rise. Allowing it to rise twice results in a better texture and fuller flavor, but you can prepare it through the first rise a day ahead, then put it in the refrigerator overnight, ready for the next day, or the day after that. The dough also freezes well, so you could bake one or two pizzas, then freeze the rest for another time.

One essential ingredient for great homemade pizza is a baking stone, or, perhaps even more practical, unglazed quarry tiles. Available at any tile supply store, these are inexpensive, and because they can be stacked, they store easily in even a small kitchen cabinet. Four 6-inch [15-cm] tiles are enough for baking one large or two small pizzas at a time; if your oven is large enough, you may want to buy eight tiles so you can bake two larger pizzas at a time; just make sure the tiles will fit on one rack with at least 2 inches [5 cm] around them for heat circulation.

MAKES ENOUGH FOR 4 LARGE THIN-CRUST PIZZAS, 10 TO 11 INCHES [25 TO 28 CM] IN DIAMETER, OR 8 SMALLER PIZZAS, 6 TO 7 INCHES [15 TO 18 CM] IN DIAMETER

1 envelope (¼ ounce) active dry yeast
[7 grams]

1 cup warm water (105° to 110°F)
[250 ml/40° to 42°C]

1 tablespoon olive oil

1½ teaspoons salt

2½ to 3 cups flour, plus more if necessary
[300 to 375 grams]

Cornmeal, for dusting

1. Sprinkle the yeast over the warm water in a large bowl and let stand until foamy, about 5 minutes.

2. Using a wooden spoon, stir the oil and salt into the yeast mixture, then gradually stir in 2½ cups [300 grams] of the flour. If the dough becomes too stiff to stir before you have incorporated the 2½ cups [300 grams] flour, turn out onto a work surface and knead in the remainder.

3. Turn the dough out onto a work surface, if you have not already done so. Knead the dough until smooth and elastic, gradually kneading in up to ½ cup [50 grams] more flour, or as necessary.

4. Put the dough in a large oiled bowl, turn to coat, and cover the bowl with plastic wrap. Set the dough aside in a warm place to rise until doubled in bulk, 30 to 45 minutes, depending on the temperature of the room.

5. Lightly dust 1 large or 2 small baking sheets with cornmeal. Gently punch down the dough. Turn it out onto the work surface and divide it into 4 pieces; if making small pizzas, divide each piece in half (see Note). Shape each piece of dough into a flat round and place at least 2 inches [5 cm]

apart on the prepared baking sheet(s). Cover with a kitchen towel or lightly oiled plastic wrap and set aside to rise until the dough has doubled in bulk, about 30 minutes. The dough is now ready to be shaped and baked according to the individual recipes.

NOTE: After the dough has risen once, it can be refrigerated or frozen. To refrigerate, divide the dough as directed, put it on the prepared baking sheet(s), cover with lightly oiled plastic wrap, and refrigerate for up to 2 days. Let come to room temperature before proceeding. To freeze, divide the dough, shape into rounds, double-wrap in plastic wrap and then foil, and freeze for up to 1 month. Thaw overnight in the refrigerator, or for about 1½ hours (still wrapped) at room temperature.

VARIATION

FOOD PROCESSOR PIZZA DOUGH Using the ingredients above, sprinkle the yeast over the water in a 2-cup [500-ml] glass measure or a small bowl with a spout, and let stand until foamy, about 5 minutes. Combine the 2½ cups [300 grams] flour and the salt in the processor bowl and pulse to mix. Stir the oil into the yeast mixture. With the machine on, slowly add the yeast mixture and continue to process until a rough dough forms. Turn the dough out onto a work surface and knead as directed above, adding up to ½ cup [60 grams] more flour, or as necessary.

WHITE PIZZA WITH TRUFFLE OIL

A WHITE PIZZA is made with just cheese, garlic, and oil for topping. Traditionally, the oil is olive oil; this upscale version adds truffle oil, too, for the best white pizza imaginable. Do be sure to use fresh mozzarella. MAKES FOUR 10- TO 11-INCH [25- TO 28-CM] PIZZAS; SERVES 4 AS A MAIN COURSE, 8 AS A SNACK

Pizza Dough (recipe follows), divided into 4 pieces, shaped into balls, and allowed to rise as directed

¼ cup olive oil [60 ml]

4 to 6 garlic cloves, thinly sliced

Cornmeal, for dusting

12 ounces fresh mozzarella, thinly sliced [350 grams]

2 tablespoons freshly grated Parmigiano-Reggiano

2 tablespoons white truffle oil

1. While the dough is rising, place a baking stone or quarry tiles (see page 187) on the lowest rack of your oven, turn the oven on to 500°F [260°C], and preheat for at least 30 minutes.

2. Meanwhile, combine the olive oil and garlic in a small bowl. Cover and set aside.

3. Lightly dust a pizza peel or the back of a baking sheet with cornmeal. Prepare one pizza at a time (unless you have a large baking stone or enough quarry tiles to accommodate two). Using a rolling pin, on a very lightly floured work surface, roll one piece of dough into a 10- to 11-inch [25- to 28-cm] round (it's fine it if is slightly irregular). Transfer to the prepared pizza peel or baking sheet.

4. Scatter one-quarter of the mozzarella over the pizza, tearing it into smaller pieces as you do so, and leaving a ½-inch [1-cm] border all around. Spoon 1 tablespoon of the garlic oil, making sure to include one-quarter of the garlic, over the cheese. Sprinkle 1½ teaspoons of the Parmesan over the top. Slide the pizza onto the hot baking stone and bake for 8 to 10 minutes, or until the edges are golden brown and crisp.

5. Drizzle 1½ teaspoons truffle oil over the pizza, and serve immediately. Repeat with the remaining ingredients to make 3 more pizzas.

FOCACCIA WITH ROBIOLA CHEESE AND WHITE TRUFFLE OIL

THIS IS AN EASY VERSION of a focaccia served in certain upscale New York City Italian restaurants. In the original, a round of pizza dough is partially baked, then split open, filled with robiola, and returned to the oven to finish baking; it comes to the table anointed with a generous drizzle of fragrant white truffle oil. Here high-quality store-bought focaccia (from a specialty bakery or gourmet market) reduces the work to a minimum. Creamy Italian robiola is available at good cheese shops and specialty food markets.

Serve this rich focaccia as a snack or for a simple lunch with a green salad and a good Pinot Grigio. Cut into small squares, it makes a great hors d'oeuvre (see the variation below).

SERVES 4 AS A MAIN DISH, 8 AS A SNACK

4 slices plain or herbed focaccia, approximately 4 by 5 inches [10 by 13 cm], **or 1 large rectangular focaccia, approximately 8 by 10 inches** [20 by 25 cm], cut into 4 pieces

4 ounces creamy robiola cheese, at room temperature [120 grams]

1 to 1½ tablespoons white truffle oil

1. Preheat the oven to 350°F [175°C].

2. Using a serrated knife, split each slice of focaccia horizontally in half. Spread the robiola evenly over the bottom halves of the focaccia and replace the tops, pressing down gently. Cut each sandwich crosswise in half.

3. Place the focaccia on an ungreased baking sheet and bake for about 3 minutes, just until the focaccia is warm throughout and the cheese is beginning to melt. Drizzle the truffle oil over the tops of the warm sandwiches, place 1 or 2 pieces on each plate, and serve at once.

VARIATION

FOCACCIA SQUARES WITH ROBIOLA CHEESE AND WHITE TRUFFLE OIL This makes a generous quantity; halve the recipe for a smaller group. Assemble the focaccia as directed (starting with 1 large rectangle or 4 slices). Cut the focaccia into 1-inch [2.5-cm] squares. Arrange on the baking sheet and bake for about 2 minutes. Drizzle with the truffle oil and serve. (Makes 80 hors d'oeuvres.)

PANINI WITH SMOKED TURKEY AND TRUFFLE MAYONNAISE

THE LITTLE SANDWICHES known as panini are sold at every café and wine bar throughout Italy and are often enjoyed as a snack to accompany an espresso or a glass of wine. Unlike overstuffed American sandwiches, these are modestly filled. MAKES 4 SMALL SANDWICHES

4 small round rolls (about 3 inches [8 cm] in diameter)

3 tablespoons White Truffle Mayonnaise or Quick White Truffle Mayonnaise (recipes follow)

6 ounces thinly sliced smoked turkey [180 grams]

Freshly ground black pepper

1 cup watercress sprigs, tough stems removed [250 ml]

1. Split the rolls in half and spread the mayonnaise over the cut sides. Arrange the smoked turkey on the bottoms of the rolls, folding it over as necessary to keep the sandwiches neat. Season the turkey with pepper to taste.

2. Arrange the watercress sprigs on top of the turkey. Put the tops of the rolls in place and press down gently. Using a sharp serrated knife, cut each panino in half and serve.

TRUFFLE MAYONNAISE

Here are several variations on a theme. Each of them is infinitely versatile and can be served as a sauce as well as a condiment. Either version of the white truffle mayonnaise is wonderful on asparagus. Of course, these are the perfect spreads for a wide variety of panini and other sandwiches. Or try any of them in egg or chicken salad. Using a flavorless oil rather than olive oil allows the truffle flavor to stand out. Mayonnaise made in the food processor will be quite thick; if you prefer a looser mayonnaise, add a few drops of water. MAKES ABOUT 1⅓ CUPS [325 ML]

BLACK TRUFFLE MAYONNAISE

2 large egg yolks

2 tablespoons fresh lemon juice

1 teaspoon Dijon mustard

1 cup soybean oil or other flavorless vegetable oil [250ml]

⅜ teaspoon salt

1 tablespoon grated fresh, flash-frozen, or canned black truffle

1. Put the egg yolks in a food processor and process for about 30 seconds. Add 1 teaspoon of the lemon juice and the mustard and process until well blended. With the machine on, gradually add about half the oil in a very thin, steady stream, until the mayonnaise is emulsified and thickened.

2. Add the remaining 1 tablespoon plus 2 teaspoons lemon juice and process to blend. With the machine on, pour in the remaining oil in a slow, steady stream. Add the salt and truffle and pulse just to blend.

3. Transfer to a bowl or jar, cover, and refrigerate until ready to use. The mayonnaise will keep for up to 3 days.

VARIATION

WHITE TRUFFLE MAYONNAISE Substitute 1½ to 2 teaspoons white truffle oil for the black truffle.

QUICK BLACK TRUFFLE MAYONNAISE Substitute 1 cup [250 ml] prepared mayonnaise for the homemade mayonnaise. Put the mayonnaise in a small bowl and stir in 2 teaspoons black truffle oil until thoroughly blended. Season with salt and white pepper to taste. Cover and refrigerate for at least 1 hour to allow the flavors to blend. Tightly covered, this mayonnaise keeps well for at least 5 days. Makes 1 cup [250 ml].

QUICK WHITE TRUFFLE MAYONNAISE Substitute white truffle oil for the black truffle oil in Quick Black Truffle Mayonnaise.

PANINI

Panini are part of the Italian "family" of sandwiches that also includes *tramezzini* and *cicchetti*, all cousins to bruschetta and crostini The word *panino* ("little bread") originally simply meant a plain roll, but now it generally implies a roll, large or small, with a filling. Tramezzini are more refined, similar to tea sandwiches—though with Italian-style filllings, of course, rather than sliced cucumbers and the like—made with thin-sliced white bread. Cicchetti are little bites that are particularly popular in the wine bars of Venice; essentially mini panini, they may be made either with small rolls or with slices of bread. All of these make great snacks or picnic food; tramezzini and cicchetti are often enjoyed with an aperitif or a glass of wine.

You can make smaller versions of any of the panini in this chapter and serve them as cocktail nibbles. They all can, of course, be made with sliced good bread, preferably an artisanal loaf, and they can be turned into open-faced sandwiches as well.

PANINI WITH BRESAOLA, ARUGULA, AND BLACK TRUFFLE PUREE

PUNGENT BLACK TRUFFLE PUREE provides a wonderful complement to the spicy Italian air-dried beef fillet called bresaola. Look for bresaola in Italian markets and the deli departments of better supermarkets. Freshly baked focaccia can be found in many gourmet markets, as well as in Italian and other bakeries.

MAKES 4 SMALL SANDWICHES

2 slices plain or herbed focaccia, approximately 4 by 5 inches [10 by 13 cm]

Extra-virgin olive oil

2 teaspoons black truffle puree or paste

2 to 4 ounces thinly sliced bresaola [60 to 120 grams]

Generous ½ cup small arugula leaves [125 ml]

1. Cut each slice of focaccia crosswise in half, then split the foccacia in half. Drizzle olive oil to taste over both cut sides of each piece. Spread ½ teaspoon of the truffle puree over the bottom of each piece. Arrange the bresaola on top, folding it over as necessary to keep the sandwiches neat.

2. Arrange the arugula leaves on top of the bresaola. Place the tops of the focaccia on the beef and press down gently. Serve.

PROSCIUTTO AND TRUFFLE BUTTER PANINI

PROCACCI, A SANDWICH BAR not far from the Piazza Santa Maria Novella in Florence, is well known for its *panini tartufati*. And no wonder—what could be more amazing than a truffle sandwich? This one is made simply with truffle butter and prosciutto. You can dress it up a bit with a basil leaf or two, but it's sublime as is. These make an elegant snack, or you can double the recipe and serve two sandwiches per person—with a glass of bubbly Prosecco—for a lovely lunch. MAKES 4 SMALL SANDWICHES

4 small round rolls (about 3 inches [8 cm] in diameter)

2 tablespoons truffle butter, at room temperature [30 grams]

3 to 4 ounces very thinly sliced prosciutto [90 to 120 grams]

4 to 8 leaves of basil, for garnish (optional)

1. Split the rolls in half and generously butter the cut sides with the truffle butter. Arrange the prosciutto on the bottoms of the rolls, folding it over as necessary to keep the sandwiches neat.

2. Top each sandwich with 1 or 2 leaves of basil, if desired. Put the tops of the rolls in place and press down gently. Using a sharp serrated knife, cut each panino in half and serve.

TRUFFLE BUTTER

Truffle butter is one of those marvelous culinary tricks you can keep to yourself and use to impress your guests anytime you are serving a simple but elegant food that needs a little lift, such as a grilled steak, simple fish, or plain vegetable. There are several ways to make your own truffle butter, depending on the truffle or truffle product you have on hand.

BLACK TRUFFLE BUTTER When you have a few black truffle "scraps" or trimmings, finely mince them and beat into softened unsalted butter, using 1 teaspoon truffle per 2 to 3 tablespoons butter. Well wrapped and refrigerated, the butter will remain flavorful for several days at least; it can also be frozen for up to 1 month.

WHITE TRUFFLE BUTTER Butter that has spent time with a fresh white truffle will take on its unmistakable fragrance. When you have just acquired a white truffle, wrap a stick or half-stick of unsalted butter loosely in waxed paper, and set it inside the container with the (paper towel–wrapped) truffle for up to 1 day. Remove the butter and wrap tightly in plastic wrap; for the most flavor, use it as soon as possible.

EASY WHITE OR BLACK TRUFFLE BUTTER Truffle butter can also be made with truffle oil. Beat ¼ to ½ teaspoon white or black truffle oil into each 2 tablespoons softened unsalted butter. Well wrapped and refrigerated, the butter will remain flavorful for several days at least.

EGGS AND CHEESE

FRENCH SCRAMBLED EGGS
WITH TRUFFLES

OMELET WITH BLACK TRUFFLES

SUMMER TRUFFLE FRITTATA
WITH ITALIAN FONTINA CHEESE

MARCH'S SHIRRED EGGS
WITH WHITE TRUFFLES AND
FINGERLING POTATOES

EGGS EN COCOTTE WITH
TRUFFLE CREAM

FONDUTA WITH WHITE TRUFFLES

TRUFFLE-CHEESE TART

PARMIGIANO-REGGIANO WITH
PEARS AND TRUFFLE HONEY

FRENCH SCRAMBLED EGGS
WITH TRUFFLES

CALLED *OEUFS BROUILLES AUX TRUFFES* **IN FRENCH,** this classic dish of scrambled eggs cooked slowly with cream, butter, and truffles to a soft, creamy mass is a must for an intimate New Year's Day brunch, accompanied by your best split of Champagne, buttery brioche, fresh-squeezed orange juice, and a pot of excellent coffee. Just don't overcook the eggs, or they will lose their magical quality. SERVES 2

4 large eggs

2 tablespoons heavy cream

½ to 1 ounce fresh or flash-frozen black truffle, thinly sliced or finely minced [15 to 30 grams]

Scant ¼ teaspoon salt

Generous pinch of freshly ground black pepper

2 tablespoons unsalted butter [30 grams]

1. Combine the eggs, cream, and truffle in a medium bowl and whisk until well combined. (If you have not "truffled" the eggs as described above, if time allows, cover and refrigerate for at least 30 minutes and up to 2 hours.) Season with the salt and pepper.

2. Melt 1 tablespoon [15 grams] of the butter in a medium skillet over low heat. Add the eggs and cook, whisking almost constantly, until they are thick, creamy, and not quite set; do not overcook.

3. Immediately remove the pan from the heat and whisk until the eggs are just set—the residual heat of the pan will finish cooking the eggs. Whisk in the remaining butter 1 teaspoon at a time. Spoon the eggs onto plates and serve immediately.

NOTE: Eggs and truffles have a well-known affinity for each other, and a favorite trick is to put the eggs in their shells in a tightly covered container with whole truffles (see page 171) and refrigerate them together for a day or so. The eggs pick up the heady perfume of the truffles right through their shells.

OMELET WITH BLACK TRUFFLES

THIS IS ONE OF THE GREAT TRUFFLE CLASSICS, and deservedly so. Serve this at an intimate brunch, or for a late-night supper. You can make the dish with "truffled eggs" (see headnote, page 200). Or, for a white truffle omelet, shave as much of a fresh white truffle as you like over the finished omelets and drizzle with a little melted butter. SERVES 2

4 large eggs

½ to 1 ounce fresh black truffle, finely chopped [15 to 30 grams]

Scant ¼ teaspoon salt

Generous pinch of freshly ground black pepper

1½ tablespoons unsalted butter [25 grams]

1. Whisk 2 of the eggs in a small bowl just until the whites and yolks are well blended. Whisk in half the truffle. Whisk the remaining 2 eggs in another bowl and whisk in the remaining truffle. (If you have not "truffled" the eggs as described on page 200, if time allows, cover and refrigerate for at least 30 minutes and up to 2 hours.) Season the eggs with the salt and pepper.

2. Melt half the butter in an 8-inch [20-cm] omelet pan or a heavy skillet with sloping sides over high heat. As soon as the butter stops foaming, add half the eggs. Using a fork held almost flat against the bottom of the pan, stir the eggs constantly until thickened and almost set, about 30 seconds. Shake the pan to loosen the omelet, and, if necessary, run the fork around the edges of the omelet to release it from the pan. Using the fork, fold one half of the omelet over, then turn it out onto a warm plate.

3. Melt the remaining butter and cook the second omelet in the same way. Serve immediately.

SUMMER TRUFFLE FRITTATA WITH ITALIAN FONTINA CHEESE

UNLIKE AN OMELET, which is cooked quickly over high heat just until very lightly browned outside and soft and creamy inside, a frittata should be cooked slowly over low heat until the eggs are set throughout but still light. If the frittata is allowed to brown—on either bottom or top—it will be tough, not delicate as it should be. A good Italian Fontina is a perfect complement to the nutty flavor of summer truffles, but another mild semi-soft cheese, such as Morbier or even a Swiss raclette cheese or Appenzeller, could be substituted. Although some frittatas are equally good hot or at room temperature, this one is best served still warm from the pan. SERVES 2

7 large eggs

1 large summer truffle (about 1½ ounces), thinly sliced [45 grams]

⅔ cup shredded mild Italian Fontina cheese [80 grams]

Salt and freshly ground black pepper

1½ tablespoons unsalted butter [25 grams]

1. Whisk the eggs in a medium bowl until well blended. Stir in the truffle and cheese. Season generously with salt and pepper.

2. Preheat the broiler. Melt the butter in a 10-inch [25 cm] skillet with a flameproof handle (see Note below) over medium heat. Add the eggs and immediately reduce the heat to low. Cook until the frittata is almost set but still a little runny in the center, 10 to 12 minutes.

3. Transfer the frittata to the broiler, setting the pan about 4 inches [10 cm] from the heat, and cook just until the top is set, about 30 seconds; do not allow the top to brown. Slide the frittata onto a serving plate or serve directly from the skillet.

NOTE: If you do not have a skillet suitable for the broiler, wrap the handle in a double thickness of aluminum foil with the shiny side out.

VARIATION

BLACK TRUFFLE FRITTATA When you are feeling flush, substitute a 1-ounce [30-gram] black truffle for the summer truffle; omit the cheese.

MARCH'S SHIRRED EGGS WITH WHITE TRUFFLES AND FINGERLING POTATOES

THIS MOST ELEGANT DISH comes from Wayne Nish, chef of the acclaimed March Restaurant in New York City. As he notes, eggs and truffles are one legendary pairing, and potatoes and eggs are another—here he combines them both. Serve as brunch or a late-night supper. If white truffles aren't in season, simply be more generous with the truffle oil. SERVES 2

8 tablespoons (1 stick) unsalted butter [125 grams]

2 small fingerling potatoes (about 1½ ounces total), preferably Ruby Crescent, halved lengthwise and cut into ¼-inch slices [45 grams/.5 cm]

Pinch of salt

About 1 tablespoon extra-virgin olive oil

2 extra-large eggs

Fleur de sel or other coarse salt

1 teaspoon white truffle oil

1 medium fresh white truffle (about 1 ounce) [30 grams]

2 tablespoons finely chopped herbs, such as basil, tarragon, flat-leaf parsley, chervil, and/or chives

1. Preheat the oven to 500°F [260°C]. Melt the butter in a small saucepan over moderate heat. Add the potatoes and the pinch of salt and simmer gently until the potatoes are tender, about 5 minutes. Remove from the heat.

2. Generously grease two 4½-inch [11-cm] nonstick ovenproof skillets or two small shallow round baking dishes with the olive oil. Crack an egg into each pan. Bake until the whites of the eggs are just set, 1½ to 2 minutes.

3. With a slotted spatula, transfer the eggs to serving plates. Drain the potatoes (reserve the butter for another use, such as cooking another potato dish) and scatter around the eggs. Sprinkle a few grains of fleur de sel over each egg and drizzle the truffle oil over them. Shave the truffle over the eggs, garnish with the herbs, and serve immediately.

EGGS EN COCOTTE WITH TRUFFLE CREAM

THE FRENCH ARE VERY FOND of eggs *en cocotte*, a term that literally means baked in a casserole, but in this case refers to eggs baked (one or two per person) in individual ramekins. Truffle cream elevates this simple dish—almost nursery fare—to a more sophisticated realm. Serve as a first course, for a light lunch with a salad, or as a late-night comfort food.

If you don't happen to have a black truffle on hand, butter the ramekins generously with truffle butter instead. SERVES 4

Softened butter, for the ramekins

¼ **cup heavy cream** [60 ml]

4 teaspoons grated black truffle

4 large eggs

Salt and freshly ground black pepper

Toasted sliced brioche or toast points for serving

1. Preheat the oven to 375°F [190°C]. Generously butter four 6-ounce [185-ml] ramekins.

2. Combine the cream and black truffle in a small saucepan over low heat and heat to just under a simmer. Remove from the heat and let cool to room temperature. (Heating the cream and letting it stand briefly infuses it with truffle flavor.)

3. Spoon 1 tablespoon of the truffle cream into each ramekin, dividing the truffles evenly. Carefully break 1 egg into each ramekin. Put the ramekins in a baking pan that holds them comfortably and add enough boiling water (it must be boiling, not just hot, so that the eggs cook properly) to reach halfway up the sides of the ramekins.

4. Bake the eggs for 12 to 14 minutes, or until the whites are just set and the yolks still soft and runny. (Check carefully, because the liquid cream may rise to the top and partially cover the whites.) Season the eggs with salt and pepper and serve with brioche toast.

FONDUTA WITH WHITE TRUFFLES

FONDUTA, THE ITALIAN VERSION OF FONDUE, is a specialty of the Piedmont and Valle d'Aosta (the source of the best Fontina) regions in the north. A rich, creamy blend of melted Fontina cheese, milk, butter, and egg yolks, it is served on its own in bowls or spooned over polenta, gnocchi, or rice. It also appears as a sauce for vegetables and savory flans, and even as a dip for bread sticks or raw vegetables. It's delicious in any case, but in late fall and early winter, white truffles are often shaved over the top as the crowning touch. Chef Fortunato Nicotra of New York City's Felidia (see page 68) is especially fond of fonduta served in roasted red onions (another Piemontese specialty) and finished with an abundance of white truffles. Lacking a fresh truffle, you can stir white truffle puree into the warm sauce just before serving.

Soaking the cheese in milk helps soften it so that it melts evenly. Traditional recipes call for melting the cheese with the milk, then stirring in the egg yolks; in our version, the cheese is gradually added to the milk-yolk mixture so there is less chance of the cheese becoming stringy. (If you want to serve the fonduta over polenta, see the recipe on page 137.) SERVES 4

---

8 ounces Italian Fontina cheese, preferably Val d'Aosta [225 grams]

1 cup milk [250 ml]

1 tablespoon unsalted butter [15 grams]

2 large egg yolks

Freshly ground white pepper (optional)

1 fresh white truffle or 1 to 2 teaspoons white truffle puree or paste

---

1. Trim off the rind and cut the cheese into ¼-inch [.5-cm] cubes or coarsely grate it. Combine the cheese and milk in a small deep bowl; the milk should just cover the cheese. Cover and refrigerate for 4 to 8 hours, or overnight, stirring occasionally.

2. Melt the butter in the top of a double boiler over barely simmering water. Drain the cheese, reserving the milk. Add the milk and egg yolks to the butter and cook, stirring constantly with a wooden spoon, until the mixture is warm to the touch. Gradually add the cheese, stirring constantly and allowing most of it to melt each time before adding more.

3. Continue to cook, stirring, until the fonduta is smooth and slightly thickened. Remove from the heat and season with white pepper, if desired. (If using truffle puree or paste, stir it into the fonduta.)

4. Spoon the fonduta into warm bowls and shave the truffle over the top. Serve immediately.

TRUFFLE-CHEESE TART

WITH ITS SILKY SMOOTH, truffle-flavored filling, this easy tart makes a great brunch or supper dish. Or serve it with a green salad for a light lunch. For a "double-truffle" variation, make the pastry shell with Truffle-Butter Tart Dough (page 58).

Note that the pastry shell is "blind baked," that is, lined with foil, filled with dried beans, rice, or metal pie weights, and prebaked before being filled and baked again. Lining and weighting the tart shell is essential for this recipe; otherwise, the shell will shrink as it bakes and will not be able to hold all the filling. SERVES 4

One 9-inch tart shell made with Buttery Tart Dough (recipe follows), unbaked

3 large eggs [23 cm]

1 cup half-and-half [250 ml]

½ teaspoon salt

⅛ teaspoon freshly ground pepper, preferably white

1 packed cup shredded truffle cheese (about 4 ounces) [120 grams]

---

1. Position a rack in the bottom third of the oven and preheat the oven to 375°F [190°C].

2. Line the tart shell with aluminum foil. Fill it with dried beans, rice, or pie weights. Bake for 15 minutes. Remove the foil and weights and bake for 8 to 10 minutes longer, or until the dough is pale golden brown. Transfer the tart pan to a wire rack and let cool slightly while you make the filling. (Leave the oven on.)

3. Whisk the eggs in a medium bowl until blended. Gently whisk in the half-and-half, salt, and pepper. Scatter the truffle cheese evenly over the bottom of the tart shell, separating any clumps of cheese. Pour the filling mixture evenly over the cheese.

4. Bake the tart for 30 to 35 minutes, or until the filling is just set in the center and the top is barely beginning to color. If the edges of the tart shell begin to brown too much before the filling is set, cover them with a strip of aluminum foil. Transfer the tart to a wire rack and let cool slightly. Serve warm or at room temperature.

BUTTERY TART DOUGH

1¼ cups all-purpose flour [155 grams]

Slightly rounded ½ teaspoon salt

8 tablespoons (1 stick) unsalted butter, cut into ½-inch [1-cm] cubes and chilled [125 grams]

2 to 3 tablespoons ice water

1. Combine the flour and salt in a food processor and pulse to blend. Scatter the butter over the flour and pulse 10 to 15 times, until the butter is in pea-sized and smaller pieces. Add 2 tablespoons ice water and pulse until the dough just starts to come together, adding up to 1 tablespoon more ice water, 1 teaspoon at a time, if necessary. Do not process until the dough forms a ball, or the pastry will be tough.

2. Turn the dough out onto a work surface, gather it into a ball, and flatten it into a disk. Wrap in plastic wrap and refrigerate for at least 30 minutes. (The dough can be made up to 1 day ahead; if necessary, let soften briefly at room temperature before rolling out.)

3. On a lightly floured surface, roll the dough out to a 12-inch [31-cm] round. Without stretching the dough, fit it into a 9-inch [23-cm] fluted tart pan with a removable bottom. Trim the excess dough with a sharp paring knife. With your fingertips, gently press against the dough all around the sides of the pan so it extends slightly above the rim of the pan. Refrigerate the tart shell for 20 to 30 minutes, until firm.

PARMIGIANO-REGGIANO WITH PEARS AND TRUFFLE HONEY

FRUIT AND CHEESE IS A CLASSIC ITALIAN DESSERT, most appropriate after any big, rich meal. Italian markets often offer two different types of Parmesan, a younger, softer one that is a little sweeter and fruitier, better for eating straight, and an older, sharper cheese, more appropriate for grating and cooking. Try to find one that is on the young side, moister and less crumbly. And for best texture and richest flavor, do be sure the cheese is at room temperature when you serve it. This perfect pairing also provides the ideal way to finish up the wine from the meal—or open a special bottle especially for the cheese course.

SERVES 4

¾ cup walnut halves [75 grams]

2 ripe flavorful pears

6 ounces Parmigiano-Reggiano, cut into 4 chunks [180 grams]

¼ cup truffle honey [60 ml]

1. Preheat the oven to 350°F [175°C]. Spread the walnuts on a small baking sheet or in a pie pan and toast in the oven, stirring 2 or 3 times, for 5 to 7 minutes, until lightly toasted and fragrant.

2. Cut the pears in half and remove the cores (the small scoop of a melon baller works well for removing the cores neatly; use a paring knife to remove the tough fibers running the length of the fruit).

3. Arrange a chunk of Parmesan and a pear half on each dessert plate. Scatter the walnuts around them. Drizzle the honey generously over the cheese and fruit, and serve.

SOMMELIER WINE SUGGESTION | Amarone della Valpolicella Boscaini Ca de Loi "Classico" 1990; Veneto, Italy

A DOZEN DELICIOUS WAYS TO USE WHITE TRUFFLE OIL

1. Drizzle it over roasted or grilled asparagus.

2. Add a few drops to warm potato salad.

3. Stir it into almost any cream soup.

4. Add a few drops to tuna tartare.

5. Brush it over the cheese for grilled cheese sandwiches (or drizzle open-faced cheese toasts with it).

6. Stir it into chicken salad.

7. Drizzle it over garlicky sautéed potatoes or oven-roasted tiny new potatoes.

8. Dress up egg salad with a splash or two.

9. Drizzle it over grilled or panfried polenta.

10. Anoint a roast chicken—or any roasted bird—with it (or carve the bird and garnish the individual servings with a drizzle or two).

11. Stir some into creamy goat cheese for topping warm croutes.

12. Drizzle it over any grilled fish—whole, steaks, or fillets.

VEGETABLES

SAUTEED ARTICHOKE HEARTS
WITH WILD MUSHROOMS

ROASTED ASPARAGUS
WITH TRUFFLE AIOLI

GREEN BEANS WITH TRUFFLE
CREAM

TRUFFLED CAULIFLOWER PUREE

TRUFFLED CORN PUDDING

ROASTED FENNEL WITH
TRUFFLE CREAM

BLUE HILL'S PAPILLOTES OF
FINGERLING POTATOES, FRENCH
LENTILS, PORCINI, AND BLACK
TRUFFLES

EMERIL'S TRUFFLED PARMESAN
POTATO CHIPS

MASHED POTATOES WITH
TRUFFLE BUTTER

MASHED POTATOES WITH
MASCARPONE AND TRUFFLE
PUREE

POTATO-CELERY ROOT PUREE

PARSNIP MASHED POTATOES
WITH WHITE TRUFFLE OIL

TRUFFLED POTATOES ANNA

TWICE-BAKED POTATOES WITH
BLACK TRUFFLE

POTATO GRATIN WITH FRESH
WHITE TRUFFLES

ZUCCHINI RIBBONS WITH
SHAVED PECORINO AND WHITE
TRUFFLE OIL

SAUTEED ARTICHOKE HEARTS WITH WILD MUSHROOMS

ARTICHOKES AND PORCINI mushrooms are a fabulous combination, but porcini can be wildly expensive. Fortunately, the fresh mushrooms are flavorful enough that just a few of them will transform a dish—here cremini are added to round out the mix. If porcini are unobtainable or out of season, you can use all cremini mushrooms and the sauté will still be tasty—or add a few dried porcini (see page 127 for instructions on "reconstituting" dried mushrooms). Serve this with roasted chicken or duck, or with pan-seared or grilled fish.

In this dish, the artichokes are "turned"—i.e., trimmed to their hearts—and the leaves discarded. But you can save the leaves to eat yourself, if you like: steam them until tender and serve them hot with melted butter or warm or cold with a vinaigrette or other sauce for dipping. SERVES 4

1 **lemon,** halved

4 **large artichokes**

2 **tablespoons olive oil**

8 **ounces cremini mushrooms,** trimmed, cleaned, and thinly sliced (see Note) [250 grams]

2 **to 4 ounces porcini mushrooms,** trimmed, cleaned, and thinly sliced [60 to 125 grams]

Salt and freshly ground black pepper

2 **garlic cloves,** minced

2 **tablespoons minced flat-leaf parsley**

2 **to 3 teaspoons white truffle oil**

1. To prepare the artichokes, fill a medium bowl with water, squeeze the juice of the lemon into it, and add the lemon halves. One at a time, using a sharp knife, cut off the stem of each artichoke. Starting at the bottom of the artichoke and working your way around it, bend back and snap off the outer green leaves until you reach the pale inner cone of leaves. Discard the outer leaves (or reserve them; see headnote). Cut off the inner cone of leaves. Using a sharp-edged teaspoon or a grapefruit spoon, scrape out the hairy choke from the center of the artichoke. Trim off all the green or tough parts from the bottom of the artichoke. As you finish each artichoke, put it in the bowl of lemon water to prevent discoloration.

2. Heat 1½ tablespoons of the olive oil in a large deep skillet over moderately high heat. Add the mushrooms, season with salt and pepper, and cook, stirring frequently, until the liquid the mushrooms release has evaporated and they are just beginning to brown, about 10 minutes.

3. Add the garlic to the mushrooms and cook, stirring, until fragrant, about 1 minute. Transfer the mushrooms to a bowl and set aside. Set the skillet aside.

4. Drain the artichokes and pat dry with paper towels. Cut each artichoke heart in half and then into thin slices.

5. Set the skillet over moderately low heat and add the remaining 1½ teaspoons olive oil, the artichokes, ¼ cup [60 ml] water, and salt to taste. Cook, stirring frequently, until the liquid has evaporated and the artichoke slices are tender and just beginning to brown, about 15 minutes; if necessary, add another tablespoon or so of water to prevent sticking.

6. Return the mushrooms to the skillet, along with any juices that have collected in the bowl, and the parsley. Cook, stirring, until the mushrooms are heated through, about 2 minutes. Season with additional salt and pepper if necessary, stir in the truffle oil, and serve.

NOTE: If using only 2 ounces [60 grams] fresh porcini, increase the cremini mushrooms to 10 ounces [300 grams].

ROASTED ASPARAGUS WITH TRUFFLE AIOLI

ROASTING ASPARAGUS, an unusual way of cooking the vegetable, gives it a sweet, nutty flavor, nicely complemented by the garlicky truffle aïoli. To celebrate the first asparagus of spring, double the recipe and serve this as a first course. Or serve the asparagus as an hors d'oeuvre, with a bowl of the aïoli for dipping. Even if you usually peel asparagus, it's unnecessary when roasting all but the very thickest stalks. SERVES 4

1¼ pounds asparagus, tough ends trimmed [600 grams]

1½ teaspoons extra-virgin olive oil

⅛ teaspoon kosher salt

⅓ cup Truffle Aïoli (recipe follows) [75 ml]

1. Preheat the oven to 450°F [230°C].

2. Mound the asparagus on a large baking sheet. Drizzle the olive oil over it, tossing to coat evenly, then season with the salt. Spread the asparagus out on the baking sheet. Roast, turning the asparagus once or twice, for 8 to 12 minutes (depending on the thickness of the stalks), until tender and beginning to brown in spots.

3. Serve on a platter or individual plates, with the aïoli spooned over the asparagus.

TRUFFLE AIOLI

Garlic aficionados find aïoli, which has been called "the butter of Provence," positively addictive. Just wait until you try it with the addition of truffle oil. Serve the creamy sauce as an accompaniment to grilled or poached fish or as a dip for grilled vegetables or chilled raw vegetables, or spoon a dollop onto lobster. It's also excellent with steamed artichokes, served hot or cold.

MAKES ABOUT 1¼ CUPS [300 ML]

1 large egg, at room temperature

1½ tablespoons fresh lemon juice

1 tablespoon white truffle oil

2 garlic cloves

½ teaspoon salt

⅛ teaspoon cayenne

1 cup soybean oil or other flavorless vegetable oil [250 ml]

1. Combine the egg, lemon juice, truffle oil, garlic, salt, and cayenne in a blender or food processor and process until blended. With the machine on, begin adding the oil in a very thin, steady stream. Once the aïoli begins to thicken, add the remaining oil in a slow, steady stream. Season with additional salt to taste.

2. Transfer the aïoli to a bowl or a jar, cover tightly, and refrigerate until ready to use. The aïoli will keep for up to 3 days.

GREEN BEANS WITH TRUFFLE CREAM

UTTER SIMPLICITY CAN MAKE the most striking impact, as evidenced by this easy recipe. Serve these spectacular green beans with any simple roast meat or chicken—even with the Thanksgiving turkey. The beans can be prepared ahead, and the truffle cream takes only a few minutes, making this especially appealing for entertaining. The versatile, fragrant cream can also be served with other vegetables, such as roasted fennel or asparagus, baked potatoes, or steamed artichokes. In larger quantity, it can even be tossed with fresh pasta for a quick, rich sauce. SERVES 4

12 ounces green beans, trimmed [375 grams]

¼ cup heavy cream [60 ml]

½ ounce black truffle [15 grams]

Salt and freshly ground black pepper

1. Cook the beans in a large pot of boiling salted water just until tender, 6 to 8 minutes. Drain thoroughly. (The beans can be blanched several hours in advance, covered, and refrigerated.)

2. Bring the cream to a simmer in a large deep skillet over moderate heat and simmer just until slightly reduced, 1 to 2 minutes. Using a cheese or nutmeg grater, grate the truffle into the cream. Season with salt and pepper to taste. Add the beans and toss to coat. Cook, tossing frequently, for a couple of minutes, until the beans are heated through, and serve.

TRUFFLED CAULIFLOWER PUREE

A SNOWY MOUND OF CREAMY CAULIFLOWER dotted with glistening bits of diced black truffle provide the perfect foil to any simple meat. The puree can be prepared a day or two in advance and reheated just before serving, making this another good choice for a celebratory meal during the busy holiday season.

SERVES 4

1 medium head of cauliflower (about 1½ pounds), trimmed, cored, and cut into florets [750 grams]

⅓ cup heavy cream [75 ml]

2 teaspoons fresh lemon juice

2 tablespoons unsalted butter, at room temperature [30 grams]

¾ teaspoon salt

Dash of cayenne

¼ to ½ ounce fresh or flash-frozen black truffle, finely diced [7 to 15 grams]

1. Fit a large saucepan with a steamer basket, add water to come to just below the basket, and bring to a boil over high heat. Add the cauliflower, cover, reduce the heat to moderate, and cook until the cauliflower is very tender when pierced with the tip of a sharp knife, about 10 minutes. Remove from the heat.

2. Combine half the cauliflower, the cream, and lemon juice in a food processor or blender. Process until the cauliflower is finely chopped. Add the remaining cauliflower and finely chop, stopping to scrape down the sides of the work bowl as necessary. Add the butter, salt, and cayenne and process until smooth. (The puree can be made up to 2 days in advance, covered, and refrigerated.)

3. To serve, gently reheat the cauliflower puree in a microwave oven or in a double boiler over simmering water, stirring occasionally. Stir the diced truffle into the puree or scatter it over the top for garnish.

VARIATION

TRUFFLED CAULIFLOWER PUREE WITH PARMIGIANO-REGGIANO When reheating the puree, stir in ¼ cup [20 grams] freshly grated Parmesan.

TRUFFLED CORN PUDDING

SINCE WE ASSOCIATE CORN WITH SUMMER and truffles with winter, they may seem like an unlikely pairing, but in fact the sweetness of the corn provides a lovely counterpoint for the earthiness of the truffle. With super-sweet hybrid corn coming to market late in the season and truffle butter always available, you can enjoy this silky-smooth custard, flecked with fresh corn kernels, with grilled meats or roast chicken practically all year-round. SERVES 4

3 large or 4 medium ears of corn

2 large eggs

¾ cup heavy cream [185 ml]

1½ tablespoons truffle butter, melted
[25 grams]

2 tablespoons minced chives

½ teaspoon salt

⅛ teaspoon freshly ground black pepper

1. Preheat the oven to 350°F [175°C]. Butter an 8-inch [20-cm] square baking dish or other 1½-quart [1.5-liter] baking dish.

2. Husk the corn, pulling off as much of the corn silk as possible. Break the ears of corn in half and, using a large sharp knife, cut the kernels off the cobs (breaking the ears in half makes this job far less messy, since it prevents the corn kernels from flying all over the place). Scrape the back of the knife blade against the cobs to remove as much of the corn "milk" as possible.

3. Beat the eggs in a large bowl until blended. Blend in the cream, then stir in the corn kernels and any corn milk. Add the truffle butter, chives, salt, and pepper and stir until well blended. Scrape the mixture into the prepared baking dish, making sure the corn kernels are evenly distributed.

4. Put the baking dish in a larger baking pan and add enough hot water to the baking pan to reach halfway up the sides of the baking dish. Bake for 25 to 28 minutes, or until the custard is just set. Remove from the water bath and let stand for 5 minutes before serving.

ROASTED FENNEL WITH TRUFFLE CREAM

ROASTING FENNEL AT HIGH HEAT slightly caramelizes the vegetable and brings out its nutty, delicate anise flavor, which is beautifully complemented by truffle cream. Serve as a very special side dish with roast pork or chicken—or with the holiday goose or turkey. SERVES 4

2 medium fennel bulbs (1¼ to 1½ pounds) [600 to 750 grams]	**Salt and freshly ground black pepper**
1 tablespoon olive oil	**¼ to ½ cup truffle cream or fonduta** [60 to 125 ml]

1. Preheat the oven to 425°F [220°C].

2. Trim the feathery fronds and stalks from the fennel bulbs. Finely chop enough of the fronds to make 1 tablespoon, for garnish. Discard the remaining fronds and stalks. Trim the tough bottom of each fennel bulb. Remove and discard any tough outer layers, then, using a vegetable peeler, slice off any tough or browned spots. Cut each fennel bulb into 8 wedges. Slice off most of the tough inner core from each wedge, leaving just enough to keep the wedges intact.

3. Heap the fennel wedges on a baking sheet and drizzle the olive oil over them, tossing to coat evenly. Season with salt and pepper. Spread the wedges out on the baking sheet, cut sides down.

4. Roast the fennel for 15 to 18 minutes, or until the edges are beginning to turn golden brown. Turn the wedges onto the other cut sides and roast for 10 to 15 minutes longer, or until tender when pierced with a knife.

5. Meanwhile, heat the truffle cream in a small heavy saucepan over low heat, stirring frequently, just until warm and fairly liquid; do not overheat.

6. Arrange the fennel wedges on a platter or individual plates. Drizzle or spoon the truffle cream over them, garnish with the reserved fennel fronds, and serve.

BLUE HILL'S PAPILLOTES OF FINGERLING POTATOES, FRENCH LENTILS, PORCINI, AND BLACK TRUFFLES

FROM MIKE ANTHONY AND DAN BARBER, chefs of New York City's popular Blue Hill restaurant, these vegetable papillotes can be served as a first course or a vegetarian main course, or a special side dish (in which case the recipe will serve 6 to 8). Be sure to let your guests cut open their own packets, so they can swoon over the wonderful aromas that will be released. SERVES 4

¾ **pound fingerling potatoes, preferably Ruby Crescent,** cut into ¼-inch slices [375 grams/.5 cm]

8 **garlic cloves,** crushed

5 **thyme sprigs**

Salt

2 **cups olive oil,** or as needed

⅓ **cup finely diced carrot** [60 grams]

⅓ **cup minced shallots** [40 grams]

2 **thick slices of bacon,** finely diced

½ **cup French lentils (lentilles de Puy),** picked over and rinsed [100 grams]

1 **bay leaf**

4 **porcini,** trimmed, cleaned, and thinly sliced

Freshly ground black pepper

1 **teaspoon sherry vinegar,** or more to taste

3 **tablespoons chopped mixed herbs, such as flat-leaf parsley, chervil, chives, and tarragon**

Pinch of freshly grated nutmeg

2 **to 3 ounces fresh or flash-frozen black truffles** [60 to 90 grams]

2 **tablespoons unsalted butter,** cut into small pieces [30 grams]

1. Combine the potatoes, garlic, 2 of the thyme sprigs, and ½ teaspoon salt in a medium heavy saucepan. Add the olive oil (it should just cover the potatoes) and bring to a simmer over moderate heat. Remove from the heat and let cool.

2. Meanwhile, combine the carrots, shallots, and bacon in a large saucepan and cook, stirring occasionally, until the carrots are softened and the bacon has begun to render its fat, 8 to 10 minutes. Add the lentils, the remaining 3 thyme sprigs, the bay leaf, a pinch of salt, and 2 cups [500 ml] water, increase the heat to moderately high, and bring to a simmer. Reduce the heat and simmer gently until the lentils are tender, 15 to 20 minutes. Remove from the heat and let cool.

3. Drain the potatoes in a strainer set over a bowl (reserve the garlic oil for another use). Remove the garlic and reserve; discard the thyme. Set the potatoes aside to drain thoroughly.

4. In a medium bowl, toss the porcini with the reserved garlic cloves, ⅛ teaspoon salt, and a generous pinch of pepper. Set aside.

5. Drain off any excess liquid from the lentils and transfer the lentils to a bowl; remove and discard the thyme sprigs and bay leaf. Add the sherry vinegar, chopped herbs, nutmeg, ¼ teaspoon salt, and pepper to taste.

6. Preheat the oven to 375°F [190°C]. Cut four 12 by 18-inch [30 by 46-cm] sheets of parchment paper or heavy-duty aluminum foil. If using parchment, fold each sheet crosswise in half and trim to a large semicircle; unfold the paper.

7. Reserve 1 ounce [30 grams] of the truffles for garnish and mince the remaining truffle(s). Add the minced truffle, potatoes, and porcini to the lentils, mixing well. Divide the vegetables among the sheets of paper, mounding them on one side of each sheet. Scatter the butter over the vegetables. Fold the other half of the paper over the vegetables. If using parchment, starting at one side, fold about ¼ inch [.5 cm] of the edges over in a series of tight pleats, twisting the final pleat to seal the packet. If using foil, fold over ¼ inch [.5 cm] of the long open side, then fold over again; fold over the two sides in the same manner.

8. Place the packets on 2 baking sheets and bake for 15 minutes, or until the packets are puffed. Transfer the packets to plates and serve immediately. Let your guests cut the packets open with scissors, then shave the reserved truffle over the top of the vegetables.

EMERIL'S TRUFFLED PARMESAN
POTATO CHIPS

TOSSED WITH MINCED BLACK TRUFFLES and Parmesan cheese, Emeril Lagasse's potato chips give a whole new meaning to the term "snack food." Serve them with cocktails, or as an accompaniment to a grilled steak or roast chicken. SERVES 4

2 pounds Red Bliss or other waxy potatoes, scrubbed [1 kg]

6 cups vegetable oil, for deep-frying [1.5 liters]

¼ cup freshly grated Parmigiano-Reggiano [20 grams]

1 tablespoon white or black truffle oil

Salt

Freshly ground black pepper (optional)

2 teaspoons minced fresh or flash-frozen black truffles

1. Fill a large bowl with cold water. Using a mandoline or a Japanese vegetable slicer, or a very sharp knife, cut the potatoes into ¹⁄₁₆-inch [2-mm]-thick rounds. Add the sliced potatoes to the bowl of water as you work, to prevent them from darkening.

2. Heat the oil in a large deep heavy pot over moderately high heat to 350°F [175°C]. Drain the potatoes and pat completely dry with paper towels. Working in batches, add the potatoes to the hot oil and cook, stirring occasionally, until golden brown, 3 to 4 minutes; be sure to allow the oil to return to the proper temperature between batches. Transfer the potato chips to paper towels to drain, then put them in a large bowl.

3. Sprinkle the Parmesan over the chips, tossing well. Drizzle the truffle oil over, tossing again, and season with salt, and with pepper, if desired. Add the minced truffles, toss to mix, and serve immediately.

MASHED POTATOES WITH TRUFFLE BUTTER

THERE ARE MYRIAD WONDERFUL VERSIONS of mashed potatoes with truffles, something of a play on heaven and earth. This is one of our favorites: rich "French-style" mashed potatoes—in other words, with generous amounts of cream and butter. Leftovers, if you should be lucky enough to have them, make great potato cakes. Shape into 2½-inch [6-cm] patties and fry in unsalted butter in a nonstick skilllet, turning once or twice, until golden brown on both sides and heated through. Top each with a sliver of truffle butter, if desired. SERVES 4

1½ pounds baking potatoes or large Yukon Gold potatoes, peeled and quartered lengthwise [750 grams]

2 tablespoons unsalted butter, at room temperature [30 grams]

½ cup heavy cream, heated [125 ml]

Salt and freshly ground black pepper

2 tablespoons truffle butter, at room temperature [30 grams]

1. Put the potatoes in a large pot, add salted water to cover by 1 inch [2.5 cm], and bring to a boil over high heat. Reduce the heat and boil gently until the potatoes are tender when pierced with a small knife, 12 to 15 minutes; drain.

2. Put the potatoes through a food mill or potato ricer back into the pot. Set the pot over low heat and beat in the unsalted butter. Beat in the cream and salt and pepper to taste, then beat in the truffle butter. Serve immediately.

LA CREME DE LA CREME: ECHIRE AND OTHER BUTTERS

When you are preparing dishes with truffles and truffle products, it only makes sense to use the best-quality ingredients, including butter. Although there are good American butters available, until recently the consensus among many chefs (especially pastry chefs) and other gourmets has been that French butter is better.

The minimum fat content of American butter, as mandated by the USDA, is 80 percent, and until recently, that is the percentage you would find in any butter produced here. Unsalted French butter, on the other hand, contains a minimum of 82 percent butterfat, which may not sound like much more but can in fact make all the difference, and some of the finest butters may contain as much as 86 percent fat. (The minimum for salted French butter, called *demi-sel*, is the same 80 percent as in the United States; however, unsalted butters are much more the rule in Europe than they traditionally have been here.)

French butter is available in many gourmet markets and upscale supermarkets: among the brands to look for are Isigny, Celles-sur-Belle, and Beurre d'Echiré, all of which have been given an AOC designation ("*Appellation d'Origine Controlée*," just like fine wine) by the French government. Echiré, considered the best of all, contains 84 percent butterfat. In addition, it is made with cream that is cultured, or ripened, giving it a unique flavor and the slight tang of crème fraîche. Recently demi-sel French butters from Brittany made with fleur de sel have also become available in some gourmet markets here.

French-style butters are increasingly being made in the United States. Several years ago, Keller's, a family firm in Harleysville, Pennsylvania, introduced Plugrá (the name comes from the French words *plus*, or more, and *gras*, fat), with a butterfat content of 82 percent. Initially it was available only to chefs and other professionals, but now Plugrá, and its sister, Keller's European-Style Butter, can be found in many gourmet markets. Keller's also comes in a salted version, which many people prefer for spreading on bread or biscuits. Egg Farm Dairy, in Vermont, is making a butter with a fat content of 86 percent. And even Land O'Lakes, long the workhorse of the kitchen, has come out with its "Ultra Creamy" butter, with 83 percent butterfat.

MASHED POTATOES WITH MASCARPONE AND TRUFFLE PUREE

CREAMY MASCARPONE IMBUES these truffled potatoes with a wonderful richness, and adding a few table-spoons of the potato cooking water gives them a silken texture. SERVES 4

1½ pounds baking potatoes or large Yukon Gold potatoes, peeled and quartered lengthwise [750 grams]

½ cup mascarpone [125 ml]

2 tablespoons unsalted butter, at room temperature [30 grams]

1 tablespoon white truffle puree or paste

Salt and freshly ground black pepper

1½ to 2 tablespoons minced chives

1. Put the potatoes in a large pot, add salted water to cover by 1 inch [2.5 cm], and bring to a boil over high heat. Reduce the heat and boil gently until the potatoes are tender when pierced with a small knife, 12 to 15 minutes. Drain the potatoes, reserving a scant ½ cup [125 ml] of the potato water.

2. Meanwhile, heat the mascarpone in a small heavy saucepan over low heat, stirring frequently, until liquefied and just warm. Remove from the heat and set aside in a warm place.

3. Put the potatoes through a food mill or potato ricer back into the pot. Set the pot over low heat and beat in the reserved potato water and the butter. Stir the truffle puree into the mascarpone, then beat the mascarpone into the potatoes. Season with salt and pepper to taste. Serve immediately, garnished with the chives.

POTATO-CELERY ROOT PUREE

POTATOES AND CELERY ROOT are a favorite combination in French cooking. Here the celeriac gives a delicate celery flavor and lighter texture to mashed potatoes. You can use either white or black truffle puree—the white highlights the sweetness of the celeriac, while the black echoes the earthy taste of the root vegetables. If you have truffle butter but not truffle paste on hand, substitute truffle butter for half the unsalted butter. Or substitute a generous drizzle of truffle oil for the puree. SERVES 4

1 pound baking potatoes, peeled and quartered lengthwise [500 grams]

1 pound celery root, trimmed, peeled, and cut into ½-inch-thick slices (see Note) [500 grams/1 cm]

¼ cup heavy cream, half-and-half, or milk [60 ml]

3 tablespoons unsalted butter, at room temperature [45 grams]

⅜ teaspoon salt

⅛ teaspoon freshly ground black pepper

2 to 3 teaspoons white or black truffle puree or paste

1. Put the potatoes in a large pot, add salted water to cover by about 1 inch [2.5 cm], and bring to a boil over high heat. Reduce the heat to moderately high and boil for 5 minutes. Add the celery root, bring back to a boil, and boil until the potatoes and celery root are very tender, 12 to 15 minutes longer. Drain well.

2. Put the potatoes and celery root through a food mill or potato ricer back into the pot. Add the cream, butter, salt, and pepper and heat over low heat, stirring, until well blended and hot. (The puree can be prepared to this point up to 1 hour ahead and set aside, partially covered, at room temperature; reheat, stirring, over moderately low heat.)

3. Stir the truffle paste into the puree. Transfer to a serving bowl and serve hot.

   NOTE: Use a sharp paring knife to peel celeriac. If peeling and cutting it up ahead of time, put it in a bowl of cold water with a squeeze of lemon juice to prevent it from darkening.

PARSNIP MASHED POTATOES WITH WHITE TRUFFLE OIL

THE SLIGHTLY SWEET EARTHINESS OF PARSNIPS adds an intriguing but subtle depth of flavor to plain mashed potatoes in this recipe from our friend Hugh Bowen of Denver, Colorado. Oddly enough, hardly anyone recognizes the parsnips. A pinch of nutmeg and final fillip of white truffle oil turns the everyday into the extraordinary. Elegant and creamy, these potatoes pair exceptionally well with roast pork, chicken, duck, or turkey.

To make sure both the potatoes and the parsnips are cooked until soft enough to mash, it is best to boil them separately, because parsnips occasionally have tough cores. If you prefer to use one pan, cook the parsnips for 5 to 10 minutes before you add the potatoes. SERVES 4 TO 6

2 large baking potatoes (about 1½ pounds) [750 grams]

2 small to medium parsnips

4 tablespoons unsalted butter [60 grams]

¼ cup heavy cream [60 grams]

¼ teaspoon salt [60 ml]

⅛ teaspoon freshly grated nutmeg

Dash of cayenne

Milk (optional)

1 tablespoon white truffle oil

1. Peel the potatoes and parsnips. Keeping them separate, cut both vegetables into 1-inch [2.5-cm] chunks. Cook in separate large saucepans of boiling salted water until soft enough to mash, 10 to 15 minutes for the potatoes, 15 to 20 minutes for the parsnips. Drain well.

2. Combine the potatoes and parsnips in one of the pans. Set over low heat and add the butter by the tablespoon, mashing the vegetables with a potato masher until smooth. (Alternatively, pass the potatoes and parsnips through a food mill or a potato ricer into the saucepan and beat in the butter.) Beat in the cream and season with the salt, nutmeg, and cayenne. If the puree seems too thick, thin with milk until it is the consistency you like. (The puree can be made ahead and set aside at room temperature for up to 2 hours, or covered and refrigerated for up to a day. Rewarm the puree in a microwave or in a small saucepan over low heat.)

3. Stir in the truffle oil and serve.

TRUFFLED POTATOES ANNA

POMMES ANNA, A CLASSIC OF FRENCH CUISINE, is a gorgeous golden brown buttery cake of layered potato slices. In the Périgord region, a similar dish called *pommes sarladaise*, after the town of Sarlat, home of one of the biggest truffle markets, is prepared with sliced truffles—the inspiration for our version of potatoes Anna. Use a mandoline or a food processor to cut the potatoes into thin, uniform slices. If you happen to own a copper pommes Anna pan, it makes a beautiful presentation, but a well-seasoned cast-iron skillet works just as well, if not better.

Note that although there is no denying that the dish is rich, some of the butter is in fact poured off after the potatoes are done (and can be reserved for another potato dish or for cooking eggs or the like). SERVES 6

½ **pound (2 sticks) unsalted butter,** cut into pieces [500 grams]

3 **pounds baking potatoes, preferably of uniform size** [1.4 kg]

1 **fresh, flash-frozen, or canned black truffle,** thinly sliced

Salt and freshly ground black pepper

1. Preheat the oven to 425°F [220°C].

2. Melt the butter in a small saucepan over low heat. Skim off and discard the milky solids that rise to the top. Stir in the truffle and set aside.

3. Peel the potatoes and cut into ¹⁄₁₆- to ⅛-inch [2- to 3-mm]-thick rounds. Pat dry.

4. Use 2 to 3 tablespoons [30 to 45 grams] of the melted butter to generously coat the bottom and sides of a heavy ovenproof 8- to 9-inch [20- to 23-cm] pommes Anna pan or a heavy ovenproof skillet, preferably cast iron. Place the pan over low heat and heat until warm. Lay a potato slice in the center of the skillet, then, starting at the center, carefully arrange the potatoes in concentric circles, overlapping them slightly, to cover the bottom of the pan. Line the sides of the pan with a band of potato slices, overlapping the slices. Drizzle about 2 tablespoons [30 grams] of the butter, including a few of the truffle slices, over the potatoes and season with salt and pepper. Repeat with the remaining potatoes and butter, reversing the direction of the potato

slices for each successive layer and seasoning each layer with salt and pepper; work quickly and shake the skillet occasionally to prevent the potatoes from sticking. It's fine if the potato slices mound slightly in the center; they will sink during baking. Drizzle the remaining butter and truffles over the final layer of potatoes.

5. Remove the skillet from the heat and cover tightly with buttered aluminum foil; press down on the foil with the palms of your hands (use a pot holder to protect your hands from the heat of the pan if necessary) to compress the layers. Place the pan in the lower third of the oven (just in case, put a baking sheet on the oven floor to catch any drips) and bake for 25 minutes.

6. Carefully press down on the potatoes again (definitely use a pot holder this time) and remove the foil. Bake, uncovered, for about 25 minutes longer, until the bottom layer of potatoes is golden brown (check by sliding a thin metal spatula down the side of the pan and peeking at the bottom layer) and crisp and the center of the potato cake is tender when pierced with a sharp knife.

7. Carefully drain off the excess butter into a container (refrigerate or freeze for another use). Use a thin metal spatula to loosen the potatoes from the skillet if necessary, then invert onto a warm serving plate. (If any potato slices have stuck to the bottom of the pan, lift them off with the spatula and replace them on top of the cake.) To serve, cut into wedges.

TWICE-BAKED POTATOES WITH BLACK TRUFFLE

"TWICE-BAKED" OFTEN MEANS TWICE AS GOOD, and when truffle is added to the equation, there's no telling how high the rating will go. Experiment with this basic recipe as your palate dictates; grating a shower of Parmigiano-Reggiano over the potatoes before their final baking is one worthy variation. You could also omit the black truffle and simply mash the potato pulp with a generous amount of truffle butter.

SERVES 4

4 large baking potatoes (2½ to 3 pounds total), scrubbed [1.1 to 1.4 kg]

1 container (8 ounces) crème fraîche or sour cream [250 ml]

1 fresh or flash-frozen black truffle, cut into thin julienne strips

Salt and freshly ground black pepper

1 tablespoon unsalted butter, melted [15 grams]

Chopped chives, for garnish (optional)

1. Preheat the oven to 400°F [200°C].

2. Prick each potato several times with a fork. Place on the middle rack of the oven and bake until soft, about 1 hour. Remove from the oven. (Leave the oven on.)

3. Slice off the top third of each potato. Scoop out the pulp from the tops and put it in a large bowl; discard the tops. Scoop out the pulp from each potato, leaving a ¼-inch [.5-cm]-thick shell, and add it to the bowl.

4. Using a potato masher, mash the potatoes. Add the crème fraîche and whisk until light and fluffy. (Alternatively, the potatoes can be whipped with an electric mixer.) Stir in the truffle and season with salt and pepper to taste.

5. Using a spoon or a pastry bag fitted with a large plain tip, fill the potato shells with the potato mixture, mounding the tops. Brush the tops with the melted butter. (The potatoes can be prepared to this point up to 1 hour in advance and kept covered at room temperature.)

6. Place the potatoes on a baking sheet and bake for 10 to 15 minutes, or until heated through and lightly browned on top (increase the baking time by a few minutes if the potatoes had cooled to room temperature). Sprinkle with the chives, if desired, and serve.

POTATO GRATIN WITH FRESH WHITE TRUFFLES

SIMPLY THE BEST SCALLOPED POTATOES EVER. Sliced potatoes are simmered in cream and milk until tender, then layered with white truffles and run under the broiler just long enough to warm the truffles and suffuse the potatoes with their flavor. Serve this with a simple roast chicken or grilled steak—or make it the centerpiece of a late supper, with a salad on the side. Served in small portions along with other vegetables as an accompaniment to a roast or a steak, this rich dish just might stretch to serve 4, but we can't guarantee it. SERVES 2

2 medium Yukon Gold potatoes (about 10 ounces) [300 grams]

½ cup heavy cream [125 ml]

¼ cup milk [60 ml]

1 tablespoon unsalted butter [15 grams]

Salt and freshly ground black pepper

½ to 1 ounce fresh white truffle [15 to 30 grams]

2 tablespoons shredded Parmigiano-Reggiano

1. Bring a large saucepan of salted water to a boil. Meanwhile, peel the potatoes. Using a mandoline or a Japanese vegetable slicer, cut them into ¹⁄₁₆-inch [2-mm]-thick or slightly thinner slices.

2. Add the potatoes to the boiling water and cook, stirring once or twice, for 3 minutes. Drain immediately.

3. Combine the cream, milk, and butter in a large deep skillet and bring to a boil over moderate heat, stirring occasionally until the butter has melted. Add the potatoes, stirring and turning them to coat, and season with salt and pepper. Bring just to a simmer, reduce the heat, and simmer gently, stirring and turning the potatoes occasionally, until they are tender, 8 to 10 minutes.

4. Meanwhile, preheat the broiler. Generously butter an 8- to 9-inch [20- to 23-cm] oval gratin dish. Spoon half the potatoes into the gratin dish, spreading them evenly. Shave most of the truffle over the potatoes; reserve a bit of truffle for garnishing the dish. Arrange the remaining potatoes on top of the truffles, being sure to cover them completely. Scatter the Parmesan over the top of the gratin.

5. Place the dish under the broiler, about 4 inches [10 cm] from the heat, for 1 to 3 minutes, or until the top is lightly golden brown and the cream is bubbling in spots. Let stand for 1 minute, then shave the reserved truffle over the top and serve immediately.

ZUCCHINI RIBBONS WITH SHAVED PECORINO AND WHITE TRUFFLE OIL

HUMBLE ZUCCHINI, so often the scourge of summer gardeners, takes an elegant turn when cut into ribbons, quickly sautéed, and crowned with a shower of cheese and truffle oil. SERVES 4 TO 6

6 medium zucchini (about 1½ pounds total) [750 grams]

1 teaspoon kosher salt

2 tablespoons olive oil

2 shallots, minced

Salt and freshly ground black pepper

A small chunk of pecorino Romano (about 2 ounces), at room temperature [60 grams]

2 teaspoons white truffle oil, or more to taste

1. Using a mandoline, a Japanese vegetable slicer, or a vegetable peeler, cut the zucchini lengthwise into long thin strips. Put it in a colander and sprinkle with the kosher salt, tossing to mix. Let stand for 15 to 20 minutes to drain.

2. A handful at a time, gently squeeze the zucchini to remove excess moisture, then transfer to a plate or bowl.

3. Heat the olive oil in a large skillet over moderate heat. Add the shallots and cook, stirring, until softened, 1 to 2 minutes. Add the zucchini, increase the heat to high, and cook, stirring and tossing, until just tender, 3 to 4 minutes. Season with salt and pepper to taste, and transfer to a serving platter.

4. Using a vegetable peeler, shave the cheese over the top. Drizzle with the truffle oil and serve at once.

SOURCES
BIBLIOGRAPHY
INDEX

SOURCES

THE BAKER'S CATALOGUE

King Arthur Flour
P. O. Box 876
Norwich, VT 05055-0876
800-827-6836
www.bakerscatalogue.com

Specialty flours, including their Italian-style flour, similar to "00" flour; fleur de sel and a variety of other sea salts; baking and cooking equipment of all kinds, including pizza peels, silicone baking liners, and mandolines

KALUSTYAN'S

123 Lexington Avenue
New York, NY 10016
212-685-3451
www.kalustyans.com

Middle Eastern and Mediterranean ingredients, including frozen fava beans, as well as an amazing range of international foods and products, including wonton wrappers

PENZEYS SPICES

P. O. Box 933
W19362 Apoloo Drive
Muskego, WI 53150
800-741-7787
www.penzeys.com

High-quality spices of all kinds

SHAFFER VENISON FARMS, INC.

RR 1 BOX 172
Hernsdon, PA 17830
800-446-3745
www.shafferfarms.com

Boneless Denver venison steaks and a wide variety of other venison products

URBANI TRUFFLES & CAVIAR

29-24 40th Avenue
Long Island City, NY 11101
800-281-2330; 718-392-5050

5851 West Washington Boulevard
Culver City, CA 90232
310-842-8850
www.urbani.com

Fresh, flash-frozen, and canned black, white, and winter truffles; truffle products of all kinds, including oils and butter, fonduta, cheese, white and black truffle puree, truffle juice, and truffle flour; fresh and dried morels and porcini, as well as many other fresh wild mushrooms; caviar, including Iranian and Caspian Sea beluga, osetra, and sevruga and American osetra; Carpegna and San Daniele prosciutto; smoked duck breasts; duck magrets and fresh duck foie gras

BIBLIOGRAPHY

Alford, Katherine. *Caviar, Truffles, and Foie Gras: Recipes for Divine Indulgence.* San Francisco: Chronicle Books, 2001.

Buchner, Otwald. *The Joy of Truffles.* Cologne: Benedikt Taschen Verlag, 1998.

Czarnecki, Jack. *A Cook's Book of Mushrooms.* New York: Artisan, 1995.

Deighton, Len. *ABC of French Food.* New York: Bantam Books, 1989.

Del Conte, Anna. *Gastronomy of Italy.* New York: Prentice Hall Press, 1987.

Derr, Mark. "With Training, a Dog's Nose Almost Always Knows." *New York Times*, 29 May 2001.

Etienne, Christian. *The Magic of the Truffle: The Favorite Recipes of Christian Etienne.* Woodbury, CT: Ici La Press, 2001.

Evans, Frank & Karen Evans, eds. *The Cookbook of North American Truffles.* Corvallis, OR: North American Truffling Society, 1987.

Field, Carol. *Celebrating Italy.* New York: Morrow, 1990.

Grigson, Jane. *The Mushroom Feast.* New York: Penguin, 1978.

Gugino, Sam. "Buried Treasure." (31 December 1997). www.winespectator.com.

Jenkins, Nancy Harmon. "White Truffle Fever Makes the Season Glow." *New York Times*, 24 December 1997.

Knickerbocker, Peggy. "Black Diamonds of Provence." *Saveur* (Dec 2001): 52-59.

Kramer, Matt. *A Passion for Piedmont.* New York: Morrow, 1997.

Montagné, Prosper. *Larousse Gastronomique: The Encyclopedia of Food, Wine & Cookery.* rev. ed. New York: Crown, 1961.

"Oregon Truffles." www.trufflezone.com.

Pébeyre, Pierre-Jean, and Ken Hom. *Trüffel.* Munich: Falken, 2000.

Renoy, Georges, and Luigi Ciciriello. *Truffles from the Heart.* Brussels: Les Editions de La Truffe Noire, 1999.

Root, Waverley. *The Food of France.* New York: Knopf, 1958; Vintage Books, 1966, 1977.

Schneider, Elizabeth. *Vegetables from Amaranth to Zucchini: the Essential Reference.* New York: Morrow, 2001.

Schneider, Sally. "Truffles in Black and White." *Saveur* (Nov/Dec 1994): 85-96.

Sogg, Daniel. "Truffle Madness." (31 January 2000). www.winespectator.com.

Strang, Jeanne. *Goose Fat and Garlic: Country Recipes from South-West France.* London: Kyle Cathie, 1991.

"White Truffles and More." www.italianmade.com.

Wolfert, Paula. *The Cooking of South-West France.* New York: Dial Press, 1983.

INDEX